MW00942200

"As a new CEO, *The Executioner* by Artie McFerrin has been invaluable. The concise principles have guided many of the initial decisions for my company, and using the right strategies has enabled me to capitalize on my company's strengths. Being able to learn from someone who has proven his exceptional entrepreneurship and leadership has made me more comfortable in making executive decisions. It is a must-read for any CEO."

—**Nancy Gaudet**, owner and CEO of Gaudet Solutions

"With *The Executioner*, Artie McFerrin has taken personal leadership development to a new level. A practical guide, this is a must-read for anyone aspiring to apply proven principles of personal leadership development. His writing on goal-setting is especially insightful and pragmatic. One of the shortcomings of many leadership books is once a description of a principle is provided, there is no guidance in how to actually execute the principle. The Executioner is full of sound explanations."

—**Dr. Richard Cummins**, director, Corps of Cadets Leadership Excellence Program at Texas A&M University

"Artie McFerrin has written a very powerful self-help book that outlines exactly how to become successful at your own dreams."

—**Chuck Royston**, mission evaluation room engineer, NASA

"This is a fascinating and extremely valuable trip inside the mind—and the success-building habits—of one of America's most successful entrepreneurs. Artie explains the phenomenal value to business and personal success of approaching all of life with an unbreakable positive mental attitude, along with deliberately brainstorming and planning multiple roads to success. There is undeniable truth to his succinct summary that you are where you are today because of what you have thought and you will become what you are in the future because of what you think. His point is fundamentally simple yet life-changing. Like a positive mental attitude coupled with a creative plan, Artie's book will change lives."

—**Bill Moore**, partner, Enoch Kever Law Firm;
former general counsel, TXU Energy

"In the "Executioner" Artie has captured the essence of what it takes to be an Entrepreneurial CEO. I have found the many examples and his principles for developing self, team and culture as the foundations for execution of a successful business strategy to be very true in my own work experiences. In his earthy and understandable style built from his own learning and experience, Artie has captured in the "Executioner" a great roadmap for being successful in business whether it is as the CEO of a start-up company, or as the leader of an established operation looking to grow and improve. I found it a good read that I could take and apply to my own personal approaches."

—**Dennis J. Seith,** CEO INEOS Olefins and Polymers USA

THE EXECUTIONER

Implementing Intangible, Elusive Success Principles

Jim

To the best Reagent I've known. Thank you for all that you have done.

ARTIE McFERRIN

Archway Publishing books may be ordered through booksellers or by contacting:

Archway Publishing
1663 Liberty Drive
Bloomington, IN 47403
www.archwaypublishing.com
1-(888)-242-5904

ISBN: 978-1-4808-0931-4 (sc)
ISBN: 978-1-4808-0933-8 (hc)
ISBN: 978-1-4808-0932-1 (e)

Library of Congress Control Number: 2014914104

Print information available on the last page.

Archway Publishing rev. date: 04/14/2015

ACKNOWLEDGMENTS

I'd like to thank Rusty Burson and my personal assistant, Tish Abbey, who both worked with me through the stages of developing *The Executioner* over six years. I also owe much to my wife, Dorothy, my son, Jeffrey, and my daughter, Jennifer, who have been doing my small stuff, which has allowed me to do what really works. I owe much to the employees, partners, and customers in my businesses, who have contributed to the great success we have had and have tolerated my long learning curve. I can't thank Archway Publishing and other friends enough for working with me to develop my mishmash writings into something that I hope is good that can benefit society.

I am very grateful for the people, employees, partners, customers, and organizations who have contributed greatly to my personal development and tolerated my learning curve: my parents; the good early development and training in the corps at Texas A&M and the continuing Texas A&M culture I still hold dear; the support and spirit of the Jaycees leadership experience; Success Motivation International; entrepreneurship, which is the leading financial force in the world; Vistage, which helps develop CEOs from good to great; and the writings and audios from the great people in the success principle world.

Nobody's success is achieved alone in a vacuum. It takes a team. I have one of the very best! My thanks to you all!

CONTENTS

Team Excellence

INTRODUCTION

He that would govern others first should be master of himself.
—Philip Massinger

I wrote *The Executioner* to help people implement the best intangible business and self-development practices that really work and matter most but seem impossible for most to do. This work is a modernized update of the principles in the 1937 success classic *Think and Grow Rich* by Napoleon Hill, with the newer, yet proven execution tools and mindsets focused on the few business practices that really work. Through his in-depth interviews with the greatest self-made people, Hill was unsurpassed in getting right the improved mindset thinking and execution needed for great success.

In today's complex and harsh business world, it's not so easy for us to chart a highly successful path. I wrote *The Executioner* solely to help people better chart this path with a clearer view resulting from my lifetime journey of implementation of the best principles and practices that matter most. I have found that these near-invisible, nonurgent, and intangible principles needed to make what really works work have been almost impossible for most to implement. We are all capable of achieving this excellence for ourselves by greatly improving our thinking, approach, practices, and habits. Much more effective methods are now available to us than have been in the past. I wrote *The Executioner* for people seeking much more success in their lives than they currently have, even though it is most applicable to independent business people, entrepreneurs and independent thinkers.

Why is this book a more doable approach to execution than most of the currently available best practices? First, it's helpful to understand that most of the great business and self-improvement materials developed over the past hundred years are from writers who have done a great job of studying people and businesses to find out what works and what doesn't. However, their findings are not from learning firsthand the entire process of actually doing, including even Napoleon Hill. Therefore, the researchers themselves never directly learned how to implement these great practices on an individual basis, and they never discovered how much personal development it requires to be able to execute these principles and practices. It took me a hundred or more times the effort to execute than what I gathered from their writings. Over the decades, I learned firsthand that what the studies don't say is what worked for those people and businesses worked because of their thinking, habits, mindset, personal growth, actions, and mastery obtained over many years (i.e., ten thousand hours of the right purposeful action over ten years to be the person capable of executing these practices that we now know from *Outliers: The Story of Success* by Malcolm Gladwell). It was only then that they could execute what really works. This is just another way of saying that they only obtained mastery after working ten years on getting their thinking, habits and actions right. Hill didn't specify the ten years, but he did demonstrate that it took many years to get the thinking right. The ten years and ten thousand hours is now a well-established principle. These practices don't work until you develop your mastery ability as a leader to execute these practices. It takes many years of the right effort under highly focused competitive conditions to develop the thinking, habits, leadership, and confidence needed to achieve the excellence desired by most. Only a small percentage of people who tried to do what really works actually did so over an entire career. The right people with the right stuff made it happen, while others couldn't. These "shortcuts" to success don't simply work well by themselves; you have to become the person who can execute them. Unfortunately, millions of people who weren't able to execute what works have learned this the hard way and have given up on trying to make these success principles work for them.

Your learning curve can be a lot smoother, clearer, surer, and faster by using *The Executioner* as a guide to develop your ability to implement these great concepts. You don't have to fit the conventional leader profile or be good at everything to succeed. We all have our own unique strengths and genius that can be used to attain the success we desire. That's what all the great success and self-help books are about, but they tend to be a little vague in making the implementation of these intangible success principles and practices more tangible and executable for most. These principles follow the exponential 80/20 principle, which is far more effective than the conventional linear 50/50 principles used by most. All of this has been left up to you to stumble through. And we all stumble. I stumbled around for three years on my own until I learned how to successfully start up a business. Then I stumbled around for 24 years before I started learning successful strategies and my CEO duties.

***The Executioner* is about a more implementable approach to excellence through success principles and practices.** This approach is about developing yourself by mastering the individual duties, which I define as CEO duties, required for mastery in your field—and not the seemingly infinite amount of stuff that nearly everyone thinks we need to know and do. After all, we are each the CEO of ourselves. It's my guide about how to accomplish the ten thousand hours over ten years of the right intangible thinking, habits, personal development, and execution needed for obtaining mastery and great achievement as outlined in *Outliers*. Mastering the basic practices of *The Executioner* can guide you in developing your thinking and actions to where you can do what really works. Anything more comprehensive will detract from your success, as it will tend to enslave you. Start from where you are with what you've got, and you'll get there soon enough with this action. Build a better you and you will build a better life and career.

I've learned that my experience of slowly developing myself on the best entrepreneurial and business-success principles over fifty years is very unique. Had I not stayed in the execution trenches long enough to learn and master these magical best practices, I would not have had the opportunity to convey these hands-on implementation principles to you.

When I say, "what really works," I am talking about focusing on the 20 percent of your efforts that produce 80 percent of value-added results. While it takes considerable personal development to even begin to master this, the results are great and seem to happen magically. Like Napoleon Hill, author of *Think and Grow Rich*, I did not develop these processes. It has taken me a lifetime of trial and error to not only discover, but organize these processes into the few essential basics that matter most. As a process engineer second to none, I'm just the messenger of a purer truth.

I've had the rewarding, successful experience of focusing on and only sweating the right mindsets that matter. Being able to implement these principles has allowed me more freedom and wealth than most Fortune 500 CEOs and entrepreneurs. You can achieve the excellence that your heart desires by being committed to these proven and doable principles and practices. It's only dependent on your improvement in successful thinking and habits.

1

A Winning Thinking Path (Getting Our Mindset Right)

Successful people are simply those with successful habits.
—*Brian Tracy, motivational author*

I'd hazard to say that no kid grows up proclaiming that he or she wants to be a leader or a CEO. A firefighter or an astronaut? Sure. A CEO? Not so much. After all, most kids don't even know what a CEO or a leader is, let alone what they do. As we mature into adults, some of us find the business world alluring, and we proceed along a career path that probably will not result in our becoming a CEO of a business unless we take the leap and start a company of our own. But many of us will become leaders, which is probably everyone reading *The Executioner*. Very few of us make it to top-tier leadership positions in global companies, but whether we're running a small group or a big one, nearly all of us who wear the leader hat share something in common: we didn't initially set out to be a leader or the CEO of ourselves. In trying to make a good living and important contributions, we just got there somehow. This first chapter will provide a great leadership thinking base, because it will provide the proven thinking and mind-set required for great achievement and leadership. It is a challenge for us to flip our thinking out of the conventional static mode of being enslaved to others' goals and over to a dynamic, nonconventional CEO mind-set. Schools, businesses, and parents typically don't teach CEO thinking or success. These first chapters will help, if this is what you want. I choose to use the acronym *CEO* to demonstrate principles, since words like *leader* and *manager* are way too vague from which to learn. The more definitive CEO and owner-thinking mindset is critical in building all leaders and will be used throughout the book, as will *entrepreneur.* It takes this strong mindset to succeed, as just an intellectual understanding of the principles won't work.

"Build your own dreams, or someone else will hire you to build theirs." *Farrah Gray*

We are the CEOs of ourselves, and it's through this mindset that we can best control our own futures. The wisest businesspeople have said for a century or more to always work as though you own the business. It's through entrepreneurs that most of these intangible concepts have been learned. It's easier to explain the concepts through the lone, total responsibility entrepreneur concept, so please bear with me on this, since so many readers will not necessarily or knowingly want to be a CEO or an entrepreneur.

In truth, everybody can be an effective CEO of themselves by gaining control of their work and doing what is best for their future. It's what it takes to be a winner and to continue to grow your winning attitude and habits. The CEO-thinking principles in this chapter are what really work. We do indeed need to perform our work as if we were the owners, as would a successful athlete or winning coach. You will live a better life by being less enslaved in doing the work for others on your terms, since no one else is that dedicated to your success, winning, or effectiveness. These proven principles of taking ownership of your own future are for everyone to use, since we're all our own CEOs in life if we choose to be. This is the point that you take full control of your own life and future and realize that there is no one else who's going to come to your rescue. It is best done by starting with the long-term, end-result perspective that you want. In that way, you have an end-result goal to be the CEO and make this concept work. Without meaningful long-term goals, you don't have much of a demanding career success goal to be the CEO of! This CEO thinking mindset will put you on the proven, right path to more success and excellence in your life, but we have to make this a habit for it to be effective. Many people will tend not to want to be a CEO of a business, but being the CEO of your life has proven to be a most effective principle.

The randomness of life impacts us on every level, and it is definitely the case in business. Take my own story of developing my successful thinking mind-set as an example. After I graduated from Texas A&M with two degrees in chemical engineering, I went to work at Shell Chemical in 1967 as a young chemical engineer who wanted to go high in the organization. I found the work interesting enough, but after the initial four years of enthusiasm, it certainly didn't light me up in neon. I didn't go to my really nice job in a great company in the morning and happily chirp, "Wow! This is great! This is what I want to do for the rest of my life!" I realized after a few years that a career in a large corporation, with all its bureaucratic hindrances to growth and innovative thinking, tended to stifle my spirit. I stuck with this slow boat until I could figure out how to do what I wanted, though, because it was a really nice job at a good salary, and I didn't know what else to do. I first realized then that I wanted the great opportunity and achievement that I had seen other young entrepreneurs accomplishing. I didn't know this when I graduated, as we never seem to know what we want or what our options are when we start our adult lives. Of course, had I possessed the conventional talents that it takes to excel at Shell, I might have embraced it. It wasn't my cup of tea, though.

As often happens in large businesses, layoffs due to budget cuts occurred in my division. It was 1971, and I was twenty-eight years old and unemployed. Since I didn't want another conventional job and

I absolutely had no idea about what kind of business to start at that moment, I ended up taking an unlimited total-commission sales job at a company called Success Motivation International (SMI), the first company of its kind, specializing in acquiring the rights to the best self-help information out at the time, condensing it, and putting it on cassette tapes. The company offered them as motivational and sales programs and seminars.

My days pounding the pavement to drum up sales entailed doing a lot of driving around. On my way to appointments, I listened to the audiotapes, which required repetitive listening in order to positively improve my brain enough to realize great improvement. They told us to listen to every audiotape six times in order to absorb the material, but I found out from the successful old-timers that I needed over a hundred repetitions to really elevate my thinking and personal development. I had seen how others at SMI had experienced a transformation to a great state with that amount of exposure, and I wanted "it," no matter how vague it was. They called it "being a product of the product." At that time, I had no concept that it took ten thousand hours of the right stuff over ten years—minimum—to obtain the "mastery" transformation as the book *Outliers* demonstrated over thirty years later ... and no one else did, either. All the sources said to persist forever, which created much self-doubt for me after years with little improvement. At home, I constantly read motivational, self-help, leadership, sales, and business books, especially the ones focusing on success and personal growth. Many of them shared common themes—practicing positive thinking, being unafraid of taking risks and failing, envisioning your own success, and taking action to turn that vision into reality, among others. Collectively, you could call what I learned *success principles*. They gave me positive direction in my personal and business life, and they essentially were reprogramming my way of thinking. However, these audios had no effect on my thinking for the first 3,000 hours and three years I listened to them. And I had yet to learn how to get into action and develop the confidence to effectively use the principles while I was in the motivation business. I was reluctant to make telephone calls and was not very gifted in speech.

I left the job at Success Motivation International at the age of 30 because I was a lousy salesman, and my savings were just about gone from having to live off of my lowly commissions. However, I have remained committed to learning and practicing the best success and business principles for the last forty-plus years.

The Arab oil embargo happened in mid-1973, and there became a huge demand for chemical engineers to help small oil and chemical businesses take advantage of the opportunity spurred by the huge spike in prices. I began helping small businesses with business and chemical engineering consulting when my friends recommended me, where I made good money (which was a huge relief for my wife) by having a hundred hours of work thrown at me each week. It was so nice to make the money that I loved every hour of getting out of the "poorhouse". At the age of 31 I also saw a niche market in the custom chemical processing and manufacturing business when I was handed a small chemical plant to manage that was losing money. I got that plant performing by overcoming many adversities in the pitiful plant, but not enough to make money because the equipment was undersized and poorly designed for what it needed to do. I told the owner, Dennis McCarthy at Saber Petroleum, an oil broker and a great person, that it wouldn't make money. He kept it open a few more months until he got the refinery that I was helping to design operating. He then transferred the people that I had working to the refinery in Corpus Christi, Texas, at the end of 1974.

I decided to start my own chemical manufacturing business full time in January 1975, right after shutting down the plant in December, and I offered to run a troublesome project for Shell that I had run at the small plant when Shell couldn't find anyone else to run it. They really didn't want to use me when they saw the rusty old building site in the middle of nowhere with high weeds and with none of the distillation equipment that it required. I had practically no money after climbing out of debt and buying reliable cars to replace our clunkers, but I believed in my vision of a viable company in an industry I knew well. I had finally overcome self-doubt by the successful action of running that small plant; I had embraced positive thinking and crystallized a vision of success both personally and for my new company, so I acted without letting self-doubt keep me on the sidelines. All the positive thinking I had exposed myself to finally had the effect I had worked so hard to achieve—a positive mind. I experienced a complete, instant transformation of overcoming self-doubt. I had no fear. From then on, I've been unstoppable, and so have others who I have known to experience this transformation.

I had become a product of the product, and I had accomplished the positive thinking that *Think and Grow Rich* is about. After this transformation, I instantly became an infinitely better engineer and executioner, even though I knew very little about running a business. This is when I became in harmony with the real world and could see opportunity. You can also achieve this transformation if you haven't already. This is the positive mental attitude (PMA) that Napoleon Hill talks about in *Think and Grow Rich*, but he obviously didn't experience it himself at the time he wrote the book. As a result, he wasn't able to quite explain it as well as he could have. Few do.

It took me less than eleven weeks to lease the property and get into a distillation operation making product with nearly no cash. Shell couldn't believe it. Those early days weren't easy, though. I had to learn everything from a novice level like every entrepreneur. No one ever learns anything wise and important until he or she has to overcome adversity to do it. Most stop learning and growing in business savvy when they stop working on their growth. One aspect of the philosophical stance I am encouraging you to consider and then adopt holds that reaching your comfort-maintaining level can stop you from growing as a person and as a CEO. If you kick back and become complacent, you'll lapse into this conventional mode without even knowing it. You won't keep pushing forward with a new vision always in mind as you go. Always pushing forward can seemingly adversely affect perceived stability in a business, but the strain of a little instability is actually good. It keeps us on our toes! I was certainly kept on my toes in those early years of running KMCO (Keenan McFerrin Company), and I still am something like a cat on a hot tin roof. I never stop moving forward, and neither should you!

Master mind group advantage

In 1998, I joined The Executive Committee (TEC)—now called Vistage International—the largest organization of CEOs in the world, dedicated solely to helping them become better, more effective, and more successful in business. Vistage gave me an independent outside view of KMCO and the other five plants that I had at that time. Without Vistage, I wouldn't have had that perspective, as I might have been distracted by my already substantial success. The input I received from my peers and Vistage speakers and consultants helped me to further develop the business to continue growing a larger, better, and more complex enterprise. In Vistage, I had finally experienced what Napoleon Hill called a master mind group in his classic book *Think and Grow Rich*. How right he was on how effective this concept is! I had previously never understood this concept. At the age of 55 I became enlightened as to the duties of a CEO and business strategy. Hill had much trouble explaining it, since he never actually experienced it himself; however, he came up with the concept to explain what so many of the successful were telling him. Once I got out of my business with everyone dependent on me, I could easily see my business with a great perspective by gaining the insight of viewing all the businesses of my master mind group. It helped me so much to see that all the people and businesses that were doing way better or worse than I was in each different aspect of business. Without using a master mind independent group, we will tend to experience the functional blindness to our own defects. We can't solve problems we cannot see.

Anytime I began to feel too comfortable, I made the conscious effort to move forward with new and challenging initiatives. Today, I can honestly say that I have never reached my comfort level because it simply is not a place I want to be. Moving forward is much more interesting and challenging. Comfort-zone ruts are overrated and enslaving to maintain. However, there is a very strong desire to slow down and coast or catch up. I say that it's probably much better to decide on an exit strategy rather than being enslaved in a drifting business. If you were the coach or owner of an NFL Super Bowl champion, would you want to take a few years off to drift, or would you want to try to win it all again? What would you think about your favorite sports team if its players stopped wanting to be champions?

Of course, it takes a lot of courage, positive thinking, goal setting, and confidence to keep the progress going and to resist the urge to slow down and try to catch up and make everything "conventionally perfect." I tell people to not lose the momentum they have in their businesses. It is very difficult to gain that momentum back when you're "dead in the water."

It's important to note that my mental reprogramming mentioned much earlier did not manifestly occur while I was working for Success Motivation International, though my exposure to the self-help literature and audiotapes were having a major cumulative effect that resulted in my PMA conversion the next year. Truly shifting from conventional to successful nonlinear thinking and habits can take many years. *Outliers* claims that no one has ever done it in fewer than ten years and ten thousand hours. I found this out for myself. It's a journey, not a quick jaunt, so as you begin your own personal cerebral trek, understand that some patience and persistence will be necessary for you to fully realize the benefits of what you're doing. We are what we think. By improving our instinctive thinking, we improve ourselves greatly. We have an opportunity to improve ourselves as much as we want, and as a result, we can improve our results to match our dream goals. Few people actually comprehend this, but you can. In the end, I think you'll find the effort was well worth it. My thoughts and actions didn't flip to the success principles until about nine months after I left SMI when I was thirty-one years old. And I didn't start learning business strategy and my CEO job until I joined Vistage at 55 years old.

My long journey after South Park High School in Beaumont, Texas, started with my education at Texas A&M, a tough, all-male military school at the time that pushed me to my very limits and honed my ability to work for the betterment of a team. It was like experiencing a fifty-hour-per-week marine boot camp and tough, full-time college at the same time. It certainly helped to make me a warrior. It was there that I began to realize that challenges were opportunities to improve and that adversity makes you stronger. I was lucky to just survive in the corps, and I did not excel in the military role. The self-confidence gained by surviving such tough experiences can't be overemphasized. Relatively everything else I've faced in business has been a party by comparison. We need great obstacles to overcome to develop ourselves; smooth seas do not make for a skilled sailor. My involvement with the Junior Chamber International, Success Motivation International, and Vistage was also pivotal, each in its own way. Vistage, as a master mind group, played and still plays an extremely important role in my life as a CEO. The path to my achievements took twists and turns, and in those early days, I had no idea that I'd become an entrepreneurial CEO. I had yet to discover the magic of entrepreneurship. Along the way, I have learned the hidden secret that embracing entrepreneurial CEO thinking is perhaps the most powerful way to grow personally and economically. I encourage you to give it a try if you haven't already!

The nonconventional leader or CEO

Not all leaders or CEOs are created equal. Obviously, we all are unique individuals with our own personalities and styles. We all share—or *should* share—a keen sense of business, a desire to grow a business, an ability to lead a team, and an innate sense of where the business needs to go to satisfy our objectives. However, the biggest difference among us is in how we think, which in turn directly influences how we lead and what we can achieve or fail to achieve for the business. Broadly speaking, there are two types of leaders or CEOs: the dynamic, nonconventional and the static, conventional, managerial. They couldn't be more different.

Let's first take a closer look at how to best define a nonconventional CEO, what obstacles get in our way as we work to change our habits and actions, and how time management plays a key role in whether we evolve as leaders in our businesses or we drift about aimlessly to the detriment of the company. Nonconventional CEOs have learned to channel their CEO thinking and business actions according to the following mandates:

- » Only sweat what matters most; that's the 20 percent of work that produces 80 percent of the value-added results.
- » Do only "good enough" on the small stuff that matters least, and make those elements your servants.
- » Recognize that trying to do everything excellently is the same as doing nothing excellently.
- » There's never enough time to do everything, but there is always enough time to do the most important thing.
- » Most entrepreneurial, growth-oriented businesses that are not old, huge, and don't have massive assembly lines are best served by dynamic, nonconventional leadership.
- » Develop the ability to accurately predict the consequences of doing or not doing something.
- » Focus on the important, nonurgent, high-value-added work.
- » Take responsibility for everything.
- » Cut through the clutter to get the right work done.
- » Overcome tough obstacles that have had the effect of developing great strength and confidence.
- » Think long term with the end result in mind, and make plans from the end back to get there; be a goal setter.
- » Think and act positively with no fear, even when things get nasty.
- » Adopt new initiatives to keep growing, helping to avoid falling into a maintaining-comfort-zone rut and losing momentum.
- » Stay goal-driven, self-motivated, and always improving.
- » Always work on improving habits and thinking with positive conditioning.

- » Constantly overcome adversity, and embrace opportunity.
- » View business as dynamic, and don't try to make it static and fixed.
- » Think and work like they are the owner of the business.
- » Earn their authority through deeds.
- » Work to build culture, people, and processes as a way to develop excellence.
- » In the military, are the fighting generals who get things done in the big wars.
- » Choose this route to become more creative, and be empowered to do more complete, wider duties. *The Executioner* is about this route.

The conventional leader or CEO

Good conventional, managerial CEOs and managers maintain in conventional businesses. They don't blaze a trail to new horizons like an excellent nonconventional leader CEO in nonlinear business, but they are essential to the leadership of most very large businesses and many small businesses. On long, complex, static assembly lines making millions of widgets, the small stuff and details are the big stuff. In this case, a business can't have managers and workers changing things on the spot or even with the approval of a couple of people. That ends up being the nature of most very large businesses.

You might argue that any CEO is the top manager in the company, that he or she is running the entire show, and that there is absolutely nothing wrong with that. But consider what we're really talking about here. Many CEOs report to boards, Wall Street, and owners who expect them to manage for them. And most CEOs have been trained to be managers. A managerial CEO will have his or her finger in every pie to micromanage every detail for others. Most will be very assertive and political. This, in turn, saps productivity and innovation from the team. Endless meetings, reports, and memos clog up the works, and most of what gets done is the maintenance of the status quo, which is the primary goal. Consequently, everybody ends up on a diet of antacids. These conventional, valuable businesses fit many needs of the world and many employees. They may or may not fit you the best.

Conventional leaders and CEOs tend to:

- » Only sweat the small stuff and only do the minimum on the dynamic big stuff
- » Realize that on a long, complex, static assembly line making millions of widgets, the small stuff is often the big stuff in a more static, conventional business
- » Be trapped in linear, conventional enslavement thinking and duties of maintaining for others
- » Be very structured and work for a very highly structured business
- » Plod from one area of small-stuff focus to the next, trying to be perfect
- » Work on mostly short-term goals and rarely long-term goals
- » Think and act quickly on repetitive, static, linear-type work and be very good at it
- » Tend to have a certain highly structured, assertive, verbal, and political profile that doesn't fit most people
- » Lack a true vision of how to creatively move the company up to the next level
- » Deal well with tangible maintaining, as maintaining is the job
- » Deal poorly with many of the more dynamic and intangible business concepts
- » Have the assertive ability to function well with large numbers of employees in a slowly changing, highly organizational structure

- » Work inside a conventional organization that discourages leadership through empowerment
- » Perform top-down management by the few
- » Answer to company owners, investors, and boards who expect them to behave and lead in preconceived management ways; even many lone entrepreneurs with much conventional experience act in this way
- » Work in conventional businesses that normally have huge volumes, own a good market share, have raw material advantages, are in a mature market where change is slow, own much of the means of production or distribution, and be branded well or some combination of the above
- » Not respond well to change
- » Spend their lives politically sweating the static small stuff for others
- » Work on winning the political game that is strong in conventional businesses
- » Gain their authority by their position, not their leadership
- » Serve as the peacetime leaders and generals who can't lead in a dynamic fighting war but are very acceptable in static peacetime
- » View business as static and not dynamic; preferring, as a result, fixed procedures and rigid policies, job descriptions, duties, and practices

Many managerial people are happy with this, oblivious that another way exists, and some really large companies must function according to most conventional business conventions by virtue of their sheer size and longtime structure that's too difficult to change. Most large businesses and other organizations need most of their workforce doing narrow, repetitive duties, as it is the nature of what they do and the way they are organized. It costs a lot more to operate in this manner, but their competition is doing the same, thinking it costs less. A great demand exists for conventional leaders in conventional businesses. That's just not my cup of tea, and it may not be yours. Nothing is truly wrong with a majority of CEOs and employees doing the static, conventional work, but this is a best-practice success principle book for the dynamic, nonlinear, exponential-growth seeking. A great many people don't have the unique strengths needed to excel as greatly as they want at conventional business. They could often do much better using their unique strengths at the most responsive and innovative companies that foster creativity and innovation at every level. Each of us has a choice of which kind of leader will best fit our strengths and goals. *The Executioner* is about achieving excellence as a nonconventional leader and not about doing static, conventional management. We each need to choose to become good at the static or the dynamic, as we can't be good at both. However, a general understanding of the other side will make us better leaders.

How I learned to do the things that matter most and that really work

A key attribute that contributed to my learning what really works is that I've always had high goals that kept me striving to continuously improve and grow for over fifty years. I never wanted to stop and coast along like most, but I have experienced that mistake. I kept growing and doing more of what I thought really mattered every year. Being very detached and not assertive or well spoken, I couldn't lead or push to accomplish much conventionally; I had to use only success principles, cooperation with willing people, and my technical ability to do everything. I had to focus on accomplishing what really mattered and keep doing it forever that way. I learned that I had to be the owner (an entrepreneur), or all the assertive people would grab all the power and use it in their static, unknowledgeable, and often political ways. From my entrepreneurial start, I learned to do all the jobs myself by necessity—which I'd not planned—so that I could get others working effectively. I designed and built the facilities, operated them, loaded the product, did the lab work, made sales, handled accounting, took care of HR, and so on. No job was beneath me. This is what it took to help me get people working effectively, and it gave me an appreciation for the people doing the work. Whatever didn't get done well was left up to me. Many thought that I loved that work. I did not. My job kept getting more difficult every year, since the buck stopped with me and because the business kept growing. For the past forty years, my job has been to do the big stuff that others haven't been able to do. I have come to believe that many of the best entrepreneurial leaders and CEOs have gone through this same process.

Although I had a seemingly good workforce after my first few years, I ended up finding myself enslaved by flaws, crises, problems, low performance, poor management, and poor business processes. This was a sign of poor leadership and management. I had to attack each of these individually, as I had no one else who could do it for me. And as I did them, I learned a lot about management, marketing, sales, accounting, and running a business that I could use to train others to do, as well. That took me 24 years to when I joined Vistage. Then I was left with the intangible big goals and CEO duties that no one else could do for me, although I was unknowingly doing a few. Because they were so intangible, nonurgent, and invisible, I took a long time to grasp what was necessary. I only started making more progress in these areas when I stopped being enslaved by the crises and small stuff that others could handle. Through the help and guidance of the CEO organization Vistage and the great sources I mention in this book, I was able to spend most of my time working on and developing my ability to execute my big goals starting at the age of 55. Most importantly, I learned what my big intangible obstacles were … and they were not what I had thought. I eventually found that the CEO duties that I couldn't delegate were the big intangible efforts needed to reach my tangible goals. It takes a nonlinear CEO to learn, see, and do these well. *The Executioner* is about implementing these CEO duties that really work and matter most.

No one else can effectively run your life, business, or success for you.

That's up to you. You are the only one who can be the CEO of yourself. This is how I was forced to learn and do the duties of a nonlinear CEO (not a linear one) over a forty-year span starting at the age of 31. If I had made billions early in my career, I would have never had the chance to learn firsthand from the ground up what I have. The approach I'm taking can't be taught by the quickly successful or the conventionally successful, since they didn't fight their way through all the nonlinear challenges enough to learn to execute the principles and practices firsthand. That really hasn't changed since 1908 when Andrew Carnegie got Napoleon Hill to agree to convey to all what the great successful people did at that time to make themselves successful. After several earlier, less-successful attempts over twenty-nine years, he finally published *Think and Grow Rich* in 1937. He did a better job than the modern writers, considering from where he started. Over twenty-nine years, he basically uncovered the universal success principles through his great in-depth interviews. He found that the most successful people built an unstoppable PMA through affirmations, were great goal setters, and utilized a master mind group. It was their personal improvement and thinking that allowed them to be so successful. It was Andrew Carnegie's idea that the success formula they documented should be taught in all schools. Over the past 106 years, we have learned a lot more and have better strategy and implementation tools.

Highly successful, entrepreneurial, nonlinear CEOs are in control of their work, consistently pursue their goals, and do not undertake tasks that others are perfectly able to competently accomplish. They set up the organization to ensure large blocks of uninterrupted time to only sweat the big stuff, and they don't allow themselves to get bogged down in crisis management (unless absolutely necessary) and other small-stuff distractions that will keep them from concentrating on that vital, most productive 20 percent that will generate 80 percent of the value-added desired results.

It sounds great to say, "Think like an entrepreneur! Only sweat the big stuff! Let other people deal with the small stuff!" But how are we to achieve this lofty goal? As noted earlier, it wasn't easy or quick for me, and it probably won't be a cinch for you, either. It is normally extremely difficult for most CEOs to develop the discipline and support needed to spend nearly all their efforts on what's truly important stuff, since they're buried in the small, urgent, and necessary stuff. I didn't start focusing on the big stuff until I was 55! The first step is to develop others to do what you're doing now. It took me a very long time before I could actually comprehend the big, nonurgent activities I needed to be doing. In *The Seven Habits of Highly Effective People,* Stephen Covey told us that the most important were the nonurgent, but I never comprehended what they were at the time. The following are among the nonurgent activities I neglected due to the frenetic press of being responsible for everything:

» A creatively effective business strategy
» A highly profitable marketing strategy regarding what really works
» Team building in hiring right and building culture
» Developing great business processes
» Performing the duties of a CEO (as I was doing manager work)
» Excellent problem solving

I first learned a lot more about what the important, nonurgent work and duties of a CEO was when I listened in 1998 to Vistage CEO speaker Walt Sutton's audio (and in person) on the duties of a CEO. Sutton's concepts were hugely enlightening. As it turned out, his duties of a CEO encompassed the 80/20 principle and focused only on what really mattered the most, although he didn't call it that. The more I worked on his duties, the more big stuff I easily did. It was magic, and I didn't even realize that I was doing such big things. I've internalized much of his wisdom and concepts by listening to his single audio over a hundred times. I've built upon them in this book after successfully incorporating them in my own business practices. These CEO duties are what matter most and what really work.

Early in our careers, my entrepreneur friends and I had no idea of what our CEO duties were. Hardly anyone does. In fact, my intended title of *The Executioner* was *The Twelve Duties of a CEO: We're All the CEOs of Ourselves.* This is perhaps a better way to think about what your job is. These twelve duties are the first eleven chapters. One chapter has two duties in it.

Sutton's approach built my confidence enough to follow the instructions to not do the urgent or the small stuff but to instead do his CEO duties. I knew it was solid gold as soon as I heard it, since I had consistently suffered by being trapped by the small stuff that I thought was my job. I assumed that management work was in fact my job, when in actuality, it wasn't. How liberating! Just about all the hard workers I know will try to handle all that's thrown at them from customers, employees, and crises, just as I did for years. It does take a lot of control and discipline to not get sucked into this small enslaving stuff that others keep dumping on us. Just keep in mind that the greatest CEOs do not allow themselves to get sucked in by the small stuff. They stay focused on the big stuff that most don't understand. The CEO's job is not "everything," and it's not "management." It took me twenty-four years as a lone chemical entrepreneur to learn this.

Another obstacle to doing the important, intangible, nonurgent work is that there's practically no one experienced in doing the nonurgent, intangible, complex big stuff because none of us grows up doing it. As I mentioned before, we're practically hardwired to think and behave in conventional ways, and business is no exception. We're just used to focusing on obviously urgent things in day-to-day business, like making sure our vendors deliver supplies or services on time, our customers are happy, employees are effective, and the company is making a profit after paying its expenses. This, of course, is vital work. It's urgent work. But it should not be *all* your work! Once you free yourself—in large part through empowerment—you'll find that the nonurgent work will begin to take up most of your time. You'll also find that the work is never completed. **Most people are hesitant to commit to spending a lot of time on doing this nearly invisible, nonurgent, intangible stuff that they're not good at and will never complete.** Your shift to a new philosophical stance will entail resisting these natural inclinations and pushing ahead in spite of them. The best part of doing the work that you're not so good at is that you won't have much competition, and you'll get better at it.

As noted, thoughtful people empowerment is key. I had others handle the small stuff for me. Keep in mind that some of the small stuff for a CEO is big stuff for others. They need to do some big stuff also. It's fine if those I empower only do "good enough" on their low-value small stuff, but they must be productive. Trying to do the best on the small stuff will cost the business a fortune and enslave it to the point that it won't be able to do what's important well. You just need for it to be good enough when it comes to the small stuff. No business can be excellent at everything. This is actually a marketing basic and where great marketing comes into play. **We can't let the perfectionistic flaw enslave us.** We have to choose what both the business and the CEO needs. We have to wisely choose the 20 percent to be really good at, as no business can be great at more than about 20 percent of all its business functions in general. Few will have the discipline to go for that level of excellence. Remember that it's the CEO's duty to focus on the important, nonurgent work, and it's not your duty to do the rest, even if you're just the CEO of yourself or your group. Hire a bookkeeper to keep the books and an assistant to empower with your many time-consuming details as soon as you can. Hire a leader to help. Trust me. The investment will be worth it if it lets you start focusing on the big stuff! It's very difficult to let stuff go, but it will become easier when you're able to grow your profits exponentially. By the way, the second title I was going to pursue was *Only Sweat the Big Stuff.* That title didn't work out, but the statement makes a strong point for the nonconventional CEO. That is the duty of a successful nonconventional CEO—and perhaps that's you. The most understandable explanation of *The Executioner* is perhaps *Only Sweat the Big Stuff* by only doing *The Twelve Duties of a CEO.*

Responsibility matters

One of the first steps needed in leadership and doing nonurgent work is for you to take total responsibility for yourself and your results. The words of Winston Churchill, "The price of greatness is responsibility," sum it all up rather nicely. The military has trained soldiers for thousands of years throughout the documented history of the world with the following fundamental principle: you cannot lead an army without taking responsibility. You cannot grow to your full potential without taking total responsibility for your past and present circumstances. And you can never fully release negative emotions without taking full responsibility for where you are and what you have or have not accomplished in life.

This goes for everybody on the planet, but it is especially important for a CEO to be able to accept full responsibility for everything around him or her. We're all the CEOs of ourselves in the nonlinear real world. One of the reasons that entrepreneurship is so effective and productive is because the good entrepreneur is forced to take so much total responsibility. It's when we end up realizing that no one else is coming to rescue us that most people start their enhanced road to success. One doesn't have to be an entrepreneur to take this approach, although being one helps.

Taking responsibility is the key to eliminating any negative emotions in your life. Think about this: it is impossible to harbor unhealthy anger, envy, animosity, and feelings of revenge toward anyone or any set of circumstances when you say, "I am responsible." Make a sign for your office! Look at it every day! Internalize the message. You truly are responsible for everything! It's a daunting realization. It's also liberating because you can plot your own course without worrying about whether you will fail or whether the risk will be too great. If you're the one at the helm, then it's your fault if you run smack into a big rock!

Maybe one of your employees embezzled money from your company. Maybe another staff member was so irresponsible that you lost your largest client. Or maybe you lost hundreds of customers because your advertising department released a controversial and inflammatory commercial. It is quite understandable to be angry in any one of those circumstances. You may need to fire some employees in those situations, as well. But ultimately, you need to accept responsibility—*full* responsibility.

Taking responsibility for hiring that person—or hiring the manager who hired that person—is liberating, as I just said. Admit that you made a mistake and move forward. That simple act frees you to move forward. It sets a positive tone throughout your organization. And it allows you to grow, unlike virtually any other thing that you can do.

In virtually every case I have seen where a person has overcome a difficult environment, the key has been taking personal responsibility—not for being abused and not for being too harshly disciplined but for how he or she chooses to respond to that negativity. Be thankful for overcoming all the past adversities in your life because that is how we build strength and confidence. You would be a very weak person if you hadn't overcome hardships. Just look at many of the people who have grown up with silver spoons in their mouths and never had to overcome hardships. They are too weak to succeed unless they subject themselves to hardships.

You are where you are and I am where I am because of who we are. Everything in your life today exists because of you, your choices, your behavior, your words, and your actions. You have freedom of choice, and because you have chosen each and every circumstance of your life, you are completely responsible for all your successes and failures. Responsibility goes hand in hand with success and happiness, as do control and freedom of action. It's my belief that you won't truly be liberated to achieve your greatest goals until you are able to take total responsibility for and control of your life and results.

Always remember that you are responsible for all your results. It's a hard lesson for even the most mature of us to learn and practice, but it does pay dividends. It's also the first step toward leadership. Take a total-responsibility attitude toward your life, time, and results. Don't blame! In the suggested audio listening at the end of the book, I recommend listening to the right audios with much repetition to assist selective programming of your mind to instinctively adopt the right thinking, principles, and practices, like responsibility.

Time is abundant for the most successful

Truly successful people view time as an abundant commodity, while the perhaps other 99 percent view it as a scarce commodity. We know this universal truth from the 80/20 principle: people at all levels, including the best CEOs, accomplish relatively little of value with 80 percent of their time. In other words, even the most productive people on earth get relatively very little from 80 percent of their time. If that's true—and I assure you that it is—there can't be a shortage of time for people to perform the important things (in your case, the nonurgent big stuff). I like to think that I get a lot of mental reinforcement, relationship building, and learning from 80 percent of my time that is spent on preparation to make the 20 percent work.

You may have a hard time believing that 80 percent—or more—of your time at work is mostly dissipated in relatively low-value activities. You'll come to see this more clearly as you develop. I am not claiming that there is an abundance of enslavement time (there's not), but trust me when I say that there is an abundance of success time. It's all about perspective and how we think about time. You can conventionally think like most, who think that there are not enough hours in the day to perform all that needs to be done. Or you can think like the truly elite winners, who realize that there is enough time to address the most important elements of every day. How you think about time makes all the difference in the world. How you think about anything makes all the difference.

The CEO's decisions in relation to time and principles should be determined more by the compass of purpose and value rather than a clock. The compass provides your life with direction, but a clock can control and enslave you. Nonconventional success comes from this freedom and direction of purpose, not enslavement in the realm of the small stuff. I encourage you to choose the compass and not the clock.

Survival and maintenance at best come from enslavement. Freedom and responsibility are what make entrepreneurship and nonconventional thinking so effective, and they are what made America and other free countries wealthy. That freedom is magic, and it includes freedom of time. We can't be free if we're enslaved by time! If we have no time, it's because we're trying to do all the small stuff. We can't truly achieve our ultimate success unless we view time in a new way, and we cannot push forward in any meaningful way until we harness time and put it to work for us by focusing our time as CEOs on what really matters. Being enslaved by time is as harmful as being enslaved by the small stuff.

Until you develop a time-is-abundant attitude and mindset, you'll struggle greatly with big goals. My advice is to take a long look at your day-to-day, twenty-four-hour activities over the course of a week. To be the best CEO you can be—and to be able to implement the duties, actions, and leadership of a CEO—you will undoubtedly need to make some changes to free up *most* of the time in your day—not just *more* time in your day. You will need to free up most of the time in your day for the nonurgent big stuff that matters most. Make time your servant, not your master. And you'll need to do this every single day. You'll need to make it a habit that you stick with over the long haul. Being a CEO is a full-time job, not a part-time job when you can get around to it.

Yes, I know. This all sounds like pie in the sky, but it really isn't. Just the same, let's assume that you're saying, "Yeah, right. Like I can really delegate responsibility to a high-level team member to handle a customer crisis that could blow up the company's bottom line." Or you're saying, "Sounds good! How do I actually do this?"

The answer to the first is that you can and should delegate all (or most) crisis management to a trusted and valued member of your team. He or she will handle the small stuff that's associated with nearly every perceived crisis, thereby freeing you up to figure out the bigger strategy of avoiding similar crises in the future and to figure out how to grow the company into its next logical level of excellence. Your duty in regards to crisis work is to oversee these efforts and continue to direct actions to resolve the root cause. The answer to the second is pretty simple. You will likely need to reassess and reexamine all your previous time-management strategies and then take steps to maximize your focus on the big stuff.

Of course, it will take time to do the high-value work and delegate or eliminate most of your low-value work, including urgent work. We can't just stop doing this work. We have to prepare an exit strategy that makes sense. Also, keep in mind that you will need to substitute the principles of what really works in *The Executioner* into the time you free up. Otherwise, other low-value activities will take up that space. They are always waiting in line to enslave you. The most helpful (a must!) way to improve your time thinking and the focus on what matters the most is to listen to great audios (suggested earlier) of this concept until it becomes a part of you. This worked for me, where my intentions to do it didn't!

The type of time-management system I'm referring to here isn't the type that most people consider when they decide to buy a planner. This is not about being so organized that you can perform double the amount of small-stuff chores and projects. That type of time-management system is quite helpful to many managers and staff, but it isn't for the CEO. As a CEO, your time is abundant to work on the big stuff according to your compass of purpose. The main thing is to know that you need a compass, and once you have one, to know that you must follow it instead of the clock every day as you take responsibility for charting the right course for your company or yourself. There's always time enough to do what is most important.

Choosing to lead or follow

We can decide to be a great worker or manager or CEO, but we need to decide which we want to be. The more conventional-management work we do, the less we become nonlinear CEOs, and the fewer great results we can achieve. No one can be a fixed, unchanging, static maintaining leader and a dynamic empowerment leader at the same time. We have to choose which one we want to be and excel at. To be a very effective CEO, we have to understand this. I chose to be the best that I could be. Most people confuse manager and leader duties by thinking that they are the same. I did. In saying this, I don't mean that we don't need conventional thinking in business or that managers are bad; the world needs good managers as badly as it needs good workers who think like workers, since most organizations are very conventional. What I mean is that if you want to achieve great success and exponential results as a CEO or leader, static manager thinking and doing are toxic for you as a dynamic CEO. It is the leadership and personal growth that comes from nonlinear CEO successful thinking that will give you the nonlinear success you want. Conventional manager thinking and doing will ruin your nonconventional success by making it conventional and toxic to the nonconventional. We just can't be a good short-term, static, conventional manager *and* be a good dynamic leader. We have to choose one if we are going to do it well. I made that choice in 1998 by following Walt Sutton's advice of manager duties being toxic to a CEO. My performance as a CEO must have gone up 1,000 percent by my liberation from doing toxic manager duties.

For a quick explanation, I'll refer to *Thayer on Leaders* by Lee Thayer, one of many books and studies on manager thinking. Thayer says that managers explain the past, make themselves indispensable, do things right, use politics, buy subordinates, are short-term thinkers, are reactive, are the bosses, are the little thinkers, limit people to narrow duties, get stressed by problems, and maintain. They are slow to change and grow. He says that leaders invent the future, make everyone else indispensable, do the right thing, eliminate politics, empower people to get things done themselves, must earn followers, think and act in the longer term, are proactive, are the coaches and the stewards, are decentralized, are big thinkers, see every problem as an opportunity, and develop. Their businesses can grow and respond quickly. That's pretty heady stuff! When it's put like that, it seems like a no-brainer to see why entrepreneurial CEOs differ so much from their counterpart managerial CEOs.

Clearly, the manager's job in most businesses is essentially to maintain a business with very little change, which is not what you want if you desire great personal growth and success. Fast growth and high profits require more dynamic, nonconventional thinking for all people in a business, even for managers. This is an area in which most people are confused. I've found that we have to be very proactive to keep ourselves from being entrapped in static, conventional manager thinking, as this thinking will happen to anyone who does enough manager chores to create those habits. And unfortunately, it's mostly the best people who try to pitch in and get everything done. Make your choice! It is very important that you know what conventional managers do and what nonconventional leaders do and that you decide which you want to be. However, if you're a nonconventional CEO in a nonconventional business, you'll need more nonconventional-thinking managers who will all help row your boat in your direction. These nonconventional managers will tend to be more coaches and team leaders than managers.

In the book *The Opposable Mind: How Successful Leaders Win Through Integrative Thinking*, author Roger Martin says that leaders have the predisposition and the capacity to hold in their heads two opposing ideas at once. And they are able to creatively resolve the tension between those two ideas by generating a new one that contains elements of the others but is superior to both. Conventional managers consider independent pieces, one-way linear relationships, and simplicity by selecting what they think is either best or least worst. Integrative thinkers (leaders) see the entire architecture of the problem.

It took me a long time to fully understand the difference between a leader and a manager. After all, in many ways, you could say a manager is, in fact, a leader. He or she heads up a department or store, managing employees, setting goals, and gauging progress toward those goals, among other things. That's conventional leadership. The true, more dynamic leader is going to focus on loftier things, like forging new directions for the business based on careful, strategic thinking.

Conventional manager duties were bad for me, and they can be bad for you, as well, if your choice is to push ahead to obtain great nonconventional goals by becoming a nonconventional leader as opposed to a conventional manager. I was enslaved by urgent and maintaining work while I was trying to be a CEO. I really wasn't doing that well in either job, although we were making a very good profit. I needed to do the CEO's job that others couldn't do, but I was hurting my business by only using 20 percent of my time to perform my vaguely perceived CEO duties. I was spending 80 percent of my time doing things others could do, and I was hurting everyone in the process. I learned firsthand how toxic that combination is. It's toxic to all. Again, I found that I got trapped in everything that everyone else did. In much of my career, I thought that I was smart enough to not get trapped like others, but I've constantly proved the hard way that I wasn't!

The CEO's responsibility—to himself or herself, employees, and the business—is to be free to build the business (or his or her own life) for the good of all in the business and for the customers. It's okay to use a business planner to do this, but most of the items you have listed should be the big stuff. Your job and your top priority are to do the CEO's job and not get enslaved by chores and crisis management. Most of your time should be free to think about and build the business, and only the CEO can perform this role. While many jobs can be handled by others within your organization, the CEO duties, which are the big stuff that others don't understand, cannot be delegated. They can only be performed by you, the CEO, with help from others. Others can't be empowered to do your CEO duties. They will rarely have your CEO thinking, perspective, and experience.

So how do you begin to eliminate enslaving, low-value activities? Obviously, it will take time to phase out the low-value work, but here are a few points to remember:

» If you can't envision Bill Gates or Warren Buffett doing the work, it's not a CEO duty. Don't do it, or phase yourself out as best you can.

» The most successful people don't appear to be slaving-away busy. They're not! Their time is abundant to do what matters most. We can't see them doing the near-invisible, nonurgent, intangible big stuff.

» You must empower your entrusted managers and leaders. This will free and unchain you from the small stuff and allow you time to concentrate on the intangible, big-picture stuff that only a CEO can do.

» Free yourself from doing most—if not all—of the small stuff. If it's not your CEO duties as outlined in this book, it's small stuff.

» Try to free your managers and workers from as much small stuff as possible by getting it done much much more effectively and good enough.

» Reduce the number of people working on the small stuff.

» Repetitively listen to the suggested audios to develop your CEO mindset, or it won't happen.

Guide and empower people toward helping you make progress on the big-picture execution and their important, nonurgent work. This is the CEO's job. Everything else is the small stuff and someone else's job, so empower others to do the small stuff and some of the big stuff you need. The CEO is not responsible for the small stuff, except trying to ensure that it's done well enough and effectively enough. Guide, lead, and encourage employees and managers, and avoid doing too much of their work for them. Start directing and leading your people instead of being enslaved by managing them or enslaving them in too much low-value work. Direct them to work on more important, nonurgent objectives. Minimize their enslaving activities. That will free up your time to allow you to keep doing the higher CEO duties.

The goal is to eliminate nearly all your low-value tasks and time drainers, as high-value work takes large amounts of uninterrupted time to learn and be performed effectively.

Peter Principle pitfalls

The Peter Principle states that in a hierarchy system, every employee tends to rise to his or her level of incompetence. Members in the hierarchy are promoted from lower levels to higher ones so long as they work competently. Sooner or later, though, they are promoted to positions at which they are no longer competent, and there they remain, being unable to earn further promotions. And since most companies rarely demote, there they stay, even though they are incompetent for that job.

The concept was first introduced by Dr. Laurence J. Peter and Raymond Hull in their late-sixties best-selling book *The Peter Principle: Why Things Always Go Wrong*. Peter wrote that "[i]n time, every post tends to be occupied by an employee who is incompetent to carry out its duties." This includes you and me! He also added that "work is accomplished by those employees who have not yet reached their level of incompetence." I'll add that much, or even most, work is also done by people trapped by the Peter Principle who are doing the work that's supposed to be done by the people a level or two below them. They continue to do their past jobs because they're so good and productive at them.

CEOs are not an exception to this rule! Maybe you were a productive manager and were rewarded with a CEO title. Maybe you were an employee who has worked your way up the ladder and now find yourself at the helm of your own ship. Whatever the case may be, you are not immune to the Peter Principle. To escape this rut, do not continue to do your past job. Even though you did it well enough to be promoted, you must look ahead and not become enslaved by your old responsibilities. You must become the well-rounded, nonlinear CEO or leader that your business needs. You'll need to stop doing what you did so well in your comfort zone before and master your new job that is outside your comfort zone.

The people who continue to get ahead are the people who are doing the work at their level or a level above them. The people who don't are doing the work a level or two below them and oftentimes doing it well. These trapped people often are very productive and do a lot of work and have good careers. What gets missed is the leadership, vision, and their future success and continued nonlinear development and success. Many high achievers who are trapped by the Peter Principle don't think that they are trapped in a rut because they're so productive and needed in a key job and making good money. Neither they nor their spouses realize that their progress is stuck in a productive rut, or comfort zone, of doing lesser leadership duties.

Most people never comprehend the Peter Principle as it applies to incompetence, themselves, or others. Very few ever know that they're trapped. What got you here won't get you there. We have to constantly change and improve what we're doing now to get "there." It takes courage to give up what we're doing well to do better. The act of constantly escaping the Peter Principle is what escapes us from linear growth and gets us to exponential growth. Ray Kroc, owner and developer of McDonald's, said, "When you're green, you're growing. When you're ripe, you rot."

What is rarely understood is that whenever we stop growing and developing, we're trapped by the Peter Principle. We're stuck in a comfort zone or rut that's bad for progress. There is a strong force in us all to think of the world, our business, and ourselves as being very static, but the real world is dynamic, just as most of the real world is nonlinear. The more success you want, the more dynamic developing toward higher and higher goals you'll need to live by. But we all have a strong tendency to think that if we ever make the next level, we'll have it made and be on our way. The real truth is that the next level is just a higher rut, and it may be where you meet Mr. Peter Principle yourself! And remember, conventional businesses love to have you trapped by the Peter Principle. You are highly productive, but because you are out of the running for future promotions, you are no threat to those who are not trapped.

I've seen the Peter Principle in effect at all times in all business and sporting levels. I've been trapped by it many times, but I was determined to break out of that trap, as I was so committed to future success, and I had high goals. I saw my dad trapped by the Peter Principle. Although he was excellent in his job as a maintenance foreman, my mother never understood why he wasn't promoted more. Now I understand. Without high goals, you're nearly certain to be trapped no matter how smart and talented you are. You can even have very profitable years and be rich as you become stagnant, enslaved, not growing and developing. But ultimately, it will cost you if you don't learn how to empower people and keep advancing while you also evolve as a CEO. Just because you were a good manager does not guarantee that you will be a great CEO in this dynamic world. Just because you were a great CEO of a small business doesn't mean that you'll be a great CEO of that business when it grows a lot unless you grow with it. The angle of the Peter Principle that I'm discussing is the part that traps the best of us.

Part of your evolution as an entrepreneurial CEO or CEO of yourself is to fully appreciate just how often the Peter Principle comes up in any business. Understand that we all get trapped by this principle, especially the very best and hardworking! It's the constant escaping of this trap that is an essential part of adopting the philosophical stance I spoke of earlier. To escape the Peter Principle, we must remain dynamic by replacing at least 20 percent (as an example) of the small stuff that we do each year with high-value 80/20 work. Stay green and growing instead of ripe and rotting, or the Peter Principle will trap you, no matter how good you are. You and I are capable of repeatedly escaping the Peter Principle. Get very good at it because you'll have to constantly escape the Peter Principle for the rest of your life if you want great success. If you want to slow down, at least think twice about it.

Empowerment of others matters

At this point, the difference between an entrepreneurial and a managerial CEO should be clear. Leaders must be free to innovate and carry out a vision for the company. To do that requires us to eschew tasks that should be empowered to others or at least delegated. If we're going to evolve as CEOs, we'll need to empower others effectively as we grow. You need to understand what your duties, objectives, strategies, goals, and plans are before you try to empower others. For me, I started off just wanting to hand off my garbage work to others. Much of the time, it wasn't anything they wanted to do or were suited to do. The results were poor. However, now that I know what is important, I only sweat the important CEO work for me and delegate the rest. This made it clear for me what to delegate or empower. Delegating is more like giving people static duties to do. Empowering is allowing people to handle dynamic, changing work by using their judgment and genius. The point is to work on the big stuff and get other people to take on some of the big-stuff responsibility. Everyone wants to think that he or she is working on important stuff, as it should be. There's a lot of necessary small stuff that all businesses need to do. It is important to do this work, although it will generate very little income, if any. Make this work your servant, not your master.

We have to hire and train can-do people who share many of our values and culture if we want to have people to successfully empower. I never had any luck getting no-can-do people or not culturally compatible, overly conventional people to do much good for me in my nonlinear world. I learned that I needed to hire more flexible people who matched my needs way in advance in order for them to grow into fulfilling our future needs. The CEO has to do the nonurgent planning years in advance to succeed greatly. Not having the right people to empower won't work very well. I've been trapped there many times. We have to think whom exactly we will need in the future. For me, it's the nonlinear thinkers who can think and work with priorities.

I also learned that I had to empower people to get results, not complete tasks. I had to delegate limits on money, time, and so on. I needed to coach, educate, and support those I'd empowered. I had to go through the stage of having them tell me what they were going to do before they did it so that I could better guide them. Then I had them report to me exactly what they did right after they did it so that I could undo it if I needed to.

Bear in mind, though, that I never want to micromanage. I only spend enough time to make sure that everyone is on the same page, and then I let the team members run with the work. If they can do decent work, I'll empower them to make decisions and be responsible. Leadership and being in harmony with them go a long way.

Develop your success thinking and habits. I discovered that repetitively listening to the right success-related audiotapes changed my thinking and habits 1,000 percent for the better, as it has others that I've known. It is the best way to develop the successful CEO thinking and habits that I have ever seen. For some reason, most people want to listen to their talk radio, TV, and read their trash novels. If you want success, you won't have much competition, but it does take time to develop your thinking, experiencing the action and learning through your mistakes.

Chapter roundup

The importance of differentiating between true leadership and simple conventional management cannot be overstated. A nonconventional-thinking CEO makes the choice to free up the bulk of his or her time to work on the big stuff, the top 20 percent of efforts that will yield 80 percent of the desired value-added results. Strategic planning, long-term goal setting, delegation, empowering the team, and taking full responsibility for everything are among the most important areas of focus for an entrepreneurial, what-matters-most CEO. Even a good managerial CEO is enslaved by the small stuff that always seems highly urgent. There is little time to envision the future success of the company and how to get there for that CEO. Instead, the focus is on maintaining the status quo and taking the least-worst option to continue operating on an even keel.

You have a choice as to which kind of CEO or leader you want to be. And that choice will largely determine your future success in life and in business. I will caution you that many people are so totally conventional and rigid that the nonconventional route will likely not be their best choice. When you clearly understand and accept that there really is a difference and then actively choose to adjust your thinking and action to move forward as a leader, you open up great potential for the growth of your business and for personal growth as a dynamic and creative person!

So, what do you do if you're already a success, but you're a conventional leader? What do you do about these dynamic CEO duties? Should you commit to mastering the duties? Obviously, everyone will not want to overly disrupt their current success. I decided to change from management that I was not so good at to CEO duties at the age of 55. If a person decides it's best not to, then they could hire outside help to assist in developing their marketing, teamwork/culture, or processes. Choose the pace and mix that fit you. I've made The Executioner a purely dynamic best practice book without mixing in management practices. It's up to you to decide how to mix the two. If you have enough flexibility and big goals, go for these CEO duties. If you lack creativity and don't have huge goals, just blend in what you need to.

Remember …

- This is a nonconventional success principle guide to getting your whole brain working in harmony to achieve your goals. Should you choose to use the linear, conventional route, you may need to use conventional books instead.
- We're all the CEOs of ourselves. This mindset is what most of the best individual performers in the world use, and it is the best thinking for high success. This thinking responsibility helps to develop our ability to do what really works.
- Getting your mindset right on each of the key concepts will define your success if you can get into the right action.
- Leaders and achievers innovate and envision with CEO thinking, and conventional managers maintain static procedures, policies, and duties.
- Leaders work on big-goal execution, and managers work to make the small stuff perfect or at least fail-safe. Learn to not mix the two.
- What-really-works leaders think in a nonconventional fashion, avoiding the plodding, step-by-step, perfectionist approach that is conventional in business.
- The 20 percent of highest-value work is nearly always nonurgent and intangible.
- The CEO's duty is to take responsibility for the highest-value 20 percent and not the rest. It can be difficult to identify for most.
- Wean yourself from the small stuff that might account for 80 to 100 percent of your present efforts after you learn what the small stuff is.

- When you do take on some of the small stuff, accept that "good enough" is all you need and get yourself liberated from it quickly.
- Perfectionism with the small stuff kills your ability to focus on the big stuff. Minimize your people's time doing the small stuff, and do it very efficiently.
- Wean your business of as much small stuff as you can. Maximize the big.
- Taking full responsibility is the mark of a good leader. Shifting blame to others is the mark of a poor leader. This does not mean not holding people accountable. Many think that a major key to business happiness is taking full responsibility and control while always maintaining a lot of freedom of action and doing the big stuff.
- Time is abundant to the nonconventional CEO if you free yourself from managerial duties to focus on the big goals.
- Be on guard against being entrapped by the Peter Principle, as we will all get caught in the nongrowth rut if we're not careful. It happens most often to the best. It's not just a loser principle like most think. This is why most of the highly productive people don't think getting trapped in their comfort zones applies to them. The Peter Principle will rob you of your growth. Always work to escape from the Peter Principle rut by only sweating the big stuff. Don't stop growing. What got you here won't get you there, so supplement some of what you do well every year with more important higher-value work. Keep growing.
- Delegating and empowering are key, but you have to hire and develop the right people who want to go in your direction to empower.
- Managerial duties are toxic to you, the CEO, because you can only be good in either focusing on the big stuff or the small stuff. Managers focus on the small stuff. No one can do both well,

as each requires its own mind-set. Walt Sutton helped me grow like I was on steroids when he got me to stop trying to do both.

- Minimize the small stuff and toxic manager thinking for others on your team. This will allow them more freedom of action to assist you.
- If you can't envision the best leaders doing the work, that duty is not a CEO duty for you.
- We are each the best CEOs of ourselves if we think like nonconventional CEOs. No one else will be constantly dedicated to our success more than we are.
- I recommend that you make your number-one duty repetitively listening to the suggested audios listed at the end of the book to build your successful CEO thinking and habits. This will greatly improve your thinking, mindset and execution. I believe that it will guarantee your success if you listen to them enough. It took me one thousand hours a year for three years to first convert to the great side. I saw no visible progress after most of that 3,000 hours. It may take some people longer. It also requires a lot of successful action to go along with the thinking (i.e., ten thousand hours of the right stuff).
- Build your CEO thinking and duty execution so that you'll be able to execute your big goals. This is easier said than done, as it takes thousands of actions and hours of thinking to make this type thinking a permanent habit in your brain.
- Learn to emulate the best, which has been the route to success over many centuries.
- The more we get our thinking and actions right, the more magically the results will come. However, we only grow and develop through our mistakes and struggles. It takes quite a struggle to make things easy!

2

Sweating the Big Stuff with the 80/20 Principle

Successful men become successful only because they acquire the habit of thinking in terms of success.
—*Napoleon Hill*

Learning to focus on what matters most will determine the level of successful execution and profit we are able to achieve in business. This chapter is about why using the dynamic 80/20 principle thinking is so effective … and how to develop this mindset. The rest of the chapters are on specifically how to implement it on what counts the most.

Now that we've looked closely at the successful CEO thinking and habits, it's time for us to drill down to the core concept of the dynamic 80/20 principle. Our ability to continuously focus on and perform that all-important 20 percent of what we uniquely bring to customers and our business that is of the most value is what we need for our maximum success. To be effective, it has to become a part of our instinctive mindset and habits.

The 80/20 principle has a storied history. Also known as the Pareto Principle, this important theory's concepts date back to 1906, when Italian economist Vilfredo Pareto created a mathematical formula to describe the unequal distribution of wealth in his country, observing that 20 percent of the people owned 80 percent of the wealth. After Pareto made his observation and created his formula, many others observed a similar phenomenon in wealth in their own countries. And others also noted that the same principle applied to business, even in their own areas of expertise. In 1937, Dr. Joseph M. Juran, a quality-management pioneer working in the United States, embraced the Pareto Principle when he wrote about management style. He essentially described the 80/20 principle as the "vital few and trivial many."

The important point here is that the principle is evident in many areas, not just business. When applied to business, the most salient aspect of the 80/20 principle holds that we need to stay focused on investing most of our time and energy on the 20 percent of whatever is most important and produces 80 percent of our desirable results, instead of dissipating our efforts on the trivial small stuff. In juggling our own daily planners, it is not important just to work hard or to work smart. It is vital to work hard and smart on the *right things* with the right thinking. You might be surprised at how few of us really accomplish this.

If you think about it in conventional terms, the idea that putting nearly all your effort on the right big things in your business will yield sixteen times the desired results than the mass amount of small stuff is rather novel. It defies conventional logic and thought processes. Thus, most very intelligent people resist the concept. Those who are open to it find that obstacles still remain, such as identifying which 20 percent of a business deserves our central focus as CEOs. For example, you could evaluate the numbers and identify which customers or products or services bring in the most revenue in the most profitable way and choose to focus on those of similar ilk. Or you could identify which future business could produce that return if you currently don't have much or any great business.

You should focus on the most profitable and productive 20 percent of what your business does and where you offer the most value. Start thinking about what that actually means in terms of your unique company. When you think of something you consider in the top 20 percent in terms of profit or in terms of the more cerebral, conventional, long-term goals arena, write it down! Just looking at customers that generate the top 20 percent of revenue isn't enough, though it serves as an easily understood illustration of how the 80/20 principle could apply to your business. We as CEOs need to take the time to actually sit down and think about our big-goals strategy. We need to channel our thinking so that it focuses on the segment of our business that is the most profitable or will lead to potential exponential growth simply by virtue of capitalizing on our niche. As a CEO, you can't get caught up in the day-to-day tasks required to maintain a business. The 80/20 principle is dynamic, and the great value is gained over time as we keep doing more and more of the most profitable business until nearly everything we do is highly profitable. What are the most productive 20 percent of actions that you do in your business? You should also focus on this. What is the most effective 20 percent of what you do personally that you need to focus on (hint: the big stuff)? As I've said, this is more easily said than done. Most everyone in business dissipates their efforts on low-value work. This is a great opportunity to escape to higher value work.

What seems so impossible for most is to intentionally minimize and only do good enough on 80 percent of what their business does. However, most keep expanding the 80 percent that they can't let go of. You still have to do the small stuff decently enough, or it will become big. Of course, I try to make the big stuff much more than 20 percent. In a nonconventional business, I've had no luck getting conventional, single-dimensional people to do the small stuff effectively because the small stuff is quite variable in small and growing businesses. In fact, we have had high level executives that think they are saving me by pouring their efforts into the small stuff that's not perfect enough. It's been a battle. These highly conventional thinkers are best suited for very conventional businesses. The highly conventional people always seem to want to spend a fortune to make the static small stuff the big stuff, as it *is* the big stuff to them. But they rarely do it effectively in a growing business, no matter how much they spend. Instead, you'll need to surround yourself with more flexible, compatible people who will help you achieve the most productive work.

Points to consider about using the 80/20 principle are as follows:

» It takes good performers to do the small stuff, and there's a lot of it.

» Not getting enslaved by the low-impact small stuff (80 percent) allows you to focus on the 20 percent with the most value. In a perfect case, you'll want to spend the maximum amount of effort on high-value work and the least amount of effort on low-value work. Employees need the judgment not to overdo the small stuff in a nonlinear-thinking business. It takes a lot of talent to figure out how to do the small stuff effectively enough so as not to get enslaved by it and allow it to hurt the big stuff. We as CEOs can always get others to do the small stuff much more effectively. The small stuff is important, and there is a lot of it, but it's not the big stuff. The goal should be to get your business to do mostly all the highly productive and profitable business—not just 20 percent.

» Only do "good enough" on the low-productive 80 percent of the business efforts. Any attempt to do more than this will hurt your profit and business strengths. Few people have enough courage or understanding to do this. You may elect to farm out some of your small stuff. Cut your percentage of time working on the small stuff. Try to do the small stuff with as little percentage of your efforts as you can.

» Minimize and control the people and cost on the small stuff. Do not assign too many people to the small stuff, as this is a common fatal flaw of making it big. Keep the small-stuff staff lean. Make it your servant and not your master, but have productive people with judgment do it.

» If you double the number of people doing the small stuff, you'll just spend twice the money and hurt your business. Find a nonconventional-thinking taskmaster who fits into your culture to get it done more and more effectively.

» You'll never get all the small stuff done perfectly. The small stuff should only be done "good enough." Define "good enough" for you. Focus on what matters most that produces the profit, value, excellence, and success.

» The practice of marketing is to find the 20 percent of customer needs that will produce 80 percent of your profits.

Your goal is to do well enough and control the cost and labor effort on the small stuff. This has caused me a lot of problems, since I have mistakenly spent years trying to get the small stuff done with too many conventional people thinking that the small stuff was our most important work.

Why don't more people focus on the highly productive big stuff to succeed? Here are four reasons to consider. Do they apply to you?

1. Hardly anyone knows what the highly productive is, since these principles are nonconventional, nonurgent, nonlinear, very intangible, and generally invisible to most. My experience is that a majority of conventional managers are pushing their stuff, whether it's low or high value. It's also complicated by the fact that there are many different, most productive 20 percents. Every person and department has its most productive 20 percent, but it may not be the most productive of the business. Few know how to use the 80/20 principle as a great feedback mechanism to keep improving productivity, growth, and results. For a caring person that's results oriented, it's a philosophy of life and business.
2. Few have yet to develop the habits, skills, discipline, and thinking needed to identify and accomplish the most productive work, since they do so little of it. The nonurgent, near-invisible, intangible big stuff doesn't appear important to most, especially

when there's urgent and necessary work being constantly thrown at them. Few ever get to do what's most important or ever get good at it. Sadly, most CEOs don't see that they in fact have all the time they need to do what is most important.

3. Most think that the more urgent and tangible small stuff that they're doing is the big stuff. Managing a crisis is a great example of small stuff that looks like big stuff, and it therefore diverts you from focusing on what you should.
4. Most are trapped and enslaved by conventional doing, thinking, and habits.

So, we have the relatively old 80/20 principle, and yet few of us have internalized the good side of it because of common obstacles. Yet if we look around, it becomes quite plain that the principle is at work in nearly every facet of reality. Consider the following points that reveal how prevalent the 80/20 principle is in many areas of our lives:

- » Twenty percent of the people in a business produce 80 percent of the results or profits.
- » Twenty percent of customers produce 80 percent of results/profits.
- » Twenty percent of the population is responsible for 80 percent of the welfare payouts.
- » Twenty percent of people cause 80 percent of accidents.
- » Twenty percent of donors generate 80 percent of charitable donations to nonprofit groups.
- » Twenty percent of your bills account for 80 percent of your expenses.

Perhaps in your own situations, those numbers are slightly different. But if you look closely, you can't help but observe that the 80/20 mathematical formula principle shows up in business, people, performance, wealth, technology, quality, crime, nature, science, and even in basic happiness. It's a bit ironic. The principle is apparently ubiquitous, but its amazing power remains oddly out of reach for many of us in business, much to our detriment. Remember, when you apply the 80/20 principle to what you focus on in business, you're charting a way to financial success and sustained personal growth. Isn't that what you want?

Understanding the nature of linear thinking

Everything that I know of in the field of success embraces the 80/20 principle. What holds us back is coherence to a linear 50/50 correlation in terms of our efforts. Let's take a closer look at what I believe constitutes linear, conventional thinking. Up until the Enlightenment and the Industrial Revolution, people believed in magic, witches, luck, evil, divine right of kings, flat earth, predestination, and other irrational ways of thinking. There was little logic, justice, or reason to life and the world. Then, by the seventeenth and eighteenth centuries, the educated had advanced their thinking to ideas of personal rights; logic; hard work; order; security; reap what you sow; justice; and orderly, logical, linear thinking. The changes in thinking represented a huge advance over the previous thinking of the Middle Ages and Dark Ages, but that thinking is still very much with us even though it is a hindrance in achieving success.

Thinking should be dynamic, not static and linear. Here's an example of how linear thinking shows up in the present. Most career-minded people still tend to believe in forty hours' pay for forty hours' work. People need stability and security in their jobs. Thinking that each hour of work is just as valuable as any other hour of work is linear thinking. This thinking leads to the conclusion that 50 percent of our time generates 50 percent of our results. This is the conventional thinking found in most businesses. What is missed is that nearly all of these efforts are, in actuality, focused on the small stuff. Nearly no big stuff is done. In other words, if you think that half of your efforts produce half of your desired results, you're thinking linearly and embracing a 50/50 principle. You're diverting your focus away from what's really important.

Linear thinking can be comfortable, desirable, and secure for many people who merely want jobs. Linear-thinking jobs can provide billions of people with the needed income for their lives. Linear thinkers also have a strong tendency to do predictive thinking, which means they won't take action unless they're assured of the result. They won't take their foot off first base until they're assured they'll get to second base. It is how perhaps most people think, including managers.

The world is filled with billions of people who—deep down—merely want to be paid a salary for performing a structured, ritualistic set of duties. There's nothing wrong with that, and they most certainly perform necessary and valuable roles within an organization and society. The linear, conventional principles provide a great deal of stability in our lives and in our businesses. Linear thinkers can have very good or even great conventional careers. A lot of linear managers, engineers, doctors, attorneys, and CEOs have much financial linear success. If that's your comfort zone, then accept it and be happy. If, on the other hand, you want to propel yourself and your business to exponential leaps in terms of success, then be very wary of linear thinking and adhering to the old notion of a 50/50 principle.

In school, we were given grades on a linear basis. The least important answer was just as important as the most important answer. Almost all schools and universities teach nearly all linear thinking to feed the mass of business with the linear-thinking people they need, and this beats the creativity out of us. Essentially, we all start out with linear thinking early in our careers. However, in the real world, success, income, excellence, performance, and achievement relationships are logarithmic, algebraic, and exponential, not linear. For this, we must get in harmony and alignment with the true principles of the universe. What amazes me is that nearly all the engineers and scientists who are well schooled in exponential math, engineering, and science principles are still linear thinkers. Of course, that included me for much of my career. And I kept my linear habits for several years after I partially understood the 80/20 principle. I lost these habits slowly, as have the others that I have known.

Linear thinking holds you back from exponential success. You won't succeed much as a nonlinear CEO if you're doing mostly linear work—and your competition is accomplishing sixteen times as much as you are with most of their effort. It's important to note that the most important 20 percent of what we do is sixteen times as productive as the other 80 percent. Look at it this way: out of 100 percent of all your efforts, the top 20 percent would get 4 percent of results for each percent of work. The lower 80 percent would get ¼ percent of results for each percent of work. That is a difference of sixteen times!

To gain a better understanding of the 80/20 principle, it may help to use some graphics. The Curve 1 in graph 1 is of the static, flat 80/20 principle as presented in books, but it's not the true picture. However, it is powerful, and its simplicity helps us in gaining an understanding of the 80/20 principle in ways that the true curve doesn't.

Graph 1
80/20 Principle
80 Percent of Results Come From 20 Percent of Input

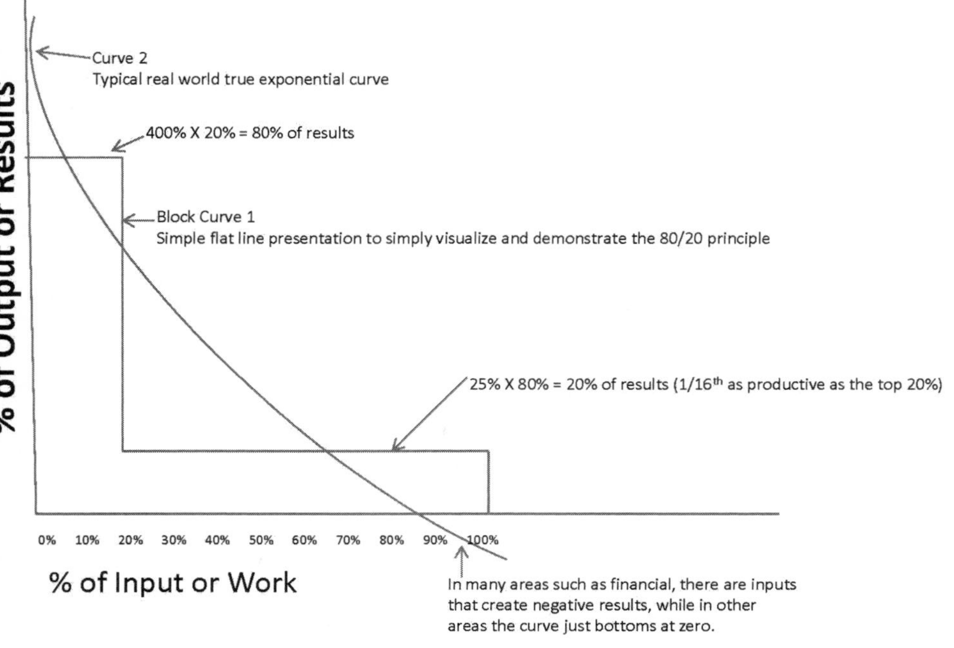

Curve 2 shows the true curve, and it is much more powerful and dynamic. It will pay you to study both curves and get this picture in your mind. In this case, a picture is worth a thousand words.

Graph 2
80/20 Principle
Salary Income –vs- Years

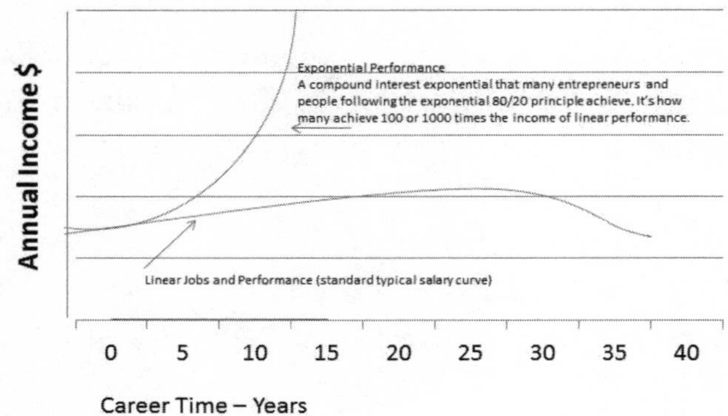

Graph 2 is one of individual income over time for conventional, linear jobs versus exponential jobs, like many ambitious entrepreneurs have. We get a different picture here, one of individual performance. People have a choice between an 80/20 principle exponential career or a linear career. Again, a picture is worth a thousand words. Do you get the picture? It's how the rich can make a hundred or a thousand times more than the average. The 80/20 exponential curve is the same one as a compound-interest curve, while the linear job curve is closer to a simple-interest curve.

In marketing, we know that no business can be exceptional at more than one philosophy or marketing business concept, which is similar to the 80/20 principle. CEOs and entrepreneurs have to find their marketing or 80/20 niches where profits and opportunities exist. Doing this most profitable approach is what the best do. They learn how to create profits and results in the real world in this manner. A business focusing on more than the big stuff will greatly dilute its results. Entrepreneurs have to survive in the real world. Linear performers survive in a linear world where they are somewhat protected by those whom they work for and their linear competition.

Very few people in business work in harmony with this principle, and those who do generally achieve far higher levels of success than those who don't. It is really quite rare for people to think like the most successful. It's rare because it's hard to change our thinking, mindsets and habits after decades of linear thinking. Just because we know this principle doesn't mean that our brains think in the 80/20-principle mode. Changing our thinking and habits is always hard, but it's very doable if we want to. I did.

It took a long time for me to change after I intellectually understood the principles. Keep in mind that the 80/20 principle is not some weird form of thinking but actually just the real-world correlation to success and economic results. It's merely a more productive way of thinking (sixteen times) in response to dynamic real-world principles in regard to our priorities and our personal success. It reflects the real world and how the universe works, not some false, static, linear concept of productivity that says that every dollar of sales is of equal value to another product's dollar of sales.

Success demands that we transform our brains (ourselves) to real-world, more productive, priority thinking that gets us rapid, dynamic growth of results instead of static, linear, limited results. I've used repetitive listening to the right audios (for example, Richard Koch's) while I drive to condition my mind to think more in keeping with the 80/20 principle. Listening to his audios for more than six hundred hours while I drove around got my mind thinking 80/20. It will likewise take you about this much time to change your mindset. His audio program (six inexpensive CDs—also available in MP3 format) worked wonders for me, and I believe that it will do the same for you. The more we work in harmony with real-world principles throughout all the areas of our own brain, the better we will do. In other words, not succeeding is all about living with false linear principles that don't actually apply in the dynamic environment we all know as reality.

For my first many years as an entrepreneur, I thought that I comprehended the 80/20 relationship, but I really didn't know or practice very much 80/20 thinking. I thought it was just a fact, and I was unknowingly practicing it with my ambition and positive thinking. At a conscious level, I knew it was important, but I couldn't see many ways that I could use it. Virtually everyone else I knew in management merely viewed the 80/20 principle as a static and stagnant fact. It has only been in the past decade that the 80/20 principle started to be more incorporated into success books. In the acknowledged success classic *Think and Grow Rich*, we have to think rich before we can become rich. That type of rich thinking and mindset is the 20 percent of what matters most that gives us 80 percent of our positive results.

Addressing the skeptics

I have tried to train highly conventional managers and workers to use the 80/20 principle, attempting to get them to focus only on what's truly important. Most often, my efforts did no good, though I did find more success with less rigid individuals who were at least open and comfortable with nonlinear thinking. The managers who didn't adopt 80/20 thinking typically thought I was an idiot for suggesting this unconventional methodology. They'd say, "How could I possibly think that I could shortcut thousands of bureaucratic chores that armies of people and 'experts' do at the big companies and in government?"

In their minds, they knew how the large leading companies in the world do things, and surely their slow, static, bureaucratic, linear, outdated, expensive ways were the best. And it's what they know and can do. They were in love with coasting through every day doing one-dimensional, static, bureaucratic chores that they knew how to do without using any creative thinking. They believed that they needed to spend nearly all their time and money to be perfect on the more conventional 80 percent of the work, and the other nonurgent 20 percent would take care of itself. They spent nearly 0 percent of their effort on the important 20 percent.

In my way of thinking, they were blind bureaucrats enslaved by management chores. I learned that it's really difficult for any of us to change our habits, even when we know we should. Of course, most don't know they should. Again, "How could a small business possibly know how to get things done right?" Of course, entrepreneurs essentially provide for nearly all the net new jobs created and economic and business growth in the world! The old dinosaur businesses are in the process of fading out over time, but they can't see that. In fact, I've noticed that all highly successful entrepreneurial businesses are much more effective at doing their work than the linear, conventional businesses. That's why anyone capable of running a growing small business can make a fortune starting from very little in any industry. Your major obstacle, besides yourself, is often the too-linear thinking of people who work for you and with you. I could develop most of the more flexible, conventional thinkers that want to grow, but not the overly structured and rigid people. It's hard to teach old dogs new tricks.

Avoid the linear snare. The more I learned about the 80/20 principle, the more I began to understand why most professionals and professional managers have such a difficult time adopting this way of thinking. Quite frankly, it's a rudimentary problem, as most of them don't have the slightest clue as to what's most important and what's unimportant. I didn't until my midfifties. To them, the urgent crisis and necessary work is most important, but we know that it's really the near-invisible, nonurgent, more intangible big stuff that seems small. The big stuff is too dynamic and intangible for most to see in their static, tangible, linear world. Richard Koch, author of *The 80/20 Principle: The Secret to Achieving More with Less*, says that we have to learn to procrastinate and be lazy on the 80 percent of the less-important work. He helped convince me to be lazy on the small stuff, as did Walt Sutton and genius authors Stephen Covey and Richard Carlson.

When non-80/20-thinking managers are provided freedom of action—freedom to delegate or to prioritize resources in areas they deem most critical—they typically throw people and money at random needs and problems linearly, without really understanding what is most important to the company's bottom line. This is why most businesses (especially large businesses) are so highly structured and the jobs are so rigid, limiting, and narrow. Very few people have the ability to decipher between what is important and what is not. They can't let everyone loose to create chaos. Therefore, decisions go through many levels of managers and departments to be approved. Most people and their work or businesses can't go through those bureaucratic barriers and be highly successful in the nonlinear world. And we're talking about *your* success, not that of a huge business. Even those of us who early in our careers had some ability to know what was important still needed to develop much more 80/20 thinking if we wanted to achieve much more.

I started off using the 80/20 principle by going after more of our most profitable business and eliminating our worst 20 percent of business as a onetime project to improve profits thirty years ago. Profits soared, but for some reason, I stopped doing it, though I did stop taking on some of the bad business from before. I didn't realize at the time that 80/20 is a dynamic way of thinking and an incredible way to approach life. The world is a dynamic and exponential world, and so is business. However, nearly everyone in business works to make it static and linear, so they slow it down to where they can do small, one-dimensional chores. But not so the most successful, as they live in a different, dynamic and successful universe and behave accordingly. Their goal is not to slow business down to a near-static linear pace like nearly everyone else. Which approach do you want?

Don't let crises distract

The 80/20 principle is also applicable in the realm of the negative in that 80 percent of the problems come from 20 percent of the sources. That's important to note when you're facing a crisis and thinking about ways to head off future crises. Bear in mind that crises are your enemy because crises can keep you from concentrating on that important 20 percent of your business, besides being bad for customer service and profits.

The hardest thing I've encountered with CEOs (including myself in the past) is to convince them that urgent and crisis work is the small stuff, not the important 20 percent. Unfortunately, it is accepted practice in most businesses that it's the critical stuff. It's human nature to attend to the crisis area first and foremost. Focusing on the daily, weekly, or monthly crisis at the business—and there can be one every hour and day—inevitably means that you will never attend to the most important 20 percent of your business. Crisis work is the small-stuff, short-term work that has to be done. Delegate this work whenever you can, and fix processes and problem solve to keep crises at a minimum.

Crisis management is toxic. The CEO's job is to minimize his or her crisis work and the crisis work that his or her business does to focus on the long-term goals. I never really comprehended this until I was in my late fifties. I've even had my managers and Vistage CEOs tell me that they don't have time to focus on the top 20 percent because every crisis they handle is important to the company, and they're right. Where they go wrong is in thinking that the crisis is their job, but that's because it's urgent, it's necessary, and they haven't developed and empowered others who can or will handle the crisis. That's the key error: thinking that they're the only ones who can put out the fires. They're failing to do their jobs as entrepreneurial CEOs when they fail to structure their companies in such a way that it truly is possible to delegate the responsibility of crisis management to competent members of their teams and to minimize these fires.

Perhaps the individual crisis is important, but it is rarely vital. A leader will have others respond to the crisis and will work to minimize those crises for them. Delegating the crises to others will allow them to take ownership of these crises. It's short-term survival work. We may have to do some crisis work, just as we will have to do a lot of unimportant necessary work, but it's not our success duty, and we also don't want others who work with us to do too much of it, either. Do everything you can to get most people doing high-value-added work. This is real leadership.

The few very successful people know that the world is dynamic, and the best business practices operate in accordance to real dynamic exponential or logarithmic principles—not static, linear principles. That's a vital concept I encourage you to take to heart. The best leaders are not inclined to do much static, linear thinking or work. They may not know the formulas well enough to know what the 80/20 principle really is, but they are in touch with the priorities of the real world. As a result, successful people are in more harmony with success principles, cause and effect, and the real world.

Wise leaders know what priorities to set, and they understand success (and failure) principles and thinking. The first job of a leader is to determine the important things that are working and to maximize them. The second job is to identify the 20 percent that is not working well and minimize or resolve it. As strange as it may seem, this is a relatively rare trait. The only way you'll have time made available for more high-value work is by minimizing or eliminating the low-value work. You also have to work hard to reduce the number of crises that come up and to delegate handling crises to the lowest-level people capable of handling them.

Anyone who wants to change his or her thinking, like I did, can do it, although it takes a lot of mental conditioning to do so. It also takes years to improve our thinking. It's best done by listening to the right audios while traveling or working out. It truly takes that much conditioning to shift the way we think from the linear to the nonlinear. The good workers just can't stand to not be very productive with the small stuff that got them to where they are. But it's the small stuff that's keeping them from doing the big stuff like it did me. It takes a PMA and courage to stop doing the low-value work you were so good at.

The other chapters are all about what the important 20 percent is and executing it. In order to do more of the top 20 percent, we'll need to stop doing something else, and that is generally the bottom 20 percent. As I've said, if you are continually enslaved by low-value activities (like crisis management), you'll never accomplish your high-value activities, no matter your intentions or talent. Keep a sustained effort to reduce your low-value activities by substituting high-value activities. If we don't substitute high-value activities, more low-value activities will just take their place. If you don't know what the bottom 80 percent is, just focus on spending more time on eliminating the worst 20 percent and sweating all the big stuff, and the picture will clarify itself. We don't even have to know or understand our strengths and weaknesses for this to work. The feedback will tell us. It's totally objective and based on reality.

Keep in mind that winners tackle the most important chores; they take on the top-level challenges. Over time, they become very bad with the small stuff and have to have assistants do these jobs. If you observe the successful, this is what you'll see. Winners understand that success really is a science. It has a formula. It's learning to instinctively think and act on sweating the big stuff while not getting consumed by the small stuff.

The shift from linear thinking to the right nonlinear 80/20 actions, mindsets, and doing takes ten thousand hours of right thinking, stress, and actions over a ten-year period (*Outliers* by Malcolm Gladwell) to fully transform us. Internalizing the 80/20 principle in our thinking is an important part of this transformation. So is taking on more work than you can do, which will force you to prioritize the work and minimize the least important, as is doing more than you are paid for. Don't let this scare you. You are only required to intensely focus on this thinking until it becomes a habit. You're going to be thinking and working on something probably ten to twelve hours a day for thirty or more years, so that focusing on doing the right thinking and doing for some of that time should be no obstacle to you at all. All you need to do is to start working on the dynamic principles and keep it up until it's a habit. Don't revert to the static small stuff or get stuck in a rut.

Our success depends on our long-term thinking over our lifetimes. While we can have great short-term improvements, as I have, our long-term success is determined by our improvement in our thinking, habits, and actions over our lifetimes. Let no one tell you otherwise. While doing the big stuff can greatly accelerate our progress, it's not a get-rich-quick solution. It's all about embracing a new way of looking at yourself and your business for long range success. You might even say that it's about learning how to be lazy enough to cease working so hard on the small stuff. All highly successful people are lazy! They're smart enough to know that working harder isn't the answer. Working on the right stuff is!

Chapter roundup

As an 80/20-principle-thinking CEO, your business duty to yourself and others is to incorporate a number of important objectives into your daily life.

» Focus on achieving excellence in that which produces most of your profits.

» Don't ruin your strengths and profits by overdoing the small stuff that only needs to be done minimally well enough. This is very difficult, as nearly everyone thinks that his or her little area needs to do all the conventional stuff perfectly. However, much of the work in sales, finance, accounting, logistics, quality, technical, shipping and receiving, operations, maintenance, construction, training, health, safety, environmental, labs, HR, ISO9000, legal, TQM, purchasing, and the like doesn't have to be done like it's what matters most. You can do much of the small stuff at perhaps half the cost of most businesses.

» Use the process principles in chapter 11 to do everything very productively.

» Think and define what "good enough" is, and then execute it.

» Any business can only be great in one primary marketing principle. Too much dilution of the business efforts by sweating too much small stuff or other incompatible principles will ruin a business's strength and profits. Our job is not to do everything as I thought for years. The successful have the ability to accurately predict the consequences of doing or not doing something while maintaining the ability to stay focused on their long-term goals.

Remember …

» Each chapter in *The Executioner* is about doing what really works in compliance with the 80/20 principle which is sixteen times as effective as linear work.

» The most successful people and businesses use the 80/20 principle by having an 80/20 principle mindset.

» The duty and responsibility of a CEO (you) is focusing on the performance of the most productive and valuable work and trying to make that most of your business.

» While the world uses billions of people to do the small stuff, your great, nonconventional success is tied to doing the most valuable.

» There is no reason why businesses can't cut their costs in half in most cases of doing low-value work.

» Work to do the necessary small stuff more effectively while minimizing the people and cost of doing it. The goal is to only do the small stuff well enough. Don't let it enslave others. Make it your servant instead of letting it become your master.

» The better we do at the small stuff, the worse we will do on the big stuff. No business can excel in everything. Therefore, our goal is excellence on what is most effective.

» Eighty percent of problems stem from just 20 percent of sources.

» Linear thinking is false, static, and conventional, holding that 50 percent of efforts generate 50 percent of results.

» The 80/20 principle mindset, the dynamic unconventional thinking CEO and innovative thinking have a lot in common.

- Nonlinear thinking is unconventional and dynamic, freeing us to focus on what matters most in the business and life.
- Crisis management is small stuff and diverts our focus from the most productive part of your business. Delegate the toxic crisis management to trusted members of your team, and minimize crises for them. This, in turn, will empower them to better handle future crises. Encourage them to use nonlinear-process execution principles (chapter 11) to deal with minimizing and handling the crises.
- Use repetitive listening to the 80/20 principle audios by Richard Koch to make this 80/20-principle thinking *your* mindset. It takes a lot of conditioning to master this thinking. Also listen to the other audios to develop the ability to execute what really works. Nothing works better than those audios that come from wisdom of the ages.
- *The Executioner* is about effectively executing your dynamic, nonlinear CEO actions with nearly all your efforts to give you mostly high-value-added innovative results It's also to help you break others' addictions to low-value work.

3

Navigating the Goal-Setting Process

The purpose of life is a life of purpose.
—Robert Byrne

Success is goal setting, and all else is commentary.
—Brian Tracy, motivational speaker and author

Every four years, soccer players, coaches, teams, and their fans from virtually every civilized country in the world turn their attention to the single-most popular sporting event on the globe: the FIFA World Cup. Officials representing the 2010 event estimated that the final tournament, which included thirty-two national teams playing sixty-four games, was viewed—via one medium or another—by a cumulative total of twenty-six billion people. Subsequent events garnered a similarly large audience. Think about that staggering number for a moment and consider that the worldwide population at the time of the 2010 World Cup was estimated at roughly seven billion.

Obviously, the twenty-six-billion figure was a FIFA estimation of the cumulative number, which breaks down to an average of approximately four hundred million viewers per match. FIFA estimated that around seven hundred million viewers watched the 2010 World Cup final. The passion those fans exhibited while watching the matches and following their teams was often beyond fanatical. From the body paint to the vuvuzela horns, and from the flag waving in the stands to the tailgating on the streets, World Cup fans are nothing short of fascinating in their fervor.

Of course, we Americans—even if we are not as crazy about soccer as the rest of the world—can relate. Super Bowl Sunday has become a de facto American holiday and is now the second-largest food consumption day in the United States behind Thanksgiving. The Super Bowl is typically the most watched American television broadcast of the year. Super Bowl XLV, played in Arlington, Texas, in 2011, was viewed by an average television audience of 111 million at any given time. And consider how many people across the United States and the globe also tune in annually to watch—or attend—college football and basketball, along with professional baseball, basketball, and hockey throughout the course of those seasons and into the playoffs or bowl games. What can we conclude from all of these numbers of fans across the planet? Quite simply, much of the world's population is absolutely obsessed and completely fixated in watching others pursue goals or cross a clearly defined goal line.

Crystallizing our long-term goals leads to excellence and ultimate success. It is universally accepted by most of the great success authors of personal development books and highly successful people in virtually all walks of life that effective long-term goal setting is key to achieving great success. I cannot stress this assumption enough. Setting goals and working steadily to achieve them without the fear of failure hanging over your head is the most important duty that you can perform to ensure your long-term success as a leader, CEO, or entrepreneur. As the above statistics attest, goals enthrall us, and yet they often elude us in our own businesses and personal lives because we don't set and actively pursue them in any meaningful way.

As an illustration, let's use a famous long-term study begun in 1979. Sure, the study is old, but the findings remain every bit as relevant today as they were when Professor Edward Banfield tracked the careers of a group of Harvard MBA students ten years after graduation. The 1989 results showed that only 3 percent of the MBA students had clearly written goals in 1979, and yet they earned ten times more than the other 97 percent of the graduates combined ten years after graduation. No other appreciable differences existed in the group.

Using the proven goal-setting process. Results like these don't seem logical for conventional thinkers, but they make perfect sense to those of us who have clearly defined goals and who have experienced the phenomenal power of goal setting. I'm one of the 3 percent, as are many of my friends. Consistently setting goals by the proven goal-setting process is the key to unlocking barriers to success, and writing those goals helps you to visualize them and change them as you evolve as a person. The same goes for growing your business. Setting goals is, or should be, a constant in your life as a CEO, and those goals will change as the business responds to the dynamic forces at work in the real world. Commit to making the most of your life.

When you realize the importance of setting long-term goals, it's like uncovering the secret ingredient to the overall magical formula for personal or professional achievement. And once you discover the potency of the goal-setting formula, you realize that virtually nothing is beyond the realm of your own possibilities. Goal setting is our own internal GPS that will lead us to our goals if our minds and actions are in harmony and alignment with our goals, reality, and who we are. You will become aware of opportunities all around you when your brain is attuned to your goals. In other words, if you're in tune with yourself and are open to establishing and setting goals that fit with your overall life plan, then the right opportunities will emerge when you look for them. Don't expect your goals to build to a great desire instantly. It takes time to complete the whole process and a lot of self-development with actions and habits before you can build an unstoppable effort that will achieve your goals. It works every time, so stick with it until it comes. It only rarely works very fast, because it takes a lot of time for most of us to develop our goals, thinking, habits, purpose, and our *why* effectively. The entire goals process is much more complex than what over 99 percent of people think. And it requires self-introspection and the right mind-set. You are equipped with the ability to be a great goal achiever. It bears noting that the first step in effective goal setting is to have a life plan in the first place! I'll discuss this more at length a little later.

For most of us, goals are something that dwell more in the abstract. Those few Harvard students who clearly defined their goals upon graduation differed from their peers in that they had enough clarity of what they truly wanted to write their goals down, taking them from the abstract to the tangible. As the study illustrated, that simple act yielded stunning results in terms of the financial and overall success of that select group of students, or at the very least, the act of crystallizing their goals to the point that they could write them down played a role in their ultimate success.

Effective goal setting is actually rare. With the importance of setting goals in mind, you might ask why so few of us actually set goals and actively pursue them. Surely intelligent and motivated people have heard and read many times that they should write down their goals so that they can attract anything that they really want in their lives, but these same people simply don't do it to the level required. From personal experience, I've found that truly unlocking the power of goal setting is much more complicated for most people than the way it is normally presented. Most people are told only a small portion of the information we need for successful goal setting. I've found that they think goal setting is very simple and easy. As a result, only very few people ever get very far in developing their goals, plans, and actions.

For example, while writing down your initial thoughts on goals is essential, that alone won't get you where you want to go. Setting goals and actively pursuing them is a bit more involved than that. You must have a plan. It's best if it is nonlinear, achievable, and crystallized into a meaningful, tangible goal that is compatible with you. Easier said than done. In fact, I've found that it's much easier to go to college and get a

PhD or an MD than to become a skilled and accomplished goal setter. With so few accomplished goal setters, the numbers seem to bear this out by a huge margin. I've also come to the conclusion that I'd rather be an accomplished high-school dropout goal setter than a non-goal-setting PhD. Planning, developing, and executing your life's plan and all the personal growth needed require a lot of time and effort over your lifetime. Highly successful goal setters spend thousands of hours on their goals in their lifetime, and they love it. Personally, I've found that we have to become the person capable of achieving the goals before we can actually achieve the goals. Otherwise, they won't work. I'm not promising a quick fix. However, getting started right can prove to be half the battle.

Focus on the long-term end result that you truly want. Each of us has our own personal obstacles that we must overcome before we can truly embrace and act on the concept of goal setting. One of the first issues that many people—including myself—must address before they can ever achieve their dreams is to gain a clear understanding of what they want and why. It's not enough to know what you don't want, and many times that's what people focus on the most. If you were to ask ten people off the street about their major goals in life, statistical analysis shows that most of those people would tell you what they don't want.

For example, the average Joe or Jane on the street would answer the question in a variety of ways, always focusing on what he or she doesn't want. "I don't want to be broke; I don't want to lose my business; I don't want to live from paycheck to paycheck; I don't want to be in constant financial stress; and I don't want to retire with nothing, like my parents." There's hardly anyone whom I meet, including CEOs, who knows specifically what he or she wants. We most all start out like this, but it's a crime if we end up like this because we'll aimlessly wander through life. We'll also wander aimlessly in our business pursuits of short-term, misguided plans no matter how knowledgeable we are.

> You read a book from beginning to end. You run a business the opposite way. You start at the end, and then you do everything you must to reach it.
> *—Harold Geneen, ITT president*

Note: What I think Harold Geneen really meant is that we successfully run a business best through reverse engineering. That's also by far the best way to do our goal setting.

Define your life purpose. I've also realized that it's not easy to define a major purpose of excellence in our lives, and it is even more difficult to believe with all our hearts that we will achieve our goals in a matter of time. There are millions of options, good diversions, enslavements, distractions, and examples from which we can choose. In many ways, it was probably much simpler in the 1920s, '30s, '40s, and earlier, when achieving your life's ambitions was often defined by owning your home and land, running your own business, or exceeding the lifestyle of your parents. Life was much tougher then, and there were few nice distractions. Today, most of us tend to think that we want a lot of things—vehicles, vacation homes, job titles, and "toys"—that aren't really of significant importance in the grand scheme of things. Growing up in a prosperous society with lots of fun diversions, most people aren't even looking to develop their goals. They are too comfortable with the nice, short-term diversions. In reality, though, the unimportant items on our typical wish list clutter our minds unnecessarily. There are a lot of people who can have very nice lives without having meaningful goals or without living purposeful lives with great goals. But not me. And maybe not you. How many people want to live a great, purposeful life?

The human brain possesses amazing powers if it is supplied with the right information. However, the human mind will not be triggered or thrust into a higher, goal-accomplishing gear without the right positive thinking and true, emotionally meaningful goals burned deep into the brain. It won't truly accept unrealistic goals, halfhearted dreams, wishy-washy visions, vague concepts, false wishes, and unimportant values. The mind will also not begin processing those goals on the highest levels if there is considerable self-doubt. This is crucial! Self-doubt and fear of failure kill more dreams and rob more people of success than anything else. Your brain will be unwilling to accept a goal if it doesn't think you can achieve it. You can overcome self-doubt by acquiring a positive mental attitude and the knowledge you need to accomplish your goal, working steadily to achieve the goal, and realizing that failure along the way won't mean you have actually failed forever. Failure is often an opportunity to learn more about how to achieve success!

As Dr. Norman Vincent Peale once wrote, "Action is a great restorer and builder of confidence. Inaction is not only the result, but the cause, of fear." Fear of failure is your best guarantee against realizing your full potential. You'll drive yourself right into a quagmire, and you'll sink in your own quicksand if you fear risk, challenges, and the adversity that will surely come when you put yourself on the firing line for something you believe in. Fear not! Take that first step to solid ground on your own unique path to success for you and your career or business. The next step will be easier! And the ones that follow will be easier still because of the momentum and zest you'll feel in your heart!

Know where you are starting from with self-understanding

I mentioned earlier that we need a life plan before we can set goals to work toward. Focusing on what you want, as opposed to what you don't want, is a vital first step. Clearing away the clutter and self-doubt is also very important. The same applies to setting goals for you and your career. You need to have a long-term life vision of where you want to go, and to do that you need to have a solid understanding of where you are at the present time. What are your current strengths and weaknesses? How about those of your business? Write them down!

It's not easy for people or businesses to have enough self-understanding to know where they're starting from or where they are going. We rarely have a tangible, definite point that we're starting from, like a map. This derails most—especially more complex—businesses, organizations, and people. Most don't have the courage or insight to own up to their weaknesses, flaws, obstacles, and problems. Few understand their strengths or weaknesses. I didn't. It takes a lot of courage to own up to the true obstacles and ugly truth standing in our way. I've found that this stops people and organizations from determining their goals. It's always our own flaws, habits, self-doubt, confidence, attitudes, knowledge, skills, experience, mindsets and thinking that stand in the way of achieving our goals. If we didn't have our own weaknesses and obstacles standing in our way, we'd already have the great success we dream about. What got us here won't get us there. It is difficult for us to evaluate all of this and know where we are starting from. But it can be done over time if we keep working, learning, and digging until we peel away enough layers of the proverbial onion to get close to the truth. I've found out that learning more about psychology helps. Working on the big, purposeful, nonconventional chapters of *The Executioner* will point out your obstacles. Working on the small stuff will only point out your small obstacles, which won't get you very far.

Start developing what you want and why. I first started writing down my overall and specific goals in earnest at the age of twenty-six, and by the age of thirty, I had a hundred-plus-page goal-setting book. At that time, I thought my goals were developed. Here's the reality: even though I had done plenty of goal setting and introspection and I had read plenty of good motivational and goal-oriented self-help books, my action, determination, and results were modest at best. I was starting to feel like I just wasn't up to the other confident, action-oriented, self-assured, goal-oriented people I was trying to emulate. I consciously believed in my goals that were too extensive and not exactly what I valued most, but I did have much self-doubt. I wasn't unstoppable. I suspect that most have felt in the past as I once did.

As I look back on those experiences now, I realize why I was not experiencing the results I coveted. For one thing, I had not yet tapped into my great creativity. My planning was very conventional, and I had yet to learn about the creative brainstorming parts of goal setting. I had too many goals, and most of my goals were just wishes or plans, although I had written them down. I also hadn't experienced what I call my positive mental attitude conversion that would allow me to overcome my self-limiting thoughts and be able to clearly see opportunity. While ambitious, energetic, and smart, I lacked a lot of self-confidence until the age of thirty-one. In addition, I lacked a well-developed, true purpose, and I wasn't taking all the necessary action I could on the big stuff to develop the inner confidence and self-development I needed to excel. The hodge podge of big and small stuff action I was doing wasn't getting me very far. I had no idea what the big, purposeful stuff was that I needed to work on, and I did not have the more implementable good strategies and best practices to work with. I was stuck on the intangible success principles. The big stuff I was trying to do was so intangible that I was very ineffective at doing it. I hadn't truly internalized or developed my goals. I hadn't made them tangible or dynamic enough, which in turn stopped my mind from responding creatively to my efforts to find the success I knew I wanted more than just about anything else. I wasn't reverse engineering my plans. I had yet to develop the unstoppable drive I needed. I only now understand that it takes time to build up the determination and drive needed to reach goals. That rarely happens quickly. It was tough to have faith in goal setting when I first did it, and I didn't feel the power. I didn't know that it takes ten years of the right stuff to get to that point. I still had time to go before I would have my conversion to mastery a few months after my 31st birthday.

Start with overcoming your own intangible obstacles. The first three years I was on my own, I was trying to commission sell and consult. I wasn't experiencing very much of the true magic of entrepreneurship or goal setting. Now I realize how much confidence-producing action my mind needed to grow and how many personal obstacles I had to overcome before goal setting could work. While I did have some hopes, wishes, and moderate goals, my plans didn't fit my experience, talent, personality, knowledge, and the real 80/20-principle world. And my major shortcomings formed a long list. At the top was a lot of self-doubt. Following that up was a lack of confidence, true positive mental attitude, faith, belief, positive habits, the right mindsets, nonlinear thinking, control, action, and leadership. While we don't have to overcome every obstacle to get our goal setting into motion, we do have to overcome enough of them to make a real difference. There is a lot more to it than most books suggest. We now know that it takes ten years of doing the right stuff to build our thinking and strength. Don't despair, as some have already done some of those years, and you're going to spend the next ten years doing twenty to thirty thousand hours of some kind of work. Why can't it be at least ten thousand hours of the right, big, success principle stuff?

Get into action on your goals. The brain needs action as a confirmation to turn on its green light to go, and failure to take action has been a weakness of mine in the past. In short, I gave myself a red light! It's easy to think about something. It's a little harder to forge a plan, and it's harder still to implement and actualize that plan. The same goes for goals. Setting the right ones is a definite proven process, and it takes time. You'll find that acting breeds more action and more confidence as you pursue your goals. Chart your course, cast off your lines, and head out into the big, broad ocean of your own unique future!

Find your overarching purpose

I mentioned a little while ago the absolute importance of having a life-plan goal in place before going about setting your other goals. Without a chart or map that designates where you are and where you want to go, it's impossible to plot a course to get you there. Thus, formulating a general plan will help you ferret out the key goals. Implementing a plan from where you are now to where you want to go is ineffective for long-term goals. In goal setting, we start from the end result of where we'll be more developed and reverse engineer our plan. Understand that effective strategic planning is reverse engineering and always evolves as we draw closer to achieving major objectives. That's a natural and highly rewarding process you want to be open to and encourage!

Hatch a plan to focus on your major goal. In the military, it's often been said that the battle plan must typically be scrapped on first contact with the enemy. But as any military leader or historian of wars will tell you, beginning with a good battle plan—or even some plan—and adjusting from there is far better than entering the battle with no plan whatsoever. It's the same way in our personal battle plan for success in business or life. You will encounter setbacks, adversities, obstacles, opportunities, and changes that will force you to adjust on the fly. But having well-planned goals, complete with action steps, is critical for your success even when you must dramatically revise them. Just as you would start out on a cross-country drive by referencing a map and making a plan, your personal life map is important to help move you from where you are now to the places you want to go.

Your life purpose drives your goals. Start with the goal that best defines your major or overarching purpose. In life, it may be charity work, excelling in an artistic discipline, or mastering a skill. Your overarching or major-purpose goal could be to achieve financial freedom, which I'll discuss at more length in the coming pages. Once we identify our major purpose, we can more easily identify other goals that will move us forward to achieving our long-term objectives. Don't be a perfectionist. Pick something to start with. It won't be what your developed goal will be, but we must have a long-term goal as a starting point to get the process started. Your major purpose could be any one of a million things that will drive you. It's not one thing. Get started and develop a great purpose in your life based on opportunity and how you develop. It's dynamic, not static. Your brain is smart enough to direct you to the right purpose on the fly. Have faith that your brain will choose wisely.

Our brains require this concise direction for us to effectively set and achieve our goals. I believe the lack of a major-purpose goal is one of the primary reasons so many people fall short in goal setting. It's not easy for people to discover their major-purpose goal, so most don't truly have a well-defined one. Others seek it in the wrong places. Unfortunately, many people never find it, because they do not know where to look. Just write a big goal down first. Being independently wealthy is a biggie, since this gives a person more freedom to follow his or her heart's desire. I've found that this works best for most people. If you're unsure of your overarching purpose, choose that one just to get you started. It will jump-start your process. It's best if it's not a rigid, static, conventional goal.

Dream big. From various studies of successful people, we can conclude that the most successful people have defined a major long-term purpose, a tangible goal that gives their lives meaning and direction. To emulate the successful, you should commit to developing a very big, major-purpose, tangible goal as your foundation. In studying and talking to many people who have created this foundation for success, I am convinced that you should err on the big side of your major goal without fear. You can always revise it. If you do not currently have a strong major purpose, don't worry. It can be developed. We nearly all start out with very weak resolve on our goals.

In retrospect, even the most highly successful entrepreneurs and CEOs typically say that they initially set their goals too small, even though they thought they set them big. Don't make this mistake. Dream big. *Really* big. And set your major long-term purpose goal without fear of failure. Your major-purpose goal must be tied to something tangible for it to be effective to the brain, although it will probably require you to spend over 90 percent of your effort on achieving intangible goals. The big battle is that you have to become the person who is capable of achieving your tangible goals before you can accomplish them.

Over my lifetime, I have seen many dedicated workers spend decades of effort toward achieving their shorter-term tangible and intangible goals that have no long-term tangible goals. It rarely worked much beyond conventional progress from what I've seen. In fact, that's what I did during my first few years out of school. Our brains need some green lights to turn on to allow us to achieve our goals. My first two green lights were overcoming self-doubt and an overarching tangible goal, although I didn't know it.

On the other hand, don't misunderstand this point: big goals don't mean unrealistic goals. Unless you are the leader of one of the largest countries on the planet, it would be unrealistic to make world peace (very intangible and complex) as your major-purpose goal. And if you are currently swimming in a cesspool of debt and on the verge of bankruptcy, becoming a millionaire in the next twelve months is probably outlandish and unrealistic. Given time, though, you could achieve financial independence, whereas you would not ever single-handedly achieve world peace.

That said, I'd rather see someone dream too big than too small because it requires that person to stretch to find a way to accomplish the major goal. For me, it took a large goal to activate my superconscious brain. Small goals did not draw out my genius. I eventually determined that my initial goals were unrealistic or not worth expending significant effort to achieve. But going through that process and making those evaluations constitutes goal development, which is always a good thing. Any of us will abandon or revise a written goal when our brains tell us that the goal isn't worth the effort after having worked at it. It's a natural process. Biofeedback and your own brain will work that out. Trust your brain. Be fearless. Do not be fearful of writing down the wrong goals, as your brain will figure that out over time. Write, write, write!

Again, my advice is to dream big … and then implement the goal, develop it, and revise it. Get started and do the dynamic process. It's up to you to be free to figure out your realistic limitations. Don't allow others to prejudge you or to determine your limits, even if they just want to help you avoid failure. I'm glad there weren't others around who knew what my written goals were when I first started. Some friends and relatives would have laughed and said that I wasn't good enough, creative enough, sharp enough, and so forth to even consider achieving those goals.

In reality, my family and friends would have been 100 percent correct in one regard. The person I was at that time was not capable of achieving those goals, but the person I became greatly exceeded those goals. I've found that to be the case with everyone. So never discourage your children, family, or friends when they try to reach the stars. Encourage them no matter how unrealistic their goals appear. They are capable of becoming great, although we all seem to think they aren't when they start. The same goes for you! Listen to your own heart, and muster the courage you need to dream big and then act on making the dream come true. Always start with the end results at a time where you will have acquired the ability to achieve whatever talent you need, and then work backward. Never, never, never do goal setting from now going forward with your current undeveloped skills and confidence. And never do goal setting with conventional, linear, 50-50 thinking. Always get into a big goal dream mind-set.

You can learn what you need to know. Most people have a difficult time grasping the fact that we aren't limited by our current capabilities. As long as you develop your mind and grow your capabilities, your goals should grow along with you, and—most importantly—your ability to achieve those goals also dramatically improves. You can achieve great goals if you have the drive to commit to following the universal success principles and only sweating the big stuff for as long as it takes. You are genetically engineered for greatness, and you are capable of developing yourself into the person who is capable of fulfilling your dreams. All the duties of a CEO and all business practices and thinking principles are learnable and doable. No one is better than you. It's just that some have started before you, and they have different talents and interests. You have as much greatness within you as you are willing to bite off.

When it comes to conventional goal setting, the vast majority of people zero in on an idealistic view of reality. They fixate on a world where they get to do what they love and get paid big money to do it. Then they focus on how to accomplish their static goals and plans from now going forward. That approach is totally wrong, although we've always been told to do this within the realm of conventional, linear thinking. Let me repeat: do *not* figure out what you love when it comes to unearthing your overarching purpose. What you think you love is not what you want; it's just a comfort zone for low achievers with little confidence to go into the unknown. It's failure thinking. Be careful about putting on blinders and missing golden opportunities that could play right into achieving your overarching purpose. What you love got you here, but it won't get you there.

Focus on what end result you truly want in the distant future,

not on what you love. Highly successful people choose their goals first and plan from the end result backward to where they are now. Don't buy into the hype that says, "Do what you love! Success will follow!" Life usually isn't like that, though it's nice to love what you're doing and to excel in a skill or discipline. Your focus should be on the end result you truly want and why, like all winners do. When you plan from what you love now, you're planning from now going forward and staying in your comfort zone, and this negates most benefits of goal setting. Effective goal setting is working backward from the end result, which will result in a much higher level of doing what you love. I realize that there are a few thousand books that mistakenly say otherwise, but doing what you love is failure thinking when it comes to goal setting. They're telling you to stay in your comfort zone and keep doing what you're doing. All of your growth and success will come from developing yourself by being out of your comfort zone. There are thousands of ways to achieve your end result. The odds of your doing one thing that you love may be a thousand to one against this single linear initial plan working. Remember, short-term and conventional goals are plans, not overarching goals that will activate your genius and superconscious mind to propel you forward to success. Obviously, this applies to your role as a CEO of a business or your personal life.

Plans aren't goals. There's a real distinction between a plan and a goal. You plan to go out for dinner or to buy a new car. Your goal actually drives who you are and what you want in life. It doesn't normally have much to do with dinner or cars. Thus, determine the great long-term results you truly want, and don't forget to ask yourself why you want what you want. Understanding *why* will force you to ask yourself deep questions that may lead you to a completely different overarching purpose. In any case, the answers to your *why* questions may surprise you. People will achieve their goals when the *why* is big enough. Suffice it to say here that you should make your entire active goal thinking tangible by committing the core concepts to paper. My advice is to plan on doing the proven total goal-setting process that works, instead of a little dab here and there that may partially work.

Once you have identified what you want—or your overarching purpose—you need to ask yourself how to get there. The arena of the *how* is all about action steps, clearly defined paths from the end result backward. Short-term plans will be part of the process. In fact, many of your action steps in the *how* part of the success equation will, in fact, be plans, not goals. The plans will lead to action that will eventually help you succeed in achieving your major-purpose goal. Be sure to reverse engineer and brainstorm your longer, short-term plans like they were goals, as this is much more effective.

It has taken me a lifetime to fully comprehend that if we don't have the right long-term goals, we'll dissipate most of our efforts in working for many short-term goals that take us in many directions, but not very far. Without the long-term developed goals, short-term successes will derail you as it as me. I've observed that that is the cause for most of the action-oriented doers stalling out in their success. I see it constantly with most people and businesses. I have stalled out in my success by actually successfully going off in different directions on the wrong two- or three-year short-term goals. It has cost me at least a decade of progress directly, but it also kept me from throwing another decade away. Lesson well learned! I've come to believe that there is only short-term planning to reach long-term big goals for the most successful. Truly successful goal setting is nearly always long-term goal setting that uses short-term plans and benchmark objectives. To me, long term is ten to fifty years. Of course, at my age, I'm forced into more five-year planning where there's less personal growth involved for me but more for others.

Chase what you know. The definitive place to look for the opportunity to achieve your major-purpose goal is nearly always right under your own nose, wherever you are now in your personal or business growth trajectory. And to find it often requires only further developing the current talents and abilities you already possess. The point is illustrated by one of the nineteenth century's most successful motivational speeches, Russell Conwell's "Acres of Diamonds." After serving in the American Civil War, Conwell developed a speech that made him a fortune and helped him to later establish Temple University.

His speech started with the true story of a farmer who sought riches. He sold his farm and traveled in search of diamonds. He ended up in Europe years later as a complete failure, walking into the sea to drown himself. Shortly after he sold his farm, the new owner discovered the largest diamond mine in the world on it.

Then there's the story Conwell tells of Sutter's Mill in California in 1848, where the owner sold the property in order to look for gold. Shortly after selling the land, the largest gold rush in history started when gold was discovered—at Sutter's Mill. Another illustration involves the Titusville, Pennsylvania, farmer who sold his farm in hopes of discovering oil. Shortly thereafter, the largest oil discovery in the world at that time was found on his farm.

Conwell's speech details many examples of similar stories, and he points out that most of the millionaires of the nineteenth century in America found their acres of diamonds right in their own backyards. The author makes the point that few people ever experience success going off in a different environment or different industry or different location or different profession to find success. In most, if not all, cases, the acres of diamonds are within our realm of expertise and in the neighborhood that we already know. The key to finding them almost always involves further developing and using the talents and strengths we already possess, and this doesn't necessarily mean chasing what we love, either. When we develop the right attitude, we'll see our acres of diamonds. We always will if we develop a great positive mental attitude and get out of the fog of self-doubt. I recommend reading the "Acres of Diamonds" speech many times to help imprint the major concepts on your mind.

Goals finally started working for me. My story certainly fits into the acres-of-diamonds concept. I found plenty of hardship when I went into sales—an industry where I was not equipped to succeed as a very detached, nonassertive nerd engineer. But I found my acres of diamonds in the chemical business—an industry I knew—the instant I had my positive mental attitude conversion and tapped into my superconscious mind. Doing so required me to embrace the 80/20 principle and to actively work to avoid miring myself in too much small stuff that kept me from thinking in a nonlinear fashion. Virtually every time I see someone change his or her course completely and stray from his or her strengths and experience, it ends in failure, so keep this in mind as you contemplate what you really want in life and for your business. While it's often tempting to think that the grass on the other side of the fence is greener when we're stalled in our current jobs or businesses, that's rarely the case. It's only our minds that are stalled. The grass is greener where you water and nurture it. Nurture your attitude to find your acres of diamonds, and rely on your known strengths and experience.

Use your annual goals as a battle plan. As soon as I had my PMA conversion accelerated by my confident chemical-processing action, I first saw the opportunity to become a custom chemical manufacturer. Then I clearly wrote my one-year and ten-year goals on less than one sheet of paper. It worked. Now I do that most every year in late December. It works. During the year, I brainstorm on major-goal strategy, and I do planning and self-improvement. These annual goals are crystallized, clear, and simple. This works for me and many others. However, I suggest that you do the entire process. Working on the whole process helps. It's like an overall war. We do all the analysis and plans, and then, on January 1, our next battle starts. We've got to take action immediately to update our goals and decisions for the year or battle that lies immediately before us.

The power of positive thinking works. To see our acres of diamonds, I think we must have a strong, positive mental attitude and must be committed to improving ourselves. The key lies within us. We won't find the answers we need anywhere else. The instant I overcame my self-doubt and experienced my spiritual-like positive mental conversion, I had a sudden realization that I really could make a business fly now. Only then could I clearly see the opportunity that best fit me and my envisioned future. That insight was instant and clear. Before, I was truly, totally blind as far as seeing my own acres of diamonds.

Through the years, I've learned that other people who don't exhibit a strong can-do positive mental attitude (PMA) can't see their acres of diamonds. They have not yet prepared their minds enough for success—much like I couldn't before my PMA transformation. I now can easily spot the people who have it and the ones that don't. People without a PMA might make good money, invest wisely, and achieve a high level of conventional success. Millions of people have done this. But they won't go as far as they could with a PMA and goals. Save yourself plenty of headaches and trust me on this: it's much easier to achieve goals with a positive mental attitude than without one. It's also a much better life with a PMA. To me, it was a hundred times easier and faster. Perhaps I'm getting too much into the next chapter, but a PMA and goal setting work hand in hand. Just using goal setting is one way that works to allow many to see their acres of diamonds. Getting in a lot of action through entrepreneurship is also very effective at helping us see our acres of diamonds, as we'll never develop without action that is outside our comfort zone.

Don't wait for everything to be just right to start acting to make your overarching purpose a key focus of your life and the goals you set. Actions speak louder than words or contemplation without follow-through. Start where you are with what you have. Begin without having developed yourself more, and then trust that you will acquire what you need if you continue to work, set goals, and sweat the big stuff. Keep the faith until it all works effectively for you. Whatever you do, do not wait until everything is right, as it will never be, and you will not subject yourself to the development needed. If you believe in yourself and don't set self-imposed limits, you'll go very far indeed!

Money matters

I mentioned earlier that a great area to look at when searching for your overarching purpose is financial freedom and security. You should have absolutely no hesitancy to make definitive financial goals. Think of money as your tangible tool that's needed, which can be used for good if you have it. Money gives you options and can help you to overcome obstacles. It's been my observation for decades that those people who are reluctant to set clear, definite, tangible financial goals never fulfill most of their other dreams. While most of the work required in obtaining success is personal improvement and achieving intangible goals, goal setting doesn't work without some major tangible goals. Working toward ultimate financial freedom and security tied to a definite amount of money is a tangible goal we can latch onto. It's something we can track and measure, and it's precisely the kind of trigger that will launch our creative minds on new paths of thought. Money is objective, and there are a million ways to obtain the money goal with a changing world. Do not limit your route to success. Money works like nothing else and gives us flexibility. It's just tangible enough for our brains to give us a green light, and it's flexible enough to use on changing goals and plans. It works much better than fixed, rigid lifetime goals that will likely change or disappear over the decades.

Every person, business, and charitable institution is extremely dependent on money. Money fuels virtually everything we do, and how we use it often goes a long way toward establishing the legacy of our lives. Money can allow you to be a better family man or woman because it provides you more time to spend with those you love, assuming that the acquisition of the money is not all-consuming, thus dragging you away from your family. It can also allow you to truly support the causes that mean the most to you: church, missions, health-related organizations, education, charity work, disaster relief, and so forth. But you cannot make a major difference in those areas unless you are free of most debt and possess enough income to pay all your bills, provide for your family, pursue your pleasures and hobbies, save for the future, and then donate your money and time to make a difference in the lives of others.

As such, the major definitive goal for most people is tied very closely to a definite amount of money as a tool. Achieving high financial goals represents financial freedom and requires personal growth that frees us to do what we really want and to pursue our lifelong goals. On the one hand, financial ruts and debt burdens normally stress and enslave us and keep us from doing and achieving our heart's desires. The idea of financial freedom, along with a clear and tangible financial goal, will nearly always trigger your brain to think outside the box, and it may also cause you to enter the genius part of the brain that most people never use. The big financial goal can set everything into motion by programming your brain for success. It will lead to great success if you carry through on developing a great purpose in your life, even if you don't have one now. Good goal setting will make the weak strong.

Ultimately, you will probably discover that your first financial goal was not what you wanted, and you will revise it. Regardless, I'm willing to bet that simply establishing that big financial goal will set your wheels in motion and force you to become active in developing your goals and creating action steps to a great life. Getting started is the hardest part of goal setting, but it is also the most important. Focusing on a clearly defined financial goal and setting projected dates from the end backward for achieving that goal will help us explore our overarching purpose in life.

Start out by deciding on a number that would provide you financial freedom, and decide what that freedom would mean to you. Ask the *what*, *why*, and *how* questions that are so vital in drilling down to a greater personal understanding about what makes you really tick as a unique individual. The age-old saying in goal setting is that "when the *why* is big enough, you'll achieve your goals." Everybody is different, but perhaps financial freedom to you might involve no debt, the house being paid off, and a specific dollar amount of investments and assets. Likewise, good health is a great goal. But then, figure out exactly what it would take for you to achieve that goal—what you would like to weigh or look like, what you would like for your blood pressure to be, and what you will do with that good health. Get specific, but start somewhere. Your goals will be developed over time, such that they will not be anything like your initial goals. Nearly no one knows what he or she really wants when starting out. Develop the habit of starting now with what you have. Trust your brain to figure it out over time. It will.

You are what and where you are because of who you are, not how much money you may or may not have. So start now on your path to success, and if it's money you need to achieve your dreams, rest assured that with the right mind-set, money will come!

Take it from the guru of positive thinking, Dr. Norman Vincent Peale: "Empty pockets never held anyone back. Only empty heads and empty hearts can do that."

Ninety percent of your obstacles are the self-improvement, intangible obstacles that you must overcome before you can perform at the higher level. I found that we have to work on all the contents of *The Executioner* every month to develop our ability to do the execution needed. Then the job becomes to more fully master them. Use all the suggested sources as they are all great and needed.

My Use of Intangible Principles

Achieving exponential goals never happened until I had my PMA mastery conversion. That's because I wasn't yet strong enough to implement the more intangible parts of The Executioner. I found that the PMA and goals are the catalyst to implement the best principles and practices. My success was executing the proven best principles and practices as I've presented. I wish I would have had such a guideline in my early years. In fact, I didn't start performing a majority of the contents of *The Executioner* until I was 55 years old.

The write stuff

In the opening of this chapter, I cited a study that tracked the financial success of a group of Harvard MBA students. Only 3 percent of those students took the time to write down their goals, and interestingly enough, members of that select few were the most financially successful. For those of us who have read a vast body of work about how to achieve personal and financial success, the finding isn't all that surprising. The brain requires information and tangible goals to spark the inspiration to move forward on a path to success, and the act of writing down a plan with integrated goals set to a specified timetable helps us get where we want to go.

Let's take an in-depth look at what I believe is one of the most difficult and misunderstood aspects of goal setting: developing our thoughts by brainstorming our dreams, likes, dislikes, priorities, fears, and wants. We need to have courage and move beyond our inhibitions and put everything in writing. Be in dream mode. Don't hesitate or deliberate much when beginning this process. Just dream big and write. Don't try to get everything perfect, and don't think conventionally. Once you have a draft, it's easy to keep developing your goals. Then you can develop initial plans, priorities, and short-term goals from all of this information. You'll perhaps start zeroing in on your true goals the hundredth time you write them during your development phase. It takes a lot of time working on goals to get past your conventional thinking for both the goals and plans. It's a dynamic process that occurs, like when we're playing sports. During the course of a game, season, playoff, or decade, we have to constantly adjust to inevitable challenges and setbacks.

Writing works *for* you, not *against* you. Writing your goals and developing them are proven programming steps required to allow your mind to work for you, enabling you to achieve more than the average person could ever accomplish. In other words, anything that you really want to achieve is possible if you can be absolutely clear about what you want and then can access your mind on a regular basis. I've found that most often when I set a goal, I won't have a strong driving desire to reach it. Nearly no one does. It can take time for that drive to build in your brain. It takes programming a lot more than one tiny speck of brain matter to achieve your goals or build up your desire and commitment. Writing and revising your goals will help with that programming. Nearly anyone who is not currently goal directed has the potential to become strongly goal directed. It's just a development process that anyone can do.

Note that when writing and developing your goals and plans, much of what you will do involves conventional, linear thinking and is not very effective outside of getting you into goal-setting action. The more you get into the creative and visual parts of the mind with both goals and plans, the more effective you will be because you will begin to tap into your genius. This is why blue-sky thinking, brainstorming, and spending a lot of mental time on the writing and dreaming process are key to successful goal setting. We all need to get past the conventional-thinking part of our brains and tap into the whole brain, which is so powerful. It's why we need to go through the whole writing-out process. If you can get excited about others achieving their goals in, say, a football game, it should be easy to be fanatical about achieving your own goals too.

Here's a great quote from Oprah Winfrey to keep in mind as you begin the process: "Create the highest, grandest vision possible for your life because you become what you believe."

Brainstorming in writing

Below, you'll find a step-by-step guide on how to best channel your thoughts and come up with an overarching purpose and accompanying goals. Give it some serious thought, and then take action and complete the lists below. Your success and that of your business may well depend on it!

Blue-sky-thinking goals guideline

Step 1:

Imagine you had no restrictions or limits on your ability to achieve anything in life—no limits whatsoever. If absolutely anything you could dream could be possible, what would your life be like? See nothing but blue skies—no clouds of doubt—and write down your long-term perspective of where you want to be in forty years (or the longest term for your age) and then reverse engineer back to where you would need to be in twenty-five years, and then in ten years. Focus on the longest time first. Don't be inhibited, as you can cross out and prioritize goals later. Focus on the perfect, long-term, blue-sky scenario. Have faith that the law of attraction, which I call the law of awareness, will allow you to achieve your goals, as it will. Somehow, get yourself out of conventional thinking and into a blue-sky-thinking mode to truly develop your goals.

Don't delay! Do it right now! And do it again later, and repeat the process in the weeks, months, and years to come!

We have to develop our goals over time, and we have to spur the brain into creative, nonlinear thought. Often, the mind will remain trapped in the conventional, linear confines we were all taught to embrace as kids. The first several written editions of our goals are rarely good, but what counts are the developed goals that you write and revise over time. If we want to achieve greatly, we'll need to advance far beyond the novice phase. Like anything else, it takes practice to develop skills. If you see setting goals as a process that will improve with practice, it might help you get over any initial inhibitions or self-doubt you have as you begin.

Major-Purpose Life Goal	10 Years	25 Years	40 Years (do first and reverse engineer)
Net Worth (Financial Independence?)			
Annual Income			
House			
Cars			
Second and Third House			
Other			
Recreation			
Vacations			
Hobbies/Sports/ Activities			
Entertainment			

Business			
Social/Friends/ Relationships			
Diet/Exercise/Health			
Family			
Spouse			
Children			
Education/Reading/ Learning			
Activities			
Mental/Education/ Spiritual			
Leadership/Positions/ Titles			
Awards/ Accomplishments/ Excellence			
Status			
Comfort			
Intangible Big-Picture Skill Goals			

I started out in Success Motivation International with their large hundred page notebook that I filled out in a few goal setting seminars and on my own. Over seven years I found that my personal goals boiled down to what I valued most. My annual goals would look something like this:

- get a dog
- go on a long family vacation
- enjoy several short vacations (London, Islands, West Coast, East Coast)
- get a beach house

- » enjoy a golf vacation
- » get more involved at Texas A&M (lots of advisory councils and such)
- » develop a good exercise and health program (working out and golf)
- » Improve the profits of each business by 20 percent (sometimes one business would be 10 percent and another 35 percent)

I do this every December when I am thinking about the new year. I write these goals down simply on a single piece of paper. This works out best for me. Keep in mind that it is a proven process to start out with evaluating everything you think you want as nearly none of us start out truly knowing what we want. It takes a true master and genius to simplify. I believe that it's our one page simplified true goal sheet, updated yearly and focused on the long term goal, that we are capable of focusing on. Then I would use the twenty approach method that's needed for dynamic development, problem solving and process development to keep the process dynamic. This is what my simplified, annual goal setting program is. Ninety-nine percent of my time is spent on the annual brainstorming that I do on my objectives. My annual goals are all aiming at my long term financial freedom goal.

Step 2:

If you only had six months to live but you'd be healthy for those six months, what would you do with that last six months of your life? What are the five most important things you would do? Write them out. You'll learn more about what is important to you.

Step 3:

When you die, what do you want your obituary to say? Write it out. Yes, I know, that sounds just a bit morbid. But it isn't, really. If you force yourself to ponder what the most important things are about you that would go into an obituary, you'll very quickly see what is truly important to you and what is less important. Do you want to be remembered as a person who gave to others? Who was so admired and loved by your family? Do you want to be remembered as a great musician or painter? Chances are, money won't factor in much, at least not on the surface. But remember that money can give you the freedom to live, love, and give back in ways that aren't possible if you spend your life enslaved by greed and others. In that sense, money will play a part behind the scenes. Don't forget that. Embrace it!

Step 4:

What would you do differently in your life if you won a $10-million lottery today? Would you help family and friends or quit your job? Travel around the world? Buy a big house? Or would you not change much in your life at all?

Step 5:

Fill this form out for each of your goals, no matter how many pages it takes. It should eventually equal the length of a short book. For intangible goals, use the same form, and try to tie each one to something tangible. Focus on the eleven big-picture-stuff chapters! Accomplishing much in these areas will allow you to achieve any goal. We have to *become* before we can *have.* Always ask how you can accomplish it while completing the answers. Write your annual personal and business subgoals down on these forms. Focus on the big stuff that you have identified at this point in the process. Doing so will trigger flashes of ideas and insights that you would not otherwise see! On the business side, the results will probably comprise your primary intangible strategic plans. The big obstacle is nearly always you—perhaps *always* you.

Specific end-result goal: ______________________________
Date for achieving:______________________________
Benefits of achieving: ______________________________

Why do I need to achieve this goal? ______________________________

____

Tangible obstacles: ____

____

Intangible obstacles (mostly your current limitations): ___________

____

Primary restraint to achieving: ______________________________

____

Intangible personal growth (or team growth) required to achieve: ___

____

____

Intangible plan (keep in mind that typically 90 percent of the efforts to achieve tangible goals are intangible, like your own thinking and habit limitations): How? What deadlines? From the end result, backward plan.

____

____

____

Tangible plan: How? Use subgoals or plans. What deadlines? From the end result backward plan.

____

____

____

Develop options. Evaluate them later.

Write twenty things you can do and approaches you can take to achieve each of your major goals (and five or ten things on minor goals). *This is where most of the power of goal setting comes into play!* I've never known any of my first five or ten thoughts to be very good. Go deep! It will probably strain your brain more than anything you've ever done. It's lifting heavy mental weights to build mental muscle. Then do this again and again. Bring out your genius and better ways to achieve your goals. Brainstorm for dynamic opportunity, creativity, and genius. I got this from Brian Tracy, who is the best in my mind, and it is pure magic. Static goals are not very effective. Give your goals this huge boost. It's this dynamic part of goals that is the most effective. This is where your freedom of action and your genius come into play, where it doesn't much with the static aspects. This is where most of my goal creativity, results and magic come from. It's that big.

1.
2.
3.
4.
5.
6.
7.
8.
9.
10.
11.
12.
13.
14.
15.
16.
17.
18.
19.
20.

Step 6:

Complete the following every day, week, or month (as many times as needed). Then do it once a year, late December or early January, when evaluating and assessing your goals and the progress you have made in achieving them. New goals are bound to surface during this process, which is what you want! The more often you take these steps, the more clearly defined your goals and strategy will become. Do not skip this step.

1. Write down your ten most important goals without looking at your previous list.
2. Write down your one major definite purpose as clearly and completely as possible.
3. Write down your major obstacle, opportunity, or goal that you need progress on now to progress.
4. Write out twenty answers, action plans, solutions, approaches, or alternatives to step 3. Keep writing until you have twenty. This is extremely difficult to do, but it will release an unbelievable amount of creativity, innovation, and results.

   The first few things nearly everyone writes are linear, conventional actions that are of little use in optimally achieving one's goals. The last few items will be very difficult to come up with, but they'll probably prove to be the best strategy. Do it at least every few days, as the first day will only tend to start you thinking, and it will put your subconscious (and superconscious) mind to work. It will be pure gold that comes out several days or weeks later.

   I can tell you that my initial plans to achieve goals are nearly always very conventional, uncreative, full of flaws, and ineffective. Don't be surprised if you feel the same way. But eventually, you will discover creative and exceptional solutions. You will have tapped into your genius, which is where goal setting will begin to work for you. Getting beyond our linear, conventional thinking is when goal setting really begins working strongly.

   In doing the twenty approaches, we activate much more of

our brain, including the creative, right-brain areas and interconnecting parts. This action in itself will make goal setting an order of magnitude sixteen times more effective. The twenty approaches to a goal will give us much more freedom of action in achieving our goals, which is needed for success. We can never do any better than our best alternative. This is how the great goal setters do it. Emulate them! There are a thousand or more ways to achieve nearly anything. If your first approach to achieve the goal gets stalled, as it nearly always will, you would have already developed many other alternatives. That freedom of action will pay great dividends for you. Choosing the better ways will greatly enhance your results. This creative approach also involves much more of your creative brain. It's what you have to do to be a great goal achiever.

5. Do step number 4 on all your major goals.
6. If this isn't working, keep writing down twenty actions until you experience a breakthrough. This really gets tough, but the last items will often be the best. Keep peeling the onion. It's a dynamic developing process, not a static process.
7. Write ten actions that you can take on your more minor goals—or even five actions on some. I've found (as have most others) that it takes a lot of blue-sky thinking and writing twenty different actions to overcome our self-limited, conventional, linear thinking and tap into our genius. We want exponential results, not linear results.
8. Short-term plans are usually an order of magnitude less effective than long-term goals, but they are necessary to have definite clarified plans to execute. They are mostly linear, conventional actions or plans required to take during a day, week, or month in order to achieve a yearly objective. Remember to reverse engineer these plans to bring out your genius.

I've found that when I wanted to achieve a short-term "goal" of

12 percent gain in our sales or profits during the year, the market and customers almost never cooperated. We'd have a 10 or 15 percent falloff and have to struggle to break even at best. The goal was out the window. Or when our business shot up 30 percent due to a good market, everyone forgot the goal and coasted. In either case, everyone would forget the goal. However, when we had a ten-year goal of going from $10 million to $40 million, I and others kept focused. We stayed on track. We realized that extra-good years have to make up for the bad ones. Keeping our eyes on the goal, we might even see the opportunity to increase our ten-year goal.

Short-term goals are, in actuality, really just plans. They're almost like a clock that governs how we spend our day at work. They are a means to an end. They are necessary, but they seem more like the frequent residents of that nefarious 80 percent of effort that fails to yield the top 20 percent of results. As a CEO, it's important for you to guard against personally getting caught up in the execution of the plans. Stay focused on the long-term goals and your overarching purpose. You are the compass, not the clock. Only rarely do the short-term, linear plans hold great power in themselves. They are just planned action steps. They may be necessary, but they shouldn't enslave us! Always work from your long-term goals backward to what you want to achieve this month or this year. Do not set short-term goals starting from the beginning, either. Successful goal setting is reverse engineering.

Remember, the process of setting long-term goals and short-term plans to get you where you want to go is definitely part of what matters most! You may feel inclined to ignore the written homework outlined in this section of the chapter. I urge you not to. True success is all about your frame of mind. It's about how you think and lead as a CEO. It's about training your mind to think in a positive, nonlinear way, and to do that requires that you tap into the ideas and insights that lurk just below the surface of your consciousness. Only writing and rewriting your goals will help tap into the creative power you'll need to reach the level of success that you envision.

Over forty years, I've averaged a 40 percent profit improvement per year, which represents well over a thousand times growth. I've done this while remaining debt-free and contributing much money and time to charity and other interests. When I set my annual goal to increase profits by five or ten million dollars, it nearly always happens. When I don't set these goals, as has happened in some years, human nature takes over, and there's rarely much profit or personal improvement. I've gotten to the point where I live according to Brian Tracy's quote of success being goals, while all other is commentary. These annual goals are more my current battle plan, but they are a way to keep my goal setting dynamic and up to date.

Chapter roundup

Consider the process of setting long-term goals your first major step forward in achieving the success you want in your life and in your business. Every journey begins with a first step, and this one is yours to take! Bear in mind that it won't be easy. Nothing worth doing ever is. However, low achievement is no picnic and it's a hassle dealing with small problems. You'll need to take time to truly think about what you want to achieve, why you want to achieve it, and how you can effectively plan to work from your end-result objective backward toward the present in a creative, nonlinear way.

Goals are magical, and if you follow the basics, your goals will come, as you'll be a magnet drawing them to you. This is hard to believe for people without much goal experience. Being an engineer, I've been rather low key. However, I've come to believe that my goals will be drawn to me, and they are. It's probably because of my awareness level, but it seems like a magnet. There is truly magic in thinking big on our goals. There's no reason that you can't find this magic like millions have done over time.

Today, goals are typically viewed in terms of materialism, which is why the focus is almost exclusively on the acquisition of great wealth to buy big houses, fancy cars, and any number of costly toys. I don't discourage you from actively seeking financial independence. In fact, I encourage it! It's a tangible goal you can track, and it's one that will trigger the creative side of your brain as you think about how to accomplish what you've set out to do. Just know that the financial freedom you seek should not solely revolve around a desire for things as much as it should revolve around your desire for true freedom to live your dreams and your ability and desire to do good for all that you value. In fact, studies of the wealthy people find that a majority of them live very modest lives. Take Warren Buffett, for example. America's most successful investor of the twentieth century and business magnate worth over $62 billion still lives in the modest house he purchased for $31,500 in 1958 in Omaha, Nebraska. In the long run, the true benefit will be a great life with personal growth, confidence, positive attitudes, happiness, fulfillment, and a huge contribution to and a relationship with others. You will also achieve more goals than you ever thought possible, but be patient. It can take quite some time to develop the abilities to achieve your goals—perhaps ten years, if you are on the fast track. Remember that it takes ten years of doing the right stuff to get the "pass" to use these shortcuts.

So, set your goals after determining what you truly want and what your overarching purpose is. Write down your ideas, and keep revising them in this dynamic, changing world. The exposure to thinking about and revising your goals a hundred times is what your brain needs. It doesn't seem to accept a one-time message, even if it's delivered ten times. Keep goals dynamic by the regular use of brainstorming, which is most effective, as is chapter 11 on problem solving and process improvement. The answers lie within you. You can reach out and touch them if you know how. Take action, and take charge. Get started on your path to your success dreams right now,

Remember …

» *Success is goal setting, and all else is commentary.* —Brian Tracy
» Most people don't set goals, but effectively setting goals and following through with action to achieve them is your path to great success.

- » Think long term, as short-term plans are often mistaken for goals and mislead us.
- » The important goals are intangible and long term but need to be tied to tangible goals.
- » When setting goals, think of what you truly want as a long-term end result, not what you think you love. Planning to do what you love as a goal is extremely self-defeating by people who don't want to pay the price of self-improvement. The place to start is with a major purpose or overarching purpose. What is your life plan? Find true north on your compass, and do not use conventional thinking on goals.
- » A desire for financial independence could constitute a viable, overarching, tangible purpose, especially if the freedom is used to focus on living the overall life of your dreams. What works for most everyone is to get your brain to tie onto a tangible goal. It gets us acting in our own interest but not necessarily being selfish. Our brains just don't work well without the right long-term tangible goals.
- » Don't be afraid to dream big. No goal is unattainable given the right nonlinear thinking and a solid adherence to the 80/20 principle. There is magic in thinking big. Large goals can be (and mostly are) easier to obtain than small goals.
- » It is our weaknesses and limitations that stop us from setting goals and achieving success. Identifying and correcting weaknesses and limitations (through personal growth) by doing what matters most pushes us toward success.
- » Self-doubt kills more dreams than anything else. With enough of the right mindsets, positive conditioning, action on the big stuff, and a solid plan on how to achieve your goals, your brain will reprogram itself to reject self-doubt in favor of a positive mental attitude.

» Brainstorming on paper when setting goals helps trigger the brain to chart a dynamic, nonlinear path. In other words, writing your goals and many options down in a comprehensive manner will give you ideas you never would have thought of otherwise. This freedom of action and choice will tap your genius and is the most effective approach to goals. The more brainstorming you do, the more success and options you will have. It's where the magic of goals really starts. When your business or goal becomes stalled, don't let it stall you. Nearly all of your initial plans will eventually stop working. The dynamic thinking will always continue on by finding better ways.

» Sweating big objectives is how we overcome weaknesses and develop ourselves through action toward obtaining big goals. We have to first become the person capable of achieving goals.

» Use the process and problem-solving chapter 11 as your advanced course in goals. These are the advanced concepts that are so great. Goal setting is problem solving and process development on what we want.

» The more mental thinking time you spend on goal setting, the stronger goal achiever you will become. Spend the time.

» Always think from the end result you want, and work backward to develop your plans. Nearly everyone else is using poor conventional thinking of where they are now and working plans going forward. Remember that goal setting is reverse engineering. You start the action plan at the end, which is when you have developed yourself to a much higher level than your current less-honed talents.

» Don't expect goals to build to a great desire instantly. It takes time and requires completing the whole process and a lot of self-development action and habits before you can build an unstoppable effort that will achieve your goals. It works every time, so stick with it until it comes. There is absolutely nothing wrong with you if you start out with a very weak effort on goals. We are all capable of developing ourselves to become unstoppable goal setters. We only have the limits that we place in our own minds.

» Work to execute the entire goal-setting process every year. Spend the time to get good at executing goals, as the process can be complex and difficult to master.

» Nothing works better than repetitive listening to the suggested audios and brainstorming your goals and plans. A strong PMA and mindset are needed.

» The three most powerful goal principles during the year to keep your goals dynamic are these:

  - Reverse engineer from the strength of person you'll be at the end.
  - Dynamically brainstorm twenty approaches to your goals regularly.
  - Sum up what goals you want for the following year each December without referring to your written goals.

» Make goal setting your magic, as have so many others.

4

Becoming Unstoppable with a Winning Attitude

The greatest discovery of my generation is that a human being can alter his life by altering his attitudes of mind.
—*William James*

Our greatest enemies, the ones we must fight most often, are within.
—*Thomas Paine*

There's a key you can use to lock self-doubt inside a jail cell. That key is positive thinking. Let's take a look at the concept in some detail, starting with Willard H. Scott. In the 1950s, Scott was a popular radio personality; in the sixties, he began balancing his radio career with jobs as the host of children's television programs; and in 1970, Scott began appearing on WRC-TV as a weekday weatherman. Scott also created and portrayed the Ronald McDonald character for a McDonald's franchise in Washington, DC, in the early 1960s. But of all the roles he played in his career, perhaps Scott was best known for being the weatherman for

The Today Show on NBC. In that position, he distinguished himself from all others in his profession in 1983 when he began wishing centenarians a happy birthday on the air.

In the decades that followed, Scott celebrated the lives of thousands of hundred-year-olds across the country. Many of them wrote him letters, telling him about their lives, loves, passions, and dreams. Scott began studying the letters and noted recurring themes as the centenarians recounted their own keys to living a long life. He wrote: "The hundred-year-olds I talk to don't claim some secret formula. Most will say they eat right, stay fit, practice moderation. Some say they have good genes. Most say faith in God plays a big part. But what strikes me is this: by and large, they are the most positive people I have ever known."

There it is. The key to longevity (and success in business) lies in the power of positive thinking. You are probably not surprised by the fact that a positive attitude can greatly contribute to a long life. "The Father of Positive Thinking," Dr. Norman Vincent Peale, set the stage for this line of thought in 1952 when he published his world-famous book *The Power of Positive Thinking*. It became a near-instant best seller and remained on the *New York Times* best-seller list for an astonishing 186 consecutive weeks! Peale believed that negativity and stress are killers of body and soul, whereas a positive outlook has rejuvenating and possibly even healing powers. At the very least, a positive disposition gives you a more optimistic view of life and of life's infinite possibilities. And that's a good thing! As entrepreneurs, as leaders of a business, we must embrace the positive even when the going gets tough.

We've heard how developing a positive attitude—and maintaining it—has helped patients overcome terminal diseases that science and medicine could not cure. We've read stories and articles about how adopting a positive mental attitude (PMA) has transformed individuals for the better and rescued fledgling businesses. The world of sports is also filled with one story after another about how athletes have used a PMA to build their careers. One of those stories involves Stan "the Man" Musial, one of the greatest hitters in the history of Major League Baseball. In twenty-two seasons with the Saint Louis Cardinals, Musial hit at least .300 seventeen times. He also won seven batting titles and three MVP awards.

In the book *Living Joyfully,* author Brian Harbour recounts the story of a pregame interaction between Musial and one of his former teammates, Wally Westlake, a career .272 hitter over the course of ten seasons (1947–56). Shortly after batting practice one afternoon, Westlake approached Musial and informed the future Hall of Famer of how good he was feeling on that particular day.

"I slept great last night," Westlake told Musial. "My breakfast this morning was great. I hit a couple of home runs in batting practice. Coach has me in the lineup, and I feel like I could get three hits today. Stan, do you ever feel that way?"

Without hesitation, Musial replied, "Wally, I feel that way every day."

Think about that. Musial played 3,026 games in a career that spanned more than two decades and went to the plate 12,712 times. He failed to produce a hit in 9,082 of those trips, but "the Man" never stepped into the batter's box without the expectation that he was going to deliver a hit, which he did 3,630 times. Even in the midst of thousands of failures, Musial's confidence never wavered, and his positive mental attitude was never shaken. A positive mental attitude made all the difference to Musial, and it can make a big difference for you, as well.

Cultivating a positive mental attitude

When self-doubt plagues us, we're inhibited and afraid to take successful actions. We let the fear of failure stop us from acting, and that in turn virtually guarantees that we won't reach the level of success that would have been possible if we had worked hard to maintain a positive mental attitude. Self-doubt can't live side by side with a positive outlook. Self-doubt is negative energy, and it's therefore toxic and incompatible with positive energy. Send it packing. It has no place in your playground. This is not real fear from external sources, but only our own self-doubt. I lived with this fear until I was thirty-one.

From personal experience, I've found that great achievement never happens for anyone until he or she can fully develop a dominant positive mental attitude like Stan Musial. Since most of us haven't overcome our self-doubt yet, we have to move ahead and overcome most of it along the way as we actively build a positive outlook on every aspect of our lives and businesses. Don't wait. Proceed from where you are with what you have, as it is this action that helps to build your PMA. I think most of us know a little about what a positive mental attitude is—and that highly successful people generally have one. Obviously, a person with a great job and financial security is going to be happy, right? Not necessarily, and that's just the point. The PMA I'm talking about goes way beyond simply being an optimist. That PMA is what Brian Tracy calls positively knowing that you will achieve your goals without the slightest self-doubt.

The stark reality is that most of us lack the perpetual PMA of the type that Stan Musial had and that is most often limited to the Hall of Famers. Sure, many people have numerous positive thoughts and a lot of talent and are very optimistic if they are decently successful already. See how that works when the chips are down, though, and you'll find that the optimism vanishes like the morning mist. That said, being an optimist doesn't mean that you've overcome self-limiting thoughts born of self-doubt. Those with a true positive mental attitude have shown self-doubt to the curb—not an easy thing to do. I've found that for myself and many who I've known, it takes a great deal of positive conditioning of our brains coupled with many hours of successful action toward our goals to transform our brains over to this dominant and unstoppable PMA state. The minute our minds are transformed, we eliminate our self-doubt. It is a wonderful thing. From that moment on, we can't be denied.

I've known more people with a PMA about religion than a PMA in any other area. I believe that this example might help explain a PMA to many. These people have an unwavering faith and complete confidence in their eternal direction, which is wonderful for their lives. We can see their glow. Most also had at least a somewhat instant transformation. Most of the better businesspeople I know personally don't possess a truly strong, unwavering business PMA, even though their dispositions and attitudes tend to be extremely positive and upbeat. I mention this because I think most people have seen or know of religious people who have overcome self-doubt and have a great religious PMA with a glow to them. You may have even made this wonderful transformation. They have experienced a conversion. In business, people with a truly unlimited business PMA have likewise experienced a conversion of eliminating self-doubt. We talked about setting goals. Well, a central goal that speaks to your overarching purpose is to stop doubting yourself and your abilities. Establish that as one of your key intangible goals, and you'll be on your way.

Acknowledge your current situation. In relation to your overall development, it may be important to understand where you are in terms of your PMA and what the rewards are for you in further developing it. In order to address the issues or to improve ourselves, we first must admit that we are not where we truly want to be and that we don't have what we truly want, whatever that is. It's not unlike the alcoholic or the sinner. You cannot make significant progress until you admit that you need to make significant progress. That is the hardest part for most people, whether it's alcoholism or a lack of a PMA. But the bottom line is that you need to take total responsibility for building your positive, nonlimiting beliefs, faith, and attitudes if you want to have far, far more success than you have now. What got you here won't get you there! And having that strong, unstoppable PMA is priceless.

Reprogram your brain to think positively. In *Think and Grow Rich*, Napoleon Hill devoted much of the book to obtaining a positive mental attitude and thinking successfully. He really got it right. In his interviews with Ford, Edison, Rockefeller, Carnegie, and more than five hundred other highly successful people starting in 1908, he drilled down to what they did to make themselves successful. These key, very elite successful were nonconventional thinkers. These elite did not focus on how to run a business tangibly. They focused on positive thinking in their reading, relationships, and the long hours of repetitive verbal affirmations they were using. They told Hill that it was their positive thinking that was so critical in their success in addition to goal setting and a master mind group. Hill had trouble explaining the PMA, since he had not had the PMA conversion himself. But Hill emphasized that the goal was to let everyone know how to succeed. He did better than anyone since. The key step forward is to submit your mind to as much positive conditioning as you can to develop a great positive mental attitude. How we think is critical to our success, just as it was a hundred years ago. It all starts here. In today's world, I've found that this is most efficiently done with repetitive listening to positive-thinking audios while you are doing something else so that it doesn't take time from your other activities. In our ever-increasingly task-filled world, listening to the success audios along with driving, working out, and so on is the easiest and most effective way I know to get the positive conditioning that it takes to achieve a PMA. It's also important to deal mostly with positive people and eliminate the negative or neutral people as much as you can. And don't watch the negative things on TV or read about negative happenings. The goal is to develop the ability to perform in a superconscious state where our subconscious, conscious, and whole minds are working together in harmony. It helps if you become more positive and action driven on the big objectives, as the small stuff beats us down. Any amount of positive conditioning and exposure is good and contributes toward our ability to do the big stuff. The more we get, the better, but never forget that the brain needs a lot of confirming action and success to give us the green light to succeed. And from experience, it is just like our brains getting its green light to go. While it won't be many readers' primary objectives to acquire PMA, the steps outlined will help all be more optimistic, and eventually they will pay off big. It paid off for me in spades when I was diagnosed with a fatal form of leukemia. My PMA just gave me the will to live every day to the fullest. I focused on the things I wanted to get done and my short-term goals (this book, among other things). I wanted to make a more positive impact. Then, when I was given a better diagnosis of survival, I saw that as an opportunity to have more time to do good things. Every day is a great day for me! I found that after I obtained my PMA and loss of self-doubt, nothing could ever stop me from obtaining most of my goals.

The moment of truth

While we all know that remaining positive is a good thing in life and in business, especially when problems or disappointments arise, we struggle against negativity and self-doubt all the time. Like me, we are all exposed to mostly neutral and negative things all the time and only small amounts of the positive. Yet, after immersing myself in self-help audios as I drove around on sales calls for two years for Success Motivation International and the year after, I was lucky enough to experience what can only be called a conversion. Let me illustrate the point for you.

Between the ages of eighteen and thirty-one, I was a high-energy, enthusiastic, optimistic, and generally positive person, and I was convinced that I owned a PMA. I did not! I had plenty of self-limiting beliefs. At the time, however, I didn't realize that all my optimistic thinking and experience had yet to transform my brain enough. From the ages of twenty-six to thirty-one, I was in love with positive thinking and personal improvement books, and I believed in success principles and the benefits of a PMA. I had listened to three thousand hours of positive-conditioning audios with the intent of eliminating self-doubt and had a book full of goals. I was made a warrior by the two years in the corps at Texas A&M and had spent three years of dedicated leadership training in the Jaycees. But it wasn't working for me yet. Though I was linearly (slowly) accomplishing many small things, the success principles and the big stuff that I loved so much were definitely not working. I still had no grasp of the 80/20 principle; I certainly wasn't applying it to my life and to my business pursuits. I was unable to put into action the concepts I knew about and believed in. This may happen to you. If it does, don't worry about it. Just be aware of it. Accept that it is natural, and never give up working toward your goals. Nothing is wrong with you, and you can still achieve your goals.

So, what was keeping me back? I unknowingly was holding on to my self-limiting thoughts and the self-doubt that resided deep in my bones. I was working on positive thinking and other success principles so that I could be financially successful and have more freedom, but I still wasn't achieving my goals. At the time, I hadn't realized that the process really takes a lot of time. Malcolm Gladwell calls the process "obtaining mastery" in his book *Outliers*. I expected the results too early, and that spawned a sense of self-doubt and failure that tried to push away what positive energy I was bringing to bear in my life and in my business.

Why a PMA mastery conversion should be your goal. About three I started KMCO, I had my positive mental attitude conversion. It came on in a flash, almost like a vision. The vision was of my ultimate success through a belief and faith in my innate abilities and in the niche market I was working to capitalize on. I somehow just knew that I was going to make it without any doubt whatsoever. I could clearly see opportunity, and I instantly became a great engineer instead of a smart engineer. I had obtained mastery in business, engineering, and in my mind, as have so many before me. I learned that mastery and an unstoppable PMA are the same thing in the success world. The point I want to make is that we can transform ourselves to another improved state. And we are not limited to one transformation. My second was a transformation to a CEO after I joined Vistage and experienced my big picture master mind group. Here I developed the right mindsets to perform the best practices. I'll cover my "doing master mind group" in the chapter about a winning culture. As I said earlier in this chapter, we as entrepreneurs don't like to play by rules that enslave and that others set for us. We set our own rules, and we invent and reinvent ourselves as we evolve over our lifetimes. Talk about living in a dynamic world of change! It's something to relish! It's one of the true joys of being the master of our own destinies.

Thomas Jefferson put his take on PMA very nicely: "Nothing can stop the man with the right mental attitude from achieving his goal; nothing on earth can help the man with the wrong mental attitude."

From the above Thomas Jefferson quote, it seems obvious to me that he had developed this dominant positive mental attitude, like I had. Achievement and leadership tend to occur to the degree that a person has developed his or her mind, thinking, and attitude to these proven positive ways. Developing our minds begins with improving our thoughts and mindsets. These thoughts lead to action, and action leads to results. The concept is simple, but it does take a lot of lifting heavy mental weights of opportunity and adversity to improve our brains (ten thousand hours!), just like it takes a lot of lifting heavy weights to build our muscles and physical strength. Acquiring a strong positive mental attitude allows our minds to lift the heavy mental weights, and it releases the genius that has been kept in chains by self-doubt.

Listen to positive messages to get your brain thinking positively. I highly recommend that while trying to implement the big stuff, you listen to the many PMA audios by the many great speakers and writers. I say audios because repetitive listening to them is generally much more effective than reading books, since we can do it while we're driving, exercising, and so on. It's this repetitive listening that will most easily transform your thinking and will have a strong effect on the many areas and connections in your brain. It will tend to get your whole brain working in harmony toward your dreams and goals. Most of the other methods that I know take too much time from our lives to do, but many also work. When Napoleon Hill did his study of the most successful self-made people, they had to spend a great deal of time repetitively reading books and developing affirmations and repeating them. They did this for thousands of hours. Hill said, "The price of ability to influence your subconscious mind is everlasting persistence in applying the principles described here." He was talking about affirmations said to oneself. He also said with regard to this, "When failure is experienced, it's the individual, not the method, which has failed." Please listen to the audios I recommend and similar ones. It's perhaps a hundred times easier and less time consuming to get this mental conditioning to develop your great genius and unstoppable attitude today. I've found that most people are so linear and conventional in their thinking that once they intellectually learn those principles, they think that they have mastered them. However, it takes over ten thousand hours over ten years of conditioning and action for our brains to transform itself to the mastery state that we seek. I did spend a lot of time and effort on verbal affirmations after having read

Think and Grow Rich. What I found was that I could basically repeat them aloud while I was driving a car. I would rewrite new affirmations every month, and after having read them a few times, I could repeat the general content from then on. These affirmations were on my thinking and confidence. However, it did not have the business and leadership content of my suggested audios, which at the time was a total mystery to me. Many good business and self-help audios lack what it takes to develop a PMA and the "what matters most" concepts.

In my personal experience, I've found that it is best to focus on the implementation of each of the major subjects of this book in order to obtain a PMA. Our brains need this executing action to support the mental conditioning training and build the confidence to transform us. It takes successful action and doing for our subconscious brains to gain enough harmony and confidence to accept the information. I found out firsthand that, in addition to the positive conditioning, it was my lack of the right action with what mattered most that held back my PMA conversion. My brain needed enough successful action to give it the green light to eliminate my self-doubt. Implementing is doing, and doing becomes a habit, and habits are very hard to break. Thus, if you are habitually positive and you habitually act on the big stuff, you'll reinforce the actions you take to continue on your path to success in life and in business.

Think positively no matter what happens. The first thing to remember regarding our thinking is that we are where we are in life today because of our thoughts. To improve our lives, we must first improve our thinking. That's what good karma has been about for more than two thousand years, as is "Love thy neighbor as thyself." It's only now that I realize how self-limiting and counterproductive my thinking was early in my career. I didn't realize how just minor poor thoughts and not enough big-stuff action can derail us so easily. We're all also exposed to too much conventional, linear thinking, too much enslavement work on the small stuff, too much negativity, and too many garbage thoughts, and not enough of the good in our real world. Never lose sight that our brains are constantly in need of a lot of positive conditioning and successful action.

Out with the negative, in with the positive

Our minds are where they are now because of the programming we have experienced all our lives. Some of that programming has undoubtedly been good. Some of it has probably even been great. But because we live in a world that is filled with very limited positive encouragement—from the news we hear on the television to the gossip we overhear in the break room—the majority of the programming you have received is almost certainly negative, self-limiting, static, neutral, trash, linear, conventional, and protective garbage. There may not be anyone in particular to blame, and we do not necessarily seek this programming. Most of this just happened to us, as it happened to me. As a result, we don't have as much positive conditioning as we need. According to *Outliers*, we need ten thousand hours of the right positive thoughts and actions for our conversion to mastery. Most of us lack the enthusiasm, self-confidence, belief, faith, trust, happiness, mental freedom, love, and leadership that we are capable of attaining. We end up having many negative emotions that we would benefit from by eliminating.

We can be thankful that we've had these experiences that have shaped us and given us perspective. We should also take comfort in the fact that overcoming our limitations and bad experiences builds character and strengthens us. Be thankful for your shortcomings, as these are opportunities to build your strengths. If we didn't have these limitations and adversities to overcome, we wouldn't be able to build the mental muscles we need. If you can improve the way you think on a consistent basis, you can improve your career and your life. Many extenuating circumstances, numerous outside sources, and plenty of people have contributed to our pasts. But if we don't improve from where we are now, we have no one to blame but ourselves. It's up to us to be proactive to condition our minds positively and to generate the actions needed to overcome our self-doubt.

Before my PMA conversion, it was almost as if my brain were a garden; while I had been continually planting the seeds of success, the weeds of self-doubt were far more in control. I lacked the right mental herbicides. I lacked confidence, and I couldn't truly see opportunity because of all the weeds and clouds of doubt. My mind would not fully invest in my personal goals, as I was always reminding myself—consciously and subconsciously—how far-fetched those visions seemed to be. I had goals, but they didn't seem realistic, and my brain wouldn't accept them. In retrospect, some of those goals were indeed unrealistic, but I didn't see it at the time, because I had a cluttered mind filled with conventional and intellectual knowledge. I didn't see how to chart a path to set new goals that were more in keeping with my ultimate vision of success. When I finally got the weeds under control, the flowers were able to grow uncontested, like the weeds once did. These concepts, including PMA, are the herbicide and fertilizer that we need to control those weeds and allow the flowers to grow uncontested.

After my PMA conversion, I understood what Napoleon Hill was talking about in *Think and Grow Rich* when he tried to explain how the most successful were able to improve their thinking to grow rich. Not having the conversion himself, I believe that Hill had trouble explaining a PMA. Hill did show that we have to have enough positive thinking exposure to overcome self-doubt to improve the way we think and become unstoppable.

Adversity equals opportunity

It's very easy to get caught up in negativity. When things go wrong, we tend to go negative. After all, adversity is tough. However, adversity is essential to building character and long-term success. With a good PMA, we'll see opportunity in adversity. Like Niccolò Machiavelli once said, "Entrepreneurs are simply those who understand that there is little difference between obstacle and opportunity and are able to turn both to their advantage."

Machiavelli was one of the most insightful Renaissance writers, and he hit the nail on the head with that quote hundreds of years ago. Being a leader or becoming a success always depends on a person's ability to overcome adversity. And that requires an unlimited PMA. Otherwise, anyone could do it. It's mostly the CEO entrepreneurs who can turn adversity into opportunity today, just like five hundred years ago. Of course, some other great CEOs, leaders, athletes, generals, and coaches have also. Adversity is as consistent as the ocean tides. It will affect some people more than others, and it will be harsher on one person than another. But adversity will affect everyone in business and in life. It takes a robust and powerful PMA to embrace adversity. And we can't overcome it effectively if we don't have a strong enough PMA to embrace it.

Adversity isn't all bad. All companies, organizations, and people experience problems, crisis, and forms of adversity. The more action and responsibility someone takes, the more frequently he or she encounters adversity. This is a crucial point! As we evolve and grow in life and in business, we as leaders and CEOs will naturally take on bigger and bigger challenges. We'll put ourselves out there, so to speak, where we can get whacked on the head more often than the person who keeps his or her head down. Thus, by our very natures, we're courting adversity, taunting it almost. "Bring it on!" we shout from the rooftop. We welcome adversity when it comes because we see it as a chance to learn from our mistakes and grow stronger. There's opportunity in adversity, not risk like the conventional thinkers believe.

As a growing and successful entrepreneur, I've had to overcome a hundred times the business adversity that most people have had to face. It's what I do. For the most part, people either become successful or fail depending on their response to the problems they encounter. If you see a problem as an opportunity, you won't get upset or depressed about it. If you see a problem as something horrible, the negativity will drag you down faster than wearing concrete boots at the beach. In my business, it has caused the more linear managers whom I have had to think that I've been doing it all wrong. They think that problems follow me and that I'm somewhat flawed. They think that they could avoid business adversity. Of course, they can avoid most adversity by doing nothing but small chores and not trying to grow, which is what they do.

For the vast majority of people, problems are viewed as something totally negative. Problems are to be avoided at all costs, even if it means not taking a risk that could launch a company or a career. As an entrepreneur, I enthusiastically look for problems to solve. The problem that people who work for others have is that they are protected from most opportunity and adversity. They are denied much of the heavy lifting that builds success muscles. As a consequence, they never develop the stamina and success muscles to break out of their conventional lives, and they therefore never reach their full potential. Granted, many folks are just as happy not to break out. They like their self-made prisons of unchallenging routines, but it's still a shame.

Don't get too comfortable. As a CEO, you face the same dangers. Things go just great. Everything is fine. And suddenly you stop pushing yourself to take on new challenges and risks that will position the company to capitalize on new opportunities for the future. If you're feeling too comfy, you probably are. Take a good hard look at yourself. Are you caught up in the Peter Principle? Are you mired in a stable comfort zone of activity and remaining pretty static and conventional by avoiding much opportunity and adversity? That's why I caution you to watch out for your comfort zone, and when you inevitably hit it, I encourage you to act in a positive way to get out of it. There seems to be a strong tendency in all of us wanting to revert to conventional thinking to "put our success on hold." The comfort zone is simply a relapse to the conventional. Do not sink yourself back into the conventional.

People with an unlimited PMA build their success muscles by combating adversity with action. Think about it this way: an athlete in training needs resistance in order to develop his or her muscles. He or she can do squats and perform the bench-press movement without any weight for hours at a time and perhaps see some muscle development. But if he or she really wants to grow and develop their muscles for peak performance, he or she needs to perform those movements under the duress of added weight.

The same principle applies to developing a PMA. As you are burdened with the weight of adversity, your muscles develop because of the actions you take. And if you are in action and growing, that means that you will inevitably suffer from growing pains. If you are constantly avoiding adversity, you are missing the opportunity to train and gain. You will then stop growing. If we never had adversity, we would never be forced to think deeply, call on our subconscious minds to do something great, and build our success muscles and confidence. Successful people with strong PMAs have the courage to seek and embrace action, adversity, and opportunity. Napoleon Hill says every adversity has the seed of an equal or greater benefit in it. This is why people with strong PMAs continue to grow, take action, develop, and use their creativity, genius, and leadership, while people without a PMA tend to let that seed that Hill referenced die in the drought of adversity.

Encourage positive thinking. In the face of adversity, I choose to be on the action, strength, fun, opportunity, and adversity side without fear. I also encourage every member of my team to respond in the same way when problems arise. When we empower the people who work for us, we give them the ability to build their success muscles by letting them face both opportunity and adversity. That's an important thing to keep in mind as you encourage a positive, performance-based culture in your company. What we can gather from virtually all the success principles and sources on personal development is that success ultimately comes from our PMAs and how we think. It is not a result of intellectual knowledge. This means that you need to only have positive, can-do people working for you. Build a positive problem-solving team, and set an example by leading them in a positive way. Write down twenty approaches that you can do to develop a more positive team. Also, write down twenty approaches that you can do to associate with more positive people and less negative people. This brainstorming can be very empowering to you.

People with a PMA and no self-doubt who have achieved this conversion have unlimited faith that they will achieve their goals and only ask how they will achieve whatever they want, and then they take action. Once you know the difference, I'm sure that you'll want a true conversion as your goal, and you won't want to stop until you get there. When my positive mental switch finally flipped, I gained a truly positive mental attitude. I then had total faith and belief in myself and my goals. I could clearly and easily see opportunity in most aspects of my business and fully respond to it. No obstacle could stop me. Others also fed off my energy and believed in me. I took the leap of faith to jump into truly entrepreneurial business, and I embraced all the challenges that went along with it. It was easy to start and run my business, although I was a novice and certainly did it the hard way. I guess that we all do, since no one knows how to run a business before he or she starts. We all learn on the fly and really only learn when we're forced to. While we're facing challenges, it's imperative that we keep a great positive outlook.

Anxiety stems from self-doubt

It's quite natural for us to worry about our lives and our businesses. After all, even if we embrace adversity and face it with positive mental attitudes, that doesn't mean that bad things won't happen that could do serious harm. You might say that we're wired to worry, and self-doubt fans that unsurprising human tendency. Worrying is negative goal setting. It's inhibiting to our abilities to drive forward toward success.

Worrying is toxic for you. I've had to learn to eliminate nearly all worrying in my life, even after my PMA conversion. When a major concern like worry hits my brain, I develop a plan for how I'll address the problem and start implementing the plan. There's nothing more I can do about it. Then I wrap myself up in either a major project or a daydream on sports or business or some movie I saw until the worry is converted to a concern. It works. I also make sure that I listen to a lot of the good motivational audios. It is very bad for us to worry, and it was very bad for me after I had my PMA. Be very proactive and committed to take action and not worry. You are the CEO of your mind and the captain of your ship. Do not worry!

Until people eliminate self-doubt and self-limiting thoughts and experience enough of the right action to convince the brain, their subconscious minds and whole brains will not tap into their genius, energy, vision, faith, belief, creativity, and enthusiasm that are necessary to succeed at peak levels. A PMA occurs only when self-limiting thoughts are overcome, allowing wonderful can-do thoughts to control us. Once self-limitations are removed and we achieve harmony in the various areas and connections of our brains, our minds are freed to blossom. This is when we get our conscious and subconscious minds in alignment with action on the right thinking, practices, habits, and principles. A PMA occurs when we get our brains in harmony, which, as we've learned, isn't so easy.

The most practical and beneficial approach to building a PMA is to saturate and train your mind by listening to lots of audio recordings pertaining to positive success principles. Listen while driving, traveling, exercising, fishing, gardening, and so on. It's very easy to do with audios, and it doesn't take any time away from your life. We all have that much time, and it takes that much time to change our flawed conventional thinking. This is how others have gotten into the creative, problem-solving, and implementation parts of the brain. These audios and other positive conditioning get through to the other parts of our brains very effectively with repetition. We have to get far past the intellectual understanding. Working on the CEO duties of a leader, *The Executioner* gives us the right action, doing, feedback, and results.

Below are ten steps you can take to effectively develop your true PMA.

1. Develop big goals in detail—it keeps the small stuff out of our minds.
2. Understand how to talk, think, and state things positively and in the present tense. I am. I do.
3. Upgrade who you spend time with. You are who you associate with the most.
4. Read books on positive thinking.

5. Eliminate most (not all) of the negative and neutral garbage of TV, radio, newspapers, and negative people.
6. Use positive, self-spoken affirmations (pictures/posters on your goals). Constantly tell yourself that you love people and your work and that you take the positive view on all adversity. Read about positive affirmations and make an audio of them to listen to. Even slight negative thoughts have a very adverse effect on us.
7. Attend self-help seminars.
8. Listen to positive audios with repetition. It's the surest and best way to self-improvement. Listening to these audios a thousand hours a year will work every time.
9. Set a goal to obtain a PMA with the absence of self-doubt.
10. Get into action and keep in action, which develops confidence and experience. The brain has to have this confirming action to give it the green light to transformation. Inaction in this area delayed my development of a true PMA.

Develop a positive mental attitude strong enough to have the courage and vision to take the leap to an opportunity that puts you at risk. Oftentimes, the people who did this were ambitious with goals, and they had to create a business or become a CEO or the equivalent to achieve their life goals.

When it comes right down to it, most if not all of us are lazy. It's human nature. We won't act for our own betterment, and we won't respond to adversity until we feel that we have to. Even then, it takes a lot of courage to put ourselves in harm's way when we'd otherwise like to sit back and stay safe. Many of us never do act. Many of us don't even get to taste the type of success I'm talking about, and I guess that's okay. Not all of us want to lead the life of an entrepreneurial CEO or of a CEO of ourselves. Still, for those of us who do, through our actions and the application of positive thinking, we have access to a world that offers rich intellectual and financial rewards. My lack of action to overcome adversity made it difficult for me to overcome my self-doubt. When I spent a year with a failing chemical plant in a mess to run, I was forced to get into a lot of overcoming-adversity action to straighten it out. This action gave my brain the confidence it needed to eliminate my self-doubt. As a result, my brain finally gave me the green light that I needed. Previously, despite all the time I'd spent on positive conditioning, it never occurred to me that it was the right action I needed to eliminate my self-doubt.

Those of us who are the most successful naturally tend to stand in front of the proverbial oncoming train, which is scary, to say the least. Talk about needing to maintain a positive mental attitude! In Sun Tzu's 2,500-year-old classic *The Art of War*, when speaking of developing his warriors to win, he said, "When people fall into danger, they are then able to strive for victory." In other words, it takes action in the face of adversity to develop a successful warrior. It builds great confidence. Entrepreneurial CEOs and leaders put themselves in the way of having to face adversity and the needed action like Sun Tzu did his warriors. The next chapter covers the action needed.

Chapter roundup

Although much has been written about the power of positive thinking, it is surprising how few of us truly possess a true positive mental attitude with the absence of self-doubt. Developing this PMA requires hard work, time, and dedication, but it is possibly the most critical ingredient to your success. The mind must be taught how to see negatives as positives and to reject the tendency to worry about problems. Remember that our brains require thousands of hours of positive thoughts to improve our thinking and to overcome the many thousands of hours of neutral and negative thoughts we're exposed to. That's the reason why repetitive listening to the suggested audios is perhaps the best thing you can do for yourself. We must overcome self-doubt to where it will not cloud all our thinking and actions. The most successful practice positive thinking in virtually every situation they face, and they come out the winners! Obtaining this transformational PMA will make you unstoppable and free your mind to where you can see opportunity and experience harmony that others can't. It is a very wonderful thing, and you can do it too!

Remember …

» A positive mental attitude with the absence of self-doubt is a truly great asset to a leader. There is magic in having a great PMA in which people who don't have it can't comprehend.

» A truly positive mental attitude transformation will ensure your ultimate success. Practically nothing can stop the person with a strong PMA with the absence of self-doubt.

» Fear and doubt prevent us from achieving what we truly want.

» Hire and develop your team to be can-do optimists. Set a good example in what you do.

» Optimism alone is only a good step on the way to a truly positive mental attitude. An optimist still is subject to self-doubt that will retard progress on the path of success.

» It takes a truly positive mental attitude to have the courage to constantly put yourself in the way of adversity and unknown opportunity. The successful action of overcoming adversity and conquering opportunity strengthens your PMA and your ability to think creatively and achieve more.

» Expect to experience a PMA conversion when all the reprogramming of your brain combined with action comes together in a flash of wonderful insight.

» Follow the ten steps to developing a truly positive mental attitude, especially the repetition of listening to the suggested audios to the point that a PMA with the absence of self-doubt is who you are. Even eliminate most of your neutral thinking. You can never do too much.

» It takes ten thousand hours of the right thinking and actions over ten years to obtain the PMA mastery transformation (*Outliers* by Malcolm Gladwell). *The Executioner* is all about the right thinking and actions. We are mostly all capable of obtaining this mastery like the best. A hundred thousand hours of hard dedicated action on the conventional and wrong stuff won't cut it. Listening to the suggested audios is a lot of what it takes. However, nothing will seem to come from this listening until these audios become your mindset. The rest is the needed action, along with doing more than paid for, creating a lot of freedom of action and advancing your ability to execute the practices described in *The Executioner.*

» Develop the habit of listening to PMA audios where it doesn't take time from your other activities, such as when you're driving or traveling or working out. It's about the only way that seems to work to obtain the necessary few thousand hours of mental conditioning needed for us. I suggest that you repetitively listen to these audios for an hour or two every day as you travel or such, where it doesn't take time from your other activities. The power is pure magic. It will transform your thinking and work every time. Don't lose faith in the listening, because most people will see little change for the first few years.

» You tend to become the people with whom you associate. Write down ten things you can do to spend more time with more positive and more successful people.

» Always be very aware of any negative or nonproductive thinking, and stop it immediately. It's that harmful. Never be negative against yourself, your family, or your team. Don't expect perfection from yourself, your family or your team. When adversity arises, deal with it positively.

» I believe that until we have had the powerful PMA transformation to mastery, the positive thinking force will be quite weak within us.

» We are mostly all capable of having the wonderful PMA transformation with the elimination of self-doubt. Be cognizant of how you think about anything.

5

Building Your Success Muscles and Ability Through Action

Action will remove the doubts that theory cannot solve.
—Tehyi Hsieh

Action is the foundation key to all successes.
—Anthony Robbins

Building your success muscles through action

Life is all about forward movement. If we're not growing and changing, we're lost in paralyzing inertia that can sap the vitality out of us. That's why action is so important and why I have emphasized it throughout these earlier pages. We only truly learn by action, through *doing*. If we are to achieve the success in life and business that we want, we have to be willing to stick our necks out and take prudent and concerted action without the fear of failure or self-doubt weighing on our backs.

The action that generates our success is the action that focuses on what matters most—that all-important 20 percent of what we do that yields 80 percent of desired results. It drives us away from stagnation, and it's also what we need to overcome adversity.

The real doers in the world thrive on action, and it's how they build their success muscles. They definitely aren't couch potatoes or passive maintainers. We've all learned that the world belongs to those who do something, and it does. Action doers are quite rare. Are you a doer or a passive looker? Are you seeking a comfort zone so that you can relax and smell the roses, or are you constantly pushing the envelope to create new challenges and new rewards? These are all very important questions to consider. There are no wrong answers. But whatever answers you come up with, it pays to know either way. It pays to know what you really want, and then it pays to actually take active steps to go out and get it. Be aware that people who succeed through action are not any smarter than most other people, and they do not make the right decisions all the time. However, a strong action orientation creates a lot of opportunity and experience that allowed them to develop so much more than their less active counterparts. In so doing, they learned from the action and grew strong and capable.

"Think for yourself. No one else is qualified." ~ *Frank Vizarre*

On the counter side, most talented hard workers doing small-stuff work do not generate much meaningful action that leads to opportunity, so they never grow and develop their action muscles and ability to achieve the great results they want. This was the case with me until I reached the age of thirty-one. Even though I was constantly working over seventy hours a week, I had no concept of the action needed and how to get into that action. I didn't even know that I was lacking this action, although I felt it. Even after three years in independent business, I was dead in the water just doing conventional, linear enslavement chores as I had done in the previous four years working for others. So were most of my smart and talented friends who also wanted to make more money.

I was trying to do what other entrepreneurs were doing that looked so easy to me, but somehow it wasn't happening. However, in the Jaycees, I did gain a lot of confidence with good leadership action.

Success and mastery requires action and effort over a long period of time on the right principles to build the strength you need. The more intangible, nonlinear action you take, the better you will get at executing, and the more you'll grow as a leader. We can all learn and develop greatly by doing this action. However, this opportunity-producing, nonconventional action is very elusive and very misunderstood. In anything new like this intangible action, we need to find a way to get into the action so that we can learn. Like a lot of things in life, taking the right action is not so easy. I found that out the hard way when I first started out. My long work hours weren't creating the action I needed to build my own strengths and create the opportunities that would grow my career. While all the positive mental conditioning, business learning, and goal setting that I had done were enough to keep me trying, they weren't enough to get me into action and build my confidence and success muscles. What was wrong? I was just doing linear, conventional, static, small-stuff work; I wasn't a true CEO entrepreneur. I was liberated when I finally got into some action with Success Motivation and the small plant where I was CEO.

I rid myself of the pervasive self-doubt that was pushing me into inertia. Then when I chose to take action without the fear of risk and failure in starting my chemical business, things continued to turn around right away. I was riding on the bull and was forced to think and make significant decisions every hour, day, week, and month. I found myself developing quickly as an entrepreneur, and my confidence soared. Once in motion, I remained in motion. After a year of this action, I had developed myself into a strong entrepreneur, as have millions of entrepreneurs who were able to develop through strong action. Please understand that at this time, my leadership, marketing, organizational, problem-solving, people, culture, and goal-setting abilities were quite weak. But I had transformed myself into a true strong, confident, entrepreneurial warrior, and I had transformed my positive mental attitude to a point that I had overcome the self-doubt that was holding me back. Once started in my entrepreneurial business, events forced me to stay in action. This action of moving forward and actively serving our customers and employees in a meaningful way was the wonderful feeling that I wanted. Everything that I had worked for over the previous seven-plus years of work and six years of college had finally started paying off, even though we only had a tiny startup business. But that tiny business was doing a very effective, much-needed job, and it was profitable. Successful action builds confidence and courage to make you unstoppable like nothing else will.

Failure to act has been one of the fundamental obstacles to success in every society since the dawn of time. Inertia is the enemy! I can't emphasize that enough. Most people don't even understand that they aren't in opportunity-generating action. I didn't for years. It's certainly not even mentioned in colleges. Action was very elusive for me and many of my friends for years. You must envision your own unique rainbow and the pot of gold that awaits you. Then you need to take the right actions to do the right things to get there. Finding out what you truly want through introspection and writing out your goals is just the beginning of a long and prosperous journey. It is those who are too afraid of failing and therefore won't act until they have some assurance of a beneficial outcome that will perpetually lag behind the dreamer with a major purpose. I was certainly like this, with action as my major weakness, like it is with so many others. It takes action for us to learn from our mistakes, to build confidence and to improve. That's how entrepreneurs can get so good so quickly. Some become multibillionaires at a young age. Check out these quotes from around the world in relation to action and inaction; they address universal truths that we should all hold dear as entrepreneurial CEOs.

» *Talk doesn't cook rice.* —Chinese proverb

» *The first step binds one to the second.* —French proverb

- » *Between saying and doing many a pair of shoes is worn out.* —Italian proverb
- » *The secret of getting ahead is getting started.* —Mark Twain
- » *As I grow older, I pay less attention to what men say. I just watch what they do.* —Andrew Carnegie
- » *When deeds speak, words are nothing.* —African proverb
- » *The best way out of a problem is through it.* —Greek proverb
- » *Action is the real measure of intelligence.* —Napoleon Hill

Action-oriented entrepreneurs have a completely different way of thinking from most people. They act on what they are thinking, and it's this action to take immediate steps that separates them from the rest of society. The nonaction-oriented entrepreneurs and managers do linear chores and use predictive reasoning, which says that the future behaves in the same way as the present and past; it usually doesn't. Using predictive reasoning requires us to be assured of success before we take action. As a result, it's nearly impossible for predictive thinkers to achieve greatly because they won't act! The action oriented see a big opportunity and take small steps toward implementing their plans and achieving long-term goals. The action doers take action with what resources and abilities they possess, while the predictive thinkers are waiting for everything to be perfect before they are willing to act. Needless to say, an action-oriented person has to possess a lot of courage, confidence, and a positive focus on goals. The entrepreneurial or nonlinear CEO must also have a positive mental attitude even when the situation at hand seems dire. Please don't think that you need to be an entrepreneur for these principles to work. But in the real world, nonlinear entrepreneurs are put in positions most often where they can best use these principles to excel and grow quickly. The good news is that practically anyone can become an action-oriented achiever if he or she wants it enough and works enough on the right stuff. In fact many, if not most, of the action-oriented high achievers were fortunate that they were exposed to the right conditions that led to their development.

Embrace entrepreneurial and leadership action

Most of us start out in work as predictive thinkers, as that is what we're all taught. And that's enough for many of us. We never take action to move beyond the conventional, predictive thinking that we have steeped in since we were kids. Most of us end up averse to risk, and we seek out the path of least resistance to maintain our comfort zones. None of that is wrong if that is what we want. Of course, many of the risk-averse people really want to develop and grow to achieve more of their lives' objectives. It's just that action truly does speak louder than words, and action is frequently risky and definitely will push most of us way out of our comfort zones. For those of us who make the leap from the conventional to the nonlinear mind-set, we are at least positioned for great success. We see this as being much less risky than what the conventional-thinking people are exposed to. We would never take the risk of being enslaved by a job with the likelihood of getting laid off later in life with few marketable skills. Yet most think that entrepreneurship is too risky. It is not. The real risk that most fear is the fear of facing mental obstacles. That was my fear. This risk is just in our own minds. In fact, the more security we seek, the less security we have. Most never understand this.

Not everyone wants to achieve at some super-high level, which is normal. My goal is to paint a picture of the optimum level with the most doable methods. It's then up to each person as the CEO of himself or herself to decide on goals and the best way to obtain them.

Besides entrepreneurship, many ways exist to get into action, although most are not effective. There are opportunities to join small or nonlinear businesses with the opportunity to advance to more leadership or gain stock or get large bonuses. You can even build your thinking and constantly seek more responsibility in the job you're in now. Or you can go to where the action is, such as Wall Street, booming oil fields, or

Silicon Valley. However, the best example I can use to discuss action is through entrepreneurship since it forces us to take action when facing adversity or opportunity.

Actions really do speak louder than words. Most entrepreneurs and leaders who are willing to act transformed themselves with the help of goals, personal development, and entrepreneurship or were put in the position of having to. Ambitious entrepreneurship forces us to take action after action, as there's usually nowhere else to turn. It's not human nature to constantly face adversity and take action if not forced to. We act, build, and gain strength on what we learn though our actions. To be successful, we need to overcome our learned tendency of overanalyzing and overplanning. If we just start, we'll be forced into the process of creating through action. If we have a developed PMA and goals, we'll have the confidence to start. If we're already in action, we will use that momentum to continue in action. Even in the conventional business world, the most successful expose themselves to much risk when they are in action as CEOs or other high positions.

Generally speaking, though, it takes something strong to force us into action. That's the way it was for me. I realized that my business practices were flawed, in spite of my efforts to do everything right, and instead of sitting around griping about it, I pushed myself even further out of my comfort zone to address the big stuff I've been talking about here. Entrepreneurship works because that's the place where most people can obtain the total responsibility, adversity, freedom of action, and being in the position of having to that makes our brains and success muscles work effectively enough to generate the action we need. I never knew or appreciated this until I had been an entrepreneur for some time. It was only after I read more about entrepreneurship that I realized that it had gotten me into action lifting the heavy weights of adversity and opportunity that built my success muscles. It is a secret that nearly no one knows outside of successful entrepreneurs. In fact, I've learned that in my business, if I can get the work to challenge the people, they will do a great job. If I have too many people to do too little work, they'll do a poor job. If I force too much disorganized work that has too many problems associated with it on them, they'll also do poorly. They are no different from me. They can be developed much like I was.

I, like most others I know, only got into independent business to obtain financial opportunity. I didn't see any other way except to go it on my own, forging my own way in a wilderness full of untapped opportunity. I saw others doing it and thought that I was at least as good as they were. I wasn't. When I set off on my journey, I had no idea how effective and powerful the entrepreneurship concept is, especially for the lone independent entrepreneur, but I gradually came to realize how empowering being on your own really is once I wasn't afraid of falling on my face from time to time. And I was not afraid to accept full responsibility for all the actions I took since I had no other choice. When we're in action, the fear disappears. Action destroys fear. Inaction magnifies it. And nonconventional exponential entrepreneurism offers much more fear and opportunity than the conventional, more static entrepreneurism.

Being an entrepreneurial CEO is not like just being an investor or in private business. I wasn't fully aware of this when I first started out. I thought all self-employed people were entrepreneurial in spirit and action, but I was wrong. A majority of people in business for themselves really aren't true nonlinear, big-stuff CEO entrepreneurs or even conventional entrepreneurs. Many are investors, partners, consultants, manager-type CEOs, lawyers, doctors, accountants, actors, athletes, specialists, commissioned salespeople, and the like. They run their own businesses or are themselves the originator of the service or intellectual property, but they still operate some in the realm of accepted conventions. Many think in a more linear fashion instead of pushing deeply into the unknown to chart a new course others may never have followed in the past. Likewise, even most true entrepreneurs are not of the big-goal-directed dynamic variety. In my case, I saw an opportunity in the custom chemical processing and manufacturing industry, and I ran and kept running with that opportunity. In other cases, like Bill Gates of Microsoft, the entrepreneur invents a new gizmo and becomes a great nonlinear CEO.

The more opportunity-producing action you do, the better entrepreneurial CEO you'll be. The closer you are to being a true lone entrepreneur working in the arena of the 80/20 principle, the more freedom of action you will have. This, in turn, will lead you to take more action that will unearth additional opportunity and the accompanying adversity that goes with it. As I've indicated already, it's basic human nature to do only the tough things that we have to do, and entrepreneurship forces us to have to. This is what it takes to greatly develop us. Being an entrepreneur is a lot like culture or having a PMA. From the outside looking in, people can't understand it. From the inside looking out, we can't explain it. The greatness and magic of implementing success principles and entrepreneurship is the real secret in the business world. It is where the most action typically is, if you will. It's where most of the economic progress in the world comes from.

The bottom line is that we simply don't develop success muscles without experiencing a lot of opportunity and adversity while having total responsibility and freedom of action. This is essentially the definition of pure entrepreneurship. Most of us have the ability to develop, but we just have to get in action and keep it going and want to. The executing action will develop any of us if we persist long enough with a good attitude (PMA and goals). We only learn by doing. None of us were good enough or smart enough to begin with. If we choose not to be an entrepreneur or a CEO with much freedom of action, it's best to think and work as closely as we can to being a CEO of ourselves and constantly seek more responsibility. Throughout history, the most successful nonentrepreneurs, generals, and CEOs essentially practiced this entrepreneurship through independent action that helped develop them. They had freedom of action and full responsibility, and they weren't afraid to take calculated risks when they deemed it advantageous or necessary.

Run or lose the race

From my own experience, I can now see that most people who want to succeed at a high level don't because of an inability to get into the action.

It's certainly not for the lack of talent or intelligence. We're all smart with ability and have a human brain that has the potential to greatly succeed. Most good workers could do very well as entrepreneurs (or CEOs) doing something where their strengths lie if they just got started in action and kept the action going that would develop them—that is, if they wanted the end result and the responsibility. Most don't, but many do want it, and many don't know if they want it or not. In my case, I learned the hard way that if you are not an assertive person, but you want to succeed greatly, it's more difficult to get into action.

Most successful entrepreneurs just stumbled into entrepreneurship by accident by trying to make a fortune or by having to make a living. They all essentially had the same talent as most people, and almost none of them understood the magic of entrepreneurship. Once started in action, they learned the experiences of life and business at a high rate that developed their abilities and business. They were forced to think like CEOs. Since this entrepreneurial action is an 80/20 principle, they theoretically developed at sixteen times the rate of others and continued developing at that rate if they continued raising their goals. The other great majority of people stayed almost stagnant, growing only very slowly, if at all, because they avoided risk, action, opportunity, and adversity. If we have a good attitude and we get on the entrepreneurial bull, most of us can ride it. Some don't have the courage or desire, and a great many do but just don't understand how to. If I've learned anything in my life, it's that each normal person has the ability to develop himself or herself greatly. While we all start with basic differences, no one is necessarily any better than anyone else.

The people who develop greatly in other fields, such as large business, education, the military, religion, and government, pretty much go through the same process of total responsibility, being put in a position of having to, developing a can-do PMA, utilizing freedom of action, and developing goals. This right-focused action using the right principles will develop any of us. In nonentrepreneur fields, only a very small percentage of people are able to put themselves in the same position as a true, lone entrepreneur. Many public and private CEOs who don't own their businesses tend to be more enslaved by owners, boards, and the system and are not given as much freedom of action as lone entrepreneurs. As a result, most aren't forced to develop in business based on the 80/20 success principle. However, they can use these success principles to drive their success. They are generally stuck doing too many toxic management duties by others, no matter how much money they make. They are often forced into developing more linearly and conventionally. Many are very financially successful and do develop as excellent leaders, although they lack the freedom of action and independent creativity needed to work on the nonurgent, intangible big stuff that would develop them more. They tend to be pressured to sweat the small stuff, but the best will sweat some of the big stuff if given a chance. The best will not allow boards, owners, or customers to micromanage them, and they will gain enough freedom of action to grow and excel more.

In my own case, I was laid off from Shell Chemical, which in turn led me to Success Motivation International. I was in a true I-had-to zone at that point, facing up to the fact that I had to earn a living but also knowing that I was missing something in the mix. In retrospect, I can see now that I wouldn't have fared all that well long term at Shell. I wanted to be very successful, but I didn't have the political, verbal, and left-brain skills to compete well with the people getting ahead in such conventional companies. But as lone, true entrepreneurs, we're nearly all given even much greater opportunity to develop in our own unique strengths, instead of the strengths that fit such large conventional businesses. This is why entrepreneurship is so effective at getting people into action and developing at lightning speed. Entrepreneurship is the best way I can explain action and being able to develop in our own unique strengths. I hope that you realize that you don't have to be an entrepreneur or CEO to make action work for you, but it does help. Brian Tracy says that you should always ask for more responsibility from those for whom you work. Constantly put yourself in the position of *doing*.

As entrepreneurs, we are forced to think like CEOs, take total responsibility, develop freedom of action when our plans don't work out, think creatively, and overcome adversity, as these are the key factors that allow people to transform themselves to higher levels. Of course, some entrepreneurs are more action-oriented, positive, courageous, ambitious, and energetic and take more advantage of the opportunities, while many are happy to be independent and make a great living instead of making a fortune. Just being an entrepreneur does not guarantee that a person will be extremely successful, as most aren't. As an entrepreneur, you are free to choose your level of work-life balance and income. So are nonentrepreneurs. You may not want to be an entrepreneur, but if you want more success than you're experiencing now, it will work best for you if you put yourself into as many of the right positions of responsibilities to get yourself into action with as much freedom as you can get.

Goals help get us into action

Your first real action hinges on setting goals and thinking big. The next entails writing down your ideas and revising them over time as you and your business evolve. Always keep your overarching, or major purpose in mind, and know why you have chosen the particular goals you included on your list. Think about the short-term plans you'll need to carry out to meet your long-term goals. Remember to always reverse engineer from your long-term goal and work backward. All the while, expose yourself to new opportunities by writing 20 approaches to your primary goals. Learn and grow strong as you navigate through the inevitable adversity that accompanies positive action. Do not exclude entrepreneurship or other opportunities that don't look great now. Stay open to opportunity. Do not choose one way like most people do. Do not limit your freedom of action, but instead think about achieving your true long-term goals. Almost none of the entrepreneurs I know had any real understanding of the opportunity they had right under their noses until years after they had happily stumbled onto the path to becoming entrepreneurs. I've found this to be true in nearly all lines of entrepreneurship for nearly everyone. There are at least a thousand ways to reach your long-term dreams, so don't choose one static way and get stuck. Always reverse engineer it. Don't exclude your future in a more opportunity-oriented field down the road.

Make no mistake about it: it flat out takes highly competitive action under pressure to develop our success muscles. And it's not so easy to put ourselves in a position to develop those muscles. Few do, but most can. We just have to put ourselves in a position of having to under stress. For instance, I know a great number of people who grew more from a work-success perspective in a military boot camp of a few months (tough having to) than they have the rest of their work lives. I believe that many of the tens of millions of people who have gone through these boot camps would agree with me.

Know that you have to. Being a lone entrepreneur with constant challenges is like being in a permanent boot camp if we remain ambitious. We're constantly forced to grow our success muscles and meet more and more challenges the faster we grow. We only grow our success muscles when we're under great stress and have to. This is what all good militaries do to develop their soldiers with their boot camps, officer training schools, military academies, and special forces training because it's the only thing that they've found that works outside of actual war to get people into action with great stress.

I developed most of my success muscles in the boot camp–like corps at Texas A&M and as an entrepreneur. Those are the heavy weights. Every other job, school, and activity was mostly learning and training, but I didn't gain many success muscles on those two-pound weights that all my competition was also lifting. You won't, either.

It's a challenge for each of us to get into the action that develops our success muscles. Most people have no concept of what it takes. I didn't. Most people who gained that muscle didn't even realize that was what they were doing when they did it. We never realize or appreciate it until later. Johann Wolfgang von Goethe once wrote, "Thinking is easy, action is difficult, and to put one's thoughts into action is the most difficult thing in the world." Oh, how true that is!

As the saying goes, talk is cheap. Actions speak louder than words. How many times have you thought of a great idea and got excited about it but then did absolutely nothing to put the idea into actual play? I'd hazard to say that you've done that more than once. I know I have. As I've said before, taking positive action was the toughest nut to crack in terms of developing my success muscles. I think part of it was that I didn't know what action to take, and part of it was the pervasive self-doubt that existed deep within me in my earlier years prior to my positive mental attitude conversion. Failing to act was holding me back on everything else. I think that action is probably the most difficult thing for most people, especially those like me who are not really assertive. We nonassertives have a strong tendency to do too much thinking and not enough action. This actually caused me much doubt in my youth when I saw a lot of assertives in action when I wasn't. The assertives tend to be mostly action with much less thinking. I say this because I've seen a lot of highly assertive people plow forward with confidence into every field. That action works for them without question, even with their weak insight. It takes *having to* for the rest of us, and maybe somewhat for the assertive.

Action fosters its own momentum. Getting started in action is really difficult. However, once started, it takes much less effort to keep the momentum going. If your action slows and you want to achieve more, keep resetting your goals higher. I never want to have that helpless feeling of being dead in the water and unable to get anything meaningful done ever again. It's so much better to gain the self-esteem, confidence, and success muscles from taking the necessary action to achieve your goals and reap the results of your efforts.

If you're working for others, keep asking for and taking on more responsibility continuously to get into action. Also, think like a CEO. This will get you going and force you to have to. Your bosses will learn to constantly give you more challenges. We literally have to find a way to put ourselves into this having-to mode if we are ambitious for success. It works. It will help develop us and help achieve our goals. You can do practically anything if you have to. Human nature is not to improve if we don't have to. If you take action on the big stuff, you'll be doing the right stuff. The problem for most is that they don't know what the "right stuff" is.

Motivate yourself through writing

Write down twenty ways in which you can get yourself into action now. Then do it again tomorrow. Ask yourself, "What are the best ways I can get started now? What actions do I need to take to realize those first vital steps toward actually achieving my long-term goals?" Figure it out from the end result backward to where you are now.

Writing down twenty ways will strain your mind and draw out much of the great creativity that is needed to succeed. As I've said, *having to* refers to facing challenges and adversity due to entrepreneurial big-picture efforts that lead you to have to act to accomplish major-purpose goals. If we're not forced to act, we generally won't. So, with this in mind, write down ten ways you can put yourself into having-to situations that will forward your progress toward fulfilling your goals. I know it might strike some of you as a bit odd, but visual stimulation with charts or signs outlining your goals and objectives will help reinforce the message. Thus, it couldn't hurt to put an index card or other sign that says "Action!" on it in your office, car, or home.

Write down twenty ways that you, as a leader, can get your people into more action. This will help you to make progress in achieving more big-picture stuff. Empower them to take more control of their responsibilities. Help develop them as you develop yourself. Get them in harmony with you. Empowerment and action go hand in hand.

Chapter roundup

It's your CEO duty to constantly create the action you'll need for great success that can't be delegated. Actions speak louder than words. It's that simple, but getting into meaningful success action is as rare as goal setting for most. When it comes to building success muscles in life and business, you first must envision yourself as a successful person.

Brainstorm and establish your goals, and write them down. Formulate your plan of action, and then act. It might sound simple, but if you look at human nature in a realistic way, the notion of acting when it puts you at risk of failure is really quite scary for most people. They shy away from adversity and challenges that take them out of their comfort zones, and as a result, they never do take on the action required to propel them to great success. They get stuck in a static position that fails to challenge them. Your key to success is your ability and willingness to act aggressively to realize your goals. Without action, all the thinking in the world won't do you a bit of good. We only learn by doing. You have the power to change your life and your company for the better.

Remember …

- » An old saying about mistakes rings true. In order for you to profit from your mistakes, you first must get out and make some.
- » Building success muscles means that you must put yourself out there and face the risk of failure. The more adversity you overcome through your actions, the stronger and better you'll be as a leader or CEO of yourself. It is doing the hard stuff in an area where you have much of the basic talent. Hardly anyone loves doing the heavy lifting with much adversity, but when you obtain mastery, you will end up loving it.
- » Acting on your goals is an essential ingredient for success in life and in business. Failure to act virtually guarantees that your goals will not be achieved. Keep developing your goals. When the *why* is big enough, you'll succeed.
- » Avoid the trap of predictive thinking. Predictive thinkers seldom act unless they know they're almost assured of a desired outcome. They refuse to take risks because of self-doubt and being afraid to fail. They also wait until everything is just right before they start, which means that they never really start. Winners start where they are with what they have.

» Taking action requires courage, and that courage builds with every new action taken and every new success you've achieved. In other words, action leads to more action, propelling you ever faster on your way to great success.

» Consistently put yourself into the position of having to act. If you do, it will force your brain to reprogram itself to be accustomed to constant challenges that will lead to success in life and business. Think in a nonlinear fashion, and cherish the dynamism of the world.

» Create your own written action plan to achieve your goals. Post an "Action!" sign in your office, car, or home to motivate you to stay in action.

» The action we need to develop greatly is a huge amount of purposeful action in doing the CEO duties. This will build your success muscles. The small stuff doesn't build the nonlinear action needed.

» Develop the people you are working with to be more action-oriented and empowered.

» Listen to the suggested audios with repetition to positively condition your mind. It took an unbelievable amount of positive thinking to make a nonassertive, detached engineer courageous and confident enough to put myself in the position of *having to*. Listening to these audios repetitively will do wonders for keeping you in action. They are truly the best tool developed since 1937 to help transform you into a great executioner. Never stop, because you always need to improve as your business and goals keep growing.

» Believe in yourself, and summon the courage to act on your dreams. Start where you are with what you have. Do everything you can to get into action, as a lack of action holds most people back. The right action will develop nearly any of us in the most amazing way. You can learn how to do nearly anything by actually doing it.

» You only learn and develop by doing. You can learn most anything you need to by the action of doing it until you master it. Action and doing what others won't is truly magic.

6

Developing Your Secret, Unfair Advantage

The successful warrior is the average man, with laser-like focus."
—*Bruce Lee*

The secret of business, especially these days, is
to focus relentlessly on your unfair advantage—
the thing you do that others don't.
—*John Rollwagen, executive*

In September 2008, Kentucky Fried Chicken made national headlines when it announced that, after being locked in a safe for sixty-eight years, Colonel Harland Sanders's handwritten Original Recipe was being temporarily relocated to a secret and secure location as KFC modernized the safekeeping of one of America's top corporate trade secrets. The relocation of Sanders's secret blend of eleven herbs and spices—written on a fading sheet of yellow paper—was quite a publicity stunt for KFC, which hired national corporate security expert and former New York City police detective Bo Dietl to oversee the transfer.

With the aid of the Louisville Metro Police Department and a Brink's, Incorporated armored car, Mr. Dietl, with the finger-lickin' good recipe locked in a briefcase that was handcuffed to his arm, transported it from KFC's corporate headquarters in Kentucky to an undisclosed location in a scene that screamed "photo opportunity." About five months later—in another carefully orchestrated publicity move that coincided with the release of the fast-food chain's first-ever value meal, KFC executives, accompanied by armed guards, returned the recipe to a newly modernized and remodeled home in Louisville. The entire relocation and return was detailed on KFC's website as part of a strategic—and rather ingenious—marketing campaign.

While many entrepreneurs easily recognize that trade secrets like the recipe for KFC's chicken are valuable, most CEOs fail to realize that every successful business possesses a unique and far-less-obvious secret critical to prospering in the marketplace. The trouble is it's not as easily grasped as a recipe for tasty fried chicken. It's typically intangible and hard to fathom, but that doesn't mean it's not there, lurking in the substrata of the company. Perhaps calling it a secret isn't quite right. But in some ways, it really is, because the driver behind what makes the company successful—whether it's delivering superior customer service or a reliable product that meets the needs of customers—is not always readily apparent. You frequently have to look for your secret, and you have to sometimes look in unconventional places—unlike good customer service or a reliable product, which are both sublimely obvious. Both are essential, of course, but the reasons for your success may go much deeper. In fact, they probably do.

Do you know what the secret to the success of your business is? Have you thought carefully about what makes you or your business or proposed business more successful than the competition? In order for you to be a truly successful CEO, you must identify your organization's secret to success, protect it, develop it, and use it as you explore areas where you want to develop new profit streams and make new big deals. Let's take a deeper look at the secret world of success within your own business or career.

Your success secret is your best weapon

What does your organization specifically do to earn its most significant source of income and that delivers its most desired and valued results? Your secret will reflect the strengths of the CEO and the people and assets of the business, and that's a good thing as long as you have a good service or product to offer and a superlative team to support you. In essence, the secret is simply what you do that is most valuable that customers are willing to pay enough for. Besides your income, it might also involve the things you do that make everything work. It is important that you know where the real value of your business is. Every person and every business is unique and has something that he or she does better than others. This includes businesses with little or no profits, which will more than likely be doing something well that others want. Surprisingly, a good many CEOs make superficial assumptions about what differentiates their companies from others in a similar industry and why theirs succeed in the face of competition. They don't dig deeper, and they should. As you evaluate yourself as a CEO and make decisions about how to improve how you go about your job, give some serious thought to the concept of your business's secret and what your customers want that you do so well. Building profits is a fun and liberating job.

The 80/20 principle applies here. Let's mine the topic for gold. As the 80/20 principle says, only the most valuable 20 percent of the actions of a typical business generates 80 percent of the profits. These sales generate sixteen times the profit of other sales. I know that I've hammered away at this quite a bit already, but it really is the crux of what I'm talking about. So is the application of this same principle to how you think and act as a CEO; the top 20 percent of the areas where your attention should be are nonurgent and often nonlinear lines of thinking that allow you to creatively address the growth of the company. This selective, top-tier thinking reaps your desired results. Your goal should be to identify what you uniquely do that is so valuable and start making that most of what you do. And then build your business and profits based on your strengths and the value you give your customers. It's possible that most of the departments in the business deliver very little value, although needed.

If you understand your secret advantage that your customers value and are willing to pay extra for, then you'll be able to capitalize on it when you explore new markets and when you go in to seal a big deal. If you know what makes you special—what *truly* differentiates you from your competitors—then you can better focus your efforts in areas where you are strong and your competition is weak. You can also concentrate on customers who will be willing to pay a premium, since what you do well will not apply to every customer. Your goal should be to do what is most valuable to your customers and keep adding more value. Still keep in mind that performing well in the chapters regarding what matters most in *The Executioner* allows you to have the ability to perform so well on your unfair, secret advantage.

Leverage your success secret. Your competitors won't know what really drives the success of your business, and so, in a sense, if you play on that secret, you'll have an advantage over the businesses competing for your customers. Like an iceberg, a competitor can only see the 10 percent of your business that's above the surface. There's the formidable 90 percent of your business that's hidden below the surface, sort of like a ramming rod on a trireme. What the competitor can't see (your success secret) gives you an advantage if you can identify it and actually use it to win customers. Just remember that you can't see your competitors' secrets, either, which means that you must take the very fact that those secrets exist into account as you plan your long-term strategies.

It bears repeating that most of the work that your business is capable of doing—and that your customers and employees want you to do—will not be profitable, desirable, or good for you. They most likely will be the strengths of your competitors. No business can be highly effective or excellent at everything. If this were not the case, virtually everyone who can manage an enterprise would be in your business, making the same products or providing the same services that you do for your customers. Your customers and employees will frequently want you to pursue business that doesn't fit your secret, or they'll push you to take on business that occupies that lowest 20 percent. The funny thing is that you probably could pursue that business and get it. But could you excel at it? Is it going to fit the 80/20 principle you seek? Not likely. A major key to making high profits is to not allow yourself to get enslaved by low-profit business or chores that don't fit your strengths. The low-profit business and small stuff will consume you, and you won't be able to pursue the valuable business. I see this all the time in business and have fallen victim to it myself. Only you, the CEO, can keep this from happening.

Most people, managers, and leaders are conventional thinkers, and they seem to think that there's a certain linear percent profit in every million dollars of sales. They see others making a profit (they think) in every type of business and think that they're just as good as them or better (they're not). But when we start doing more of that 80 percent of business that produces 20 percent of our successful results, our business suffers no matter how well we do it. In the real, nonlinear world, each person and business has great talents in certain areas and poor talents in others. The CEO has to mesh these strengths and weaknesses into what customers want and will pay enough for. The CEO's duty is to make sure that his or her business is focused on doing what it's really good at and to be certain that customers are willing to pay a fair price for whatever service or product is on offer. The 80/20 principle works just the same with conventional business or any other business. That duty cannot be delegated, as others won't have your perspective or wisdom. The CEO then must continue developing business in that and associated areas to grow the company for the future. Of course, to do this means minimizing and eliminating much of what the company does not produce well or efficiently. Over time, we can cut all of this low-value-work cost in half. We can simplify it, reduce it, become more efficient, and only do good enough at it.

Find your success secret. In an effort to truly determine your company's secret, ask yourself the following questions:

» What do we do that customers need so much that they are willing to pay enough to enable us to make a good profit?

- What are we really good at? Does it translate into profits? Why or why not?
- What do we need to get better at so as to better develop our secret?
- What is the 20 percent of our business that makes 80 percent of our profit? (You should have already figured this out by now, but it's worth asking again.) How can we improve and refine our advantage?
- What is the most profitable thing we do? Why?
- What is the most productive thing we do? Why? Least productive?
- What is the least profitable 20 percent that we do that we should consider not doing? Why is it the bottom 20 percent?
- How can we cut our 80 percent low-value-added work in half?
- What should we charge more for that might produce more results?
- Do we have a labor, utility, raw material, or location advantage we can use?
- Which customers or types of customers will most value our secret?
- Should we raise our prices to flush bad business and highlight good business?
- Is part of our secret our ability to develop strong personal relationships and the ability to make deals and sell? This is the primary secret of many people and businesses.
- What is most valuable to our customers from how we do our business?
- What is the best way for us to serve our customers quickly, easily, rightly, and economically?
- Wouldn't our business be more productive and offer much greater value to our customers if we operated by the 80/20 principle?

In answering those questions, you also must honestly assess your company's position and size in the marketplace. It's no shame to be a small company looking for a very specific niche. In fact, it is often a major benefit. Your more-established competition is probably overly bureaucratic, with old, inefficient processes. Your smaller competitors probably have far different strengths (faster, closer, cheaper, relative) than you and a lot of weaknesses. That can give you an advantage that you can use. I believe that each person who reads this book has unique strengths that can be developed into his or her secret, unfair advantage. Keep in mind that every customer basically only wants things fast, easy, right, and of good value. And a good or great relationship is valued by most.

Know your weaknesses. When assessing your company to truly identify why it's successful—assuming that it is, of course—be keenly aware of its weaknesses. If you find areas of weakness, look at them carefully to make a decision regarding whether improving those weaknesses will enhance your ability to serve your most valuable contribution. You may be weak in an area that serves the lowest 20 percent of your customer base. If so, eliminating customers in the lowest 20 percent of your business would eliminate that weakness problem with no muss or fuss! We can't be strong in everything. Trying to be good in everything is a huge flaw in business strategy that causes us to be weak in success. It takes a strong CEO to keep the business focused on what mattered most.

If you do run a small company, take pride in it. Small companies are normally faster, more innovative, creative, and flexible and have lower capital costs and lower overhead than larger companies and corporations. Smaller companies are decentralized, can typically develop better relationships with clients and customers, can be more creative, give better service, generally have simpler processes, and are better suited to handle small jobs and short runs. Smaller companies have lower labor costs because they are free to hire more of the 20 percent of people who produce 80 percent of the value-added results. They are often at the right location. They can also use temporary employees, can respond faster to changes, and are often closer to the markets. Perhaps most importantly, smaller companies can often determine their secret and begin working to further develop it and the other big stuff much more easily than bigger companies.

Many small, decentralized, innovative, principled businesses can have a few thousand workers, while some very small businesses can operate as conventional large businesses. Small businesses are normally disadvantaged in purchasing power, large-volume raw materials, high-volume products, owning a market, high capital-intensive businesses, and branding.

Work your secret, and never forget that it conforms to the 80/20 principle. All the dynamically successful businesses and people use the 80/20 principle to continually develop their secret. Your strengths are much stronger than you think. Knowing your secret, along with all the big stuff, will allow you to better know how to effectively use the 80/20 principle to build your business.

Developing your secret success muscles

When you discover your success secret, it doesn't mean that it is developed enough to fully leverage, though it may well be. If it isn't, you've still found a key opportunity, an area to focus on as you chart your present and future course for the company. Just know that your success secret is as dynamic as everything else, so it is bound to evolve as you and your company grow. With that in mind, consistently work hard to further develop and improve your secret within yourself and your business. You also may need to understand enough about accounting, law, finance, management, and psychology to fully develop your secret. You may need to improve your accounting so that you can better understand what you do that is most valued. Another great method is to raise your prices and let the customers reward you for what you do well and get you out of what you don't do well. We never have it made. Your secret may be only worth an extra $50,000 a year now, but it doesn't mean that you can't make it worth a hundred or a thousand times more.

The point is that just knowing and using your secret isn't all there is to it. If it were that easy, everybody in business would be rich and successful. No, once we identify our success secret, we must become its master and build from there. It's just like a young, talented athlete or musician who must continue to develop his or her talent—hopefully in an area where there is high demand and people willing to pay a good price for that talent. You likewise have a unique talent. The most successful find their niche and then develop it. Set a goal to obtain a high level of mastery in your secret.

Stick to your success secret. Once you find your secret, do not stray far from it. Your general secret and strengths will not normally change significantly over time, but you must continue to develop them over the years because change is inevitable. A simple rule of thumb for protecting your secret and staying focused on it is to not start operating your business like a large conventional company or in a different manner than you have in the past. You may be tempted to do so, but this potentially could be a huge mistake. The way you run your business is most often the secret that drives your success. If you work for a large business, develop your personal and department secret.

As you move forward, you'll find that you'll have to tweak what drives the success of your business or career to account for the changes that always occur in life and business. Just stick with what you do best and refine from there. Always strive to add value to your secret. Look for new ways to harness the power of your secret, but be careful not to force big changes that aren't coming about naturally. If you land a new, big deal you've worked hard to seal that requires changes, that's great. If you find yourself superimposing change for the sake of change itself, watch out.

I've seen successful small businesses hire consultants who came in and reorganized the business like a large centralized business and bankrupted them. Consultants will always want to help you with their secret, which will not be *your* secret. This will end badly. Don't try to be everything to everybody or to do everything for everyone. Serve your customers, but don't be a slave to them or let them micromanage you and become something you are not, which they will want to do. Work to keep your strengths that make your secret to success work as your business grows. This will always be a challenge. It takes more control to do this than I thought at first. You will get too far from your secret from time to time. Just be aware of this, and always try to get back on track.

Stand firm with customers. Do not misunderstand me when I suggest that you not do everything your customers ask for. You should, of course, strive to achieve customer and employee satisfaction. But when you start letting all kinds of random requests by customers, employees, and salesmen dictate what you do, you'll unknowingly change your secret and lose profitability and effectiveness. Do not let others ruin your business; only you can stop them. They will all have a tendency to try to get you to operate like they do or have done, trying to be helpful. It's what they do and believe in. If your customers were not bad at what they're paying you for, you wouldn't have the business. Most of those ways will damage your success secret. So will lowering your prices or agreeing to do more work without charging more. Resist this.

In reality, customers essentially only want four things: they want what you do to be fast, easy, right, and of good value. If you get out of your niche, you may not be any of these things, and your customers will notice in a heartbeat. Then they'll get angry with you, even when it was they who nudged you away from the core of what drove your success in the first place. The CEO's job is to keep the business doing what it's good at and have the discipline to not let others get it too far away from that. This is a good time to point out that without a really good CEO, no nonconventional business has a chance to be successful for very long.

Once I eventually understood this, it helped our business tremendously. How can we expect our employees or others to learn this lesson without our guidance? Keep in mind that it's only your CEO thinking that can really see the secret and have the right perspective on the business. Realize that few CEOs clearly know their secret. It took me years to understand that I even had one. This secret is basically the core of intangible and tangible value you bring your customers in terms of the service or product you deliver—and how you go about it to make the process easy, efficient, economical, and as hassle-free as possible when problems inevitably arise. Your secret is a major part of your marketing strategy, as well, because you're going to leverage it when soliciting prospects operating in the sphere occupying the most productive part of your business.

Poor pricing can destroy your success secret. As you go forward, keep price in mind. The reason you're targeting prospects in the most profitable and productive part of your business is that you want to be able to freely charge them a fair premium for what your service or product is worth. You don't want to compete with the lowballers and cheapskates on price.

Thus, you've got to be sure to charge customers enough when fulfilling their desires. Much of your secret is getting enough value out of your secret. If you go on the cheap to build volume at the cost of profit margin, you will possibly lose your secret to success. I am going to assume that you aren't a denizen of the discount, like the dollar store or Walmart. Instead, I'm assuming you offer a service or product that can command or be built to command a high price if marketed to the right set of customers. As the CEO, you must understand what your service and secret to success are worth, and then you must make sure that you charge the customers a fair price to make it a win-win for all. You will destroy your own success if you don't, and you'll be competing with others on price with too many of the wrong customers. I have seen many small and newer businesses destroyed by listening to their salespeople and lowering their price on their secret.

Naturally, we can't overcharge. If we do, we'll reduce or eliminate the value we give customers. In this regard, it is vital that you prevent your sales staff and managers from giving your service or product away too cheaply, as most will surely want to do. Salespeople and managers generally want to make sales at any price to really please and serve the customer and get the order. CEOs tell me all the time that their salespeople essentially work for the customer and not for them. That's why marketing exists! But as CEO, you'll need to get a fair value from your most valuable asset. Remember that you will need to have a profitable business to serve customers and employees in the long run and grow with them. It's the CEO's job to keep the profits up and to get close to full value for the product or service. It's always a battle for every business to get close to full value. A good, more obvious example of a business that knows its success secret and gets full value for it is Starbucks. Starbucks customers are willing to pay a higher price for their coffee because of the quality, taste, image, environment, and custom options. Starbucks would ruin its unfair advantage if it matched McDonald's prices.

Anyone can give away the product or service under customer pressure. The novice CEOs who don't have a good understanding of their secret and a good strategy generally do just that. It takes truly understanding your secret and its value to withstand the customer pressure and to use relationships and selling strengths in order to establish good prices or terms. Fair pricing is always a battle. It's been my observation over the years that only outstanding managers and salespeople with the support of good CEO leadership and understanding are strong enough to keep prices balanced. It is very difficult to do so. But even the cream of the crop of the management staff do not have CEO thinking. They have a management mentality, not a CEO and marketing focus. That's why as the CEO or leader, you need to maximize your success secret, enabling you to leverage it when you explore new potential sources of business.

Others won't have your niche, because your niche fits your personality, knowledge, secret, ability, leadership, culture, people, weaknesses, and business model. It is unique to you and your strengths. It's what you do that customers value most. It's what generates the most money for you in most cases, so stick to it! You may need to raise the price on your secret to some if your margins have fallen. This happens. But do whatever it takes to develop and maintain it. This normally means constantly measuring the top 20 and 40 percent of your actions that make the most money, and then doing more of that. Do less of the bottom 20 percent and 40 percent of your business. This is true feedback you can measure with accuracy and assurance. You are not in business to break even or lose money.

Stick with what you know. Likewise, it is extremely important to learn not to enter other peoples' niches if they don't fit your own business climate. Compete with others, but only in areas where they are weak and you are strong. Knowing my secret was very empowering and built my self-confidence and profits. It's what highly profitable businesses do. It was the top 20–50 percent of what I did that generated 80 percent of my profits. Then I started doing more and more of that business until it became 60 or 70 percent of our business and very profitable. It worked for me, and it will work for you. Please keep it in mind that if we had a 100 percent highly profitable business, we might still have 70–80 percent low-value work going into these products. We all have genius areas where we are strong and areas where we are weak. Why intentionally choose to operate in an area where you are weak and where the profits are bound to fall short of those you could earn in areas where you are strong? A CEO with wisdom will make money in most any market. The chapters of this book are an accumulation of the business wisdom of the ages.

There is a catch, though. Everyone who is a serious worker who's committed to success has unique strengths that are valuable. But realize that each of us also has strengths that have little commercial demand and value to others. Many of our strengths don't correlate to what drives our success, though some obviously do. That is an absolutely crucial point! You can't leverage *all* your strengths for increased profit, just *some* of them. When it comes to your business, let the actual numbers tell the story. Your value lies in what your customers will pay for at a good price point to fit their needs. In other words, just because you do something really well doesn't mean somebody wants to pay enough for it. So, in a very real sense, identifying your secret for success is all about identifying where others place the most value on what you do best.

Along these same lines, we have to become good at a lot of things we're currently not good at. That may sound like a contradiction. After all, I've just said that you need to ditch the areas of business in which you are weakest and that don't pay much. I've said to stick with your strongest areas. So you may ask, "Isn't getting good at doing something I'm not currently good at the same thing as operating in an area where I'm weak?" You would be right to ask that question. Indeed, without careful thought, you could end up doing that very thing. No, what I'm talking about is that once you see where your strengths that others value enough truly lie, you can then thoughtfully assess how to build on those strengths and broaden them. The broadening process inevitably means that you'll have to get good at something you're not currently good at. That's not serving areas of weakness. It's serving marketing strength! It's like the Peter Principle—what got us here won't get us there. You can build your strengths where they will do you the most good. Likewise, you can elect not to use your strengths where they won't help you.

Don't be afraid to grow strong. Our business strengths are often not what we think. We need feedback from a free market to find out what we do that's so valuable to others. We also need that feedback to determine what we need to improve on that we're not so good at, as that could well develop into an as-yet-undiscovered advantage. It's a dynamic world, and the most successful people keep adapting to the changing needs we all experience in life and in business. This is why free markets work so well. The type of knowledge and personal development we need to do this is wrapped up in the best business practices presented. Losers do what they like and want to do. Winners do what others are unwilling to do and keep adapting. Your secret may be something that you hate and are not good at. The fact that you're willing to do this hated work makes you valuable to others. Then you'll need to get good at it!

In my niche of custom chemical processing, I found that I could make the smaller-volume specialty chemicals with less capital cost and get into operation much more quickly than others. I could build the right equipment, get good productivity from a decentralized organization, and give the customers what they wanted. In my business, my customers need us to be a decentralized organization to do the work that their centralized organizations are not economically good or fast at. In our organization, people are empowered to do their work without going through layer after layer of bureaucracy. Our customers' businesses are designed to make huge quantities of products, but they aren't well equipped to do small quantities.

Find your niche. Small businesses everywhere mostly succeed by being decentralized businesses doing what the big businesses don't do well. There is always a need. I found that we could be best at batch processing in certain chemistries in which all our people had been developed. When we got too far away from our secret, we couldn't do very well. I also found out what value we could get for this work—and which businesses and industries valued and needed us and which didn't. I also had to figure out how to keep out the markets of other small businesses where they ha successful niches. Our tangible secret is typical of an entrepreneurial business, and it reflects my strengths and weaknesses.

Of course, the real intangible secret is my entrepreneurial drive to learn and get ahead exponentially (80/20), combined with my creativity, work ethic, knowledge, PMA, technical ability, problem solving, goals, leadership, teamwork, and working on the high-value work of sweating the big stuff. It's we who get ahead and develop our secrets who use our strengths. It's not a product, process, scheme, hot business, or someone else making you a success. In the end, we only succeed to the level of our personal and business development of doing the best business practices. Most of my competitors were more conventional and did not do much of of the best business practices, which also helped me. The tangible is just the manifestation of the intangible. There is not enough space in this book to cover all of what great marketing entails. Great marketing uses the 80/20 principle to focus on what you can best offer the customers what they want most. You may need to learn more about marketing. Much of that can be more of what matters most for you.

Go with what you know. Find your niche. Stick with it. Identify what makes you successful in your niche, and leverage this secret advantage as you explore new and exciting ways to grow your business to maximize profit. Follow the examples of successful businesses like Starbucks and McDonald's that stick to their unfair advantage. Developing your advantage is marketing, and great marketing conforms to the 80/20 principle. Sales is mostly a more linear function, which is not a CEO duty. Of course, the more good marketing we work into sales, the more effective sales will be.

Chapter roundup

As an entrepreneur or CEO, you will find your secret, unfair advantage if you truly spend your efforts sweating what matters most and keep from getting tied up in the small stuff. That's not an easy task, but you can definitely do it given the right focus and a sufficient length of time to fully absorb the central concepts at work here and make them your mindset.

Finding your success secret and working it is a small concept that yields large results. But like other concepts we have covered—and ones yet to be addressed—the secret works hand in hand with the other principles and practices that matter most. Strategy is so general that few businesses, or people, are ever able to develop a great one. It was so general for my first years as an entrepreneur that I didn't have much of a good handle on what I truly needed to concentrate on. When I first discovered the secret to what had been driving my success, I had already been making what I thought was a good profit in my specialty chemical business. When CEO and motivational speaker Walt Sutton introduced me to the concept of the secret with his audio at a Vistage meeting, it was like a lamp got turned on in my head. I suddenly realized that my job as CEO had been missing a key element. I didn't realize what my real potential was. This secret is such that it can be easily done by most nonlinear CEOs.

While I was sort of generally using my strengths for 20 percent of my business, I was dissipating much of the other 80 percent on going-nowhere business. You want to use your secret advantage on nearly all your business like I do now, not just 20 percent. Knowing my secret has been like a compass to me, which is extremely liberating. The compass gives my team and me unwavering direction. All I have to do is to stick with what's working and not let others in the business vary from it too much. When we get off course, we just seek to get back to true north. It's nice to be steering your boat in the right direction and know that you are, in fact, on the right course. Business is always good for us. Developing your unfair advantage is marketing. Other areas of marketing can also help quite a bit. After you have developed your highly profitable business, you'll surely continue to develop your market.

Remember …

- Your company's secret advantage to success lies in what is most valued by its customers. It's your job to clearly identify what that is and to always build on it to serve your customers. Don't enslave yourself fighting for crumbs.
- Your unique secret gives you an advantage over your competition. Leverage that secret in terms of what customers are willing to pay. Continue to develop it, as it requires building and developing. Raise prices to test the market, but don't overcharge.
- The market will determine what it values most about what you do. Use the real numbers as a measure of your strengths in a given area.
- The origins of profits from the top 20 percent of your business are a good indicator of where your key to success is hidden. Find out what you do best for this segment of your business, and try to do it for 100 percent of your business.
- Look to your accounting department to show you what business draws in the most profits. Also, look at customer service, personal relationships, value, and innovation as potential drivers behind your success. Think! If you identify what your customers value most about your business, you can focus on doing more of the same for them. Most likely, it will be doing a lot of what matters most.
- Secrets to success are always transitory. Remain flexible, and adapt to changing circumstances.
- Your secret, unfair advantage gives you a clear advantage over your competitors. Just remember not to compete much where your competitors have an unfair advantage. Situational awareness is essential!

- Charge fair value for your unfair advantage, and do not ruin it by cutting your price. You will always be under that pressure from nearly all sides.
- Always continuing to develop and build your dynamic, unfair advantage is very satisfying and builds your business, confidence, courage, excellence, people, and profits.
- Listen to the audio of this book repeatedly to develop the mindset to build this marketing and profitability. Success is not a one-time, static event. It is an ever-increasing, dynamic way of life. Be successful every day and year of your life. Keep that static, linear thinking from taking over. It is your duty, and it cannot be delegated, as only you will have the vision of your true business by which to judge.

7

Building Your Financial Wisdom and Toughness for Long-Term Survival

If you can find a path with no obstacles, it probably doesn't lead anywhere.
—Frank A. Clark

Running a business presents a multitude of challenges for us as CEOs. Starting a new business from scratch is even more of a challenge, but the potential rewards in both pursuits are many. We are in the position of leader, charting a course into the unknown as we carry out our vision for our future. For long-term business survival, we must learn how to play some defense. Business is not all offense after making money. In my time in business, I can easily see that the nonsurvivors never developed good financial thinking and habits. This chapter is more targeted toward the nonconventional entrepreneurs that start out with their own money and perhaps some money from family, friends or a partner. The typical business school entrepreneur will start out with much debt and other stockholders.

I attempt to address both, but less so with the business school entrepreneur whose thinking is nearly always very conventionally flawed.

Getting started right financially and surviving major financial obstacles that will arise are some of what matters most. It's fair to say that until you've experienced starting a company or executing a business turnaround, you won't fully understand what it takes. Many in the developed world have grown up in a prosperous home and society, which tends to make us ill-equipped for tough financial survival. Likewise, people growing up without much money or a strong financial background will also face their financial weaknesses. Nearly no one starts out with good financial wisdom, knowledge, experience, and habits as a CEO or leader. Then we tend to get trapped in our own business and have few, if any, benchmarks to compare ourselves to. We simply don't have the tools, and so we're not sure how to respond or what to do when the chips are down. We are forced to learn on the fly. To me, business (entrepreneurial) survival when you first start is like being dumped into a huge jungle with nothing. There's no one to help you but yourself, and you've never even been in the jungle. There is very little time and money to work with, and you are a novice.

My advice is to get out of a financial survival mode as soon as you can and work to never have to go into that mode again. Fighting to survive will tend to stifle your growing business. Strong and proven financial mindsets, as well as a lot of confidence and good habits, are needed for this survival. Learning how to survive tough times is a duty and responsibility that cannot be underestimated or delegated. While there aren't many guidelines to follow, I do have some advice that may help you when you inevitably face difficult financial times in your own business and when you need to get very lean quickly. I figure if you learn the survival basics required when you launch a business, you'll be able to survive anything. Think of it as playing a good defensive game. So let's focus on the financial challenges you're likely to face for survival during your career or when starting a business, and use those as a learning tool for survival in all times. A good look at surviving those first three or four years as a start-up will arm you with what you need to know going forward. Even if you never start a business, the exercise can be a great way to learn financial survival and success in nearly any circumstance.

My main experience in business survival mode has come from being an independent entrepreneurial survivor for over forty years and from my boot camp–like experience in the corps at Texas A&M. I especially learned a lot in the early years, when I started with essentially nothing. Since then, I have also spent a considerable amount of time watching and studying many CEOs and businesses that have survived during tough times and gone on to excel. Likewise, I've observed many more businesses that have gone bankrupt because the CEO never acquired good financial habits or thinking. Nearly every individual and business I've seen that has gone under did so because of this mismanagement and poor financial habits at the top, although the CEOs might not readily admit as much. Mostly this is through their instant-gratification habits, trying to buy survival and success, or not facing up to financial reality every month and year.

I understand that many business owners who have gone belly-up typically place the blame on a down economy, a downturn in the market, or some other downward trend. But guess what? Every business—from the most successful to the least—experiences a major downturn every so often, as well as many other crises, adversities, and problems. And of course, if the economy is bad nationally, regionally, or locally, it's bad for everyone, not just one particular organization. So how do some businesses survive and go on to thrive when others fold shop? Don't guess luck, as I've rarely seen luck play much of a role. No, it goes much deeper than that.

I think that an easy way to gain some financial wisdom is to watch some of the business shows on TV. I'd recommend *Shark Tank* and *The Profit* and any others you can find. It's good to see examples of others to compare ourselves to.

Building yourself a financial lifeboat

To survive in difficult times—or virtually any other times, for that matter—a business must stay lean, efficient, and productive, while also bringing in new business, generating income, and keeping a strong workforce within the organization. In order to accomplish those objectives, a CEO must be prepared to survive. We all start with a plan to succeed, but few of us make a plan to survive because we don't think we'll need one. Experience has shown me that nearly every one of us will face do-or-die survival moments more than once in our careers if we're an entrepreneur or a CEO. Of course, nearly everyone starts off weak with poor financial habits. We just need to be aware that we have to build as much survival strength and better habits as we can as fast as we can. We need to rely on our success muscles and keep building them. Just because you might be making a lot of money now doesn't mean you don't need to build more financial wisdom.

Remember that 80 percent of new businesses ultimately do not make it past their first few years of operation. While various studies show different statistics, it's quite obvious that the conventional financial thinking that most of us start with is not cutting it in terms of keeping companies afloat. From my viewpoint, we need to better develop our flawed financial mindsets and habits that we all start with in this unforgiving entrepreneurial (or CEO) jungle to survive. Luck rarely plays a role.

Over the long run, it takes a tremendous amount of positive mental attitude, discipline, courage, time, and effort to survive well in business or in our lives. And it most definitely takes survival skills that are practiced and proven when you're on your own and you are forced to pay the bills and meet the payroll every week and month. There's normally no one else to come to your rescue. Taking full responsibility and facing the adversity head-on will give you strength in the long run. Try not to feel too overwhelmed when the storm finally sweeps in and the wind pipes up!

Operate lean. When I began my business, I wasn't the best CEO. In fact, I wasn't really good at all. None of us are. Like most first-time CEOs, I made many mistakes along the way, as I had zero experience. But one thing I did well right from the start—and ultimately this proved to make all the difference in the world for me—was to stay in a survival frame of mind. I stayed very, very lean, saved enough, and made enough of an income to overcome my numerous mistakes and survive, which allowed me to stay in business long enough that I could develop into a much better CEO and finally start making terrific profits. In other words, I stayed lean from the outset, and that gave me time to grow. You can do the same thing with your company—but only if you watch every penny and spend wisely. I had an advantage, as I grew up without money and had Depression-era parents who saved and spent nothing on anything above the basics. I was lean-thinking to a fault in most people's eyes. My wife, Dorothy, also had the same background, which made it even easier for me.

When business turned down for me—as it will for practically everyone—I had enough time and resources to develop more business and to correct some of my flawed personal and business practices. At that time, my major flaw was that I didn't know how to hire and manage the right people, and I was enslaved by nearly everyone I hired. The reality is that no one slips on a CEO hat for the first time with the necessary know-how and experience to perform the role exceptionally well ... or even reasonably well. In most instances, new CEOs will make some costly mistakes, and in virtually all cases, new businesses and growing organizations will experience financial strife.

Start lean. It literally always pays to have as much financial cushion as possible in order to survive long enough to develop yourself, your team, and your cash flow. That cushion should mostly come from creative economizing, lean practices, saving, and minimizing debt. I essentially started out with nothing more than credit. As I look back on it now, I realize that I was practicing exactly what successful people do in terms of being a business survivor. Emulation is the number-one characteristic of the rich, according to many. I simply had more time to develop and respond because of my long-term financial economizing habits; I maintained a more positive attitude than most others because of my success training and positive focus; and I kept working on improving myself, my business, and my survival cushion. In studying other businesses and speaking at length with other CEOs who have endured extremely difficult financial struggles, I've discovered that nearly all of them who carried on and stayed afloat practiced the same long-term, future-oriented, financial-economizing thinking methods.

Focus on the future. It's a proven success principle that the further people think into the future, the more successful they are, the better decisions they tend to make, and the more financially secure they will eventually become. Long-term-perspective thinkers practice good financial habits even long after they have made it. They possess the discipline to save and to practice delayed gratification for the best long-term results. They are economizers and savers in good times and bad. Likewise, they strive for excellence in good times and bad. At the opposite end of this spectrum is the instant-gratification segment of society, and it is—unfortunately—a large segment. That is why such a large percentage of the population struggles with debt; it's why so many people live above their means; it's the ailment of the shopaholics, alcoholics, and addicts; and it's the path to financial devastation for even many talented, well-meaning people. However, we can change, as millions have, if we get our thinking and goals right. It's wrong to put your family, yourself, employees, suppliers and customers through bad self-imposed financial hardships.

To me, it only makes sense that if people want to be financially successful, they *must* learn to practice the financial habits and attitudes of the financially successful and *must* avoid the practices of the financially downtrodden or destitute. While anyone can develop positive habits, changing your financial habits can be as difficult as changing any other bad habit—from eating disorders to smoking and from alcoholism to worrying too much. Intellectual knowledge of good financial habits isn't enough. The smoker knows that inhaling tobacco isn't healthy, but a smoker continues to smoke until he or she is wise enough to quit or disease sets in to force the change. Then the smoker quits because he or she must. Beyond being addicted, the smoker has settled into a pattern. To stop smoking, he or she must dramatically change patterns, thought processes, actions, and habits. While there may not be a chemical addiction involved with poor financial habits and thinking, it is not easy to program your mind to overcome years of frivolous spending or wasteful tendencies.

One of my few real positive attributes when I started out as an entrepreneur was the conservative savings habit I had always taken fully to heart. It's the same habit that allowed me to become an entrepreneur while others were burdened with high monthly payments that prevented them from going into business for themselves. I had yet to learn so many other disciplines. My financial conservative brainwashing worked to allow me enough time to improve much of my ill-suited, conventional management habits. It can do the same for you. This may be a tougher habit to break than smoking, drinking, or eating disorders.

Get rid of your financial bad habits. Doing long-term goal setting helps keep us on the financial path to success, as it leads to good financial and survival thinking. Short-term thinking promotes spending money now for things you want but don't need. In fact, every business that I've been aware of that was selling a proven product that went under did so by trying to buy success or by not facing up to or stopping ongoing monthly losses. The businesses that were trying to sell unproven products are another story. As an entrepreneur, my learning was accelerated because I always had to change and adapt on the fly because of the constant demands involved in running a business. Throughout my life, I have discovered that practically no one ever changes his or her thinking or habits unless it is absolutely required to survive. I once thought that only I was so hardheaded in that regard, but I have since discovered that it is practically everyone. Change happens faster when we have to do it because there is no other option. Over time, we get good at it.

The most successful people place themselves in situations where they must change, which also takes plenty of faith and courage. I have said this in earlier chapters, and I will repeat the message: if you wrap your mind around the very basic notion that change requires a strong impetus, you'll be more than on your way to harnessing your inner power. You'll know you have to actually put your neck on the chopping block to force change of any kind in your life. In doing this, you will make a lot of mistakes, but that's the only way that you truly learn and develop. When you do, you'll have made a hugely important shift in how you think about life and business. It takes a pretty strong PMA to have the courage to do it.

Change fosters potential for financial growth. I have also discovered that entrepreneurs have the capacity to develop faster than others because the nature of their business endeavors forces them into situations where they must change and adapt. This is a lesson that virtually all entrepreneurs learn. I learned more financially in a week as an entrepreneur than I did in five years working for others. My advice to save, economize, minimize debt, keep a positive mental attitude, and shed any financial bad habits you might have may sound like just plain common sense, and it is! Listen to the suggested audios. They have much financial wisdom in them, which helps us make that wisdom a part of our thinking and actions. My point is that even when we know we should be doing something that seems so obviously sensible, we often don't for some strange reason. Trust me! I've been there!

The entrepreneur or CEO can't delegate responsibility for the company's financial survival or prepare it for a time when the financial fur hits the proverbial fan. From the start of your business or career, your goal must be to conserve money in order to provide yourself with the greatest amount of time to move into a position of relative safety and profitability and to weather those inevitable financial storms that are brewing just over the horizon. There's also an added benefit in minimizing the money spent because it forces you to become creative and allows you to develop your business in a much more effective and profitable way. This is the approach of most of the survivors and the most successful entrepreneurs. In fact, this method results in your being the low-cost supplier, and it forces you in creative ways to give good service and value to your customers, which is cheap when you start with a shoestring budget. However, conventional thinking makes us think that we can buy success. But we can't hire someone else to ensure our survival. It's our hands-on duty that cannot be delegated.

The profiles of the nonsurvivors in business share many common characteristics. The entrepreneur who goes belly-up is nearly always one who invests too much money at first, goes into too much debt, tries to buy success, creates too much overhead, uses no creativity to cut capital and operational costs, and plans for everything to happen perfectly from the start. This method does not promote creativity, and it fails to draw out the genius that the CEO has within his or her mind. Of course, nothing new works well from the beginning. Part of Murphy's law is that nothing works right the first time. Count on tough financial times. Just know that with the right actions coupled with an eye on the future, you can get through them. Indeed, they'll make you stronger.

Give yourself staying power. Starting or expanding a business is a struggle. Or perhaps a better description would be to call it a grueling, long relay race that you must find a way to do well enough to survive. You are at the starting line of the race with your cash reserves, which will hopefully be bolstered by your profits. But those profits are not a proven performer, so you must enter this race counting primarily on your own resolve and your cash reserves. Your opponents—time and obstacles—are much more proven and far more consistent than your profits. So you must run this race carefully. It's not a sprint, so don't worry about starting impressively. Your goal is to survive—at the end of the week, month, and year—and to elude obstacles along the way. To do that, you must keep a reserve in your tank. You're running a marathon. Eventually, the hope is that your profits will continue to build as the race goes along, which will allow you to sprint past your opposition. But do not try to sprint moneywise until the time is right or start using too much leverage as most business schools recommend. Pace your expenses because time is an amazingly consistent opponent. Your first goal is to survive. To do that, always balance your books and stop the bleeding. Every established business that I've known that went under allowed their expenses to exceed their income for a year or two or even longer, betting that things would get better. They waited too long to cut their payroll.

Inevitably, you'll need more time than you originally thought to build your business. And the obstacles will likely be greater than you imagine. Murphy's law often applies when beginning a business: anything that can go wrong probably will. And to carry that law a little further, it's also Murphy's law and it's been my personal experience that some of the worst things will go wrong at the most inopportune moments. If you expect this to happen, it won't surprise you when it does. You'll have included responses to such adversity in your action plan.

Make sure that time is on your side. It's also a business guideline that it will take you three times longer to get your business on its feet than you estimate, and it will cost you twice as much as you initially planned. I'm not sure I've ever met an entrepreneur who didn't agree 100 percent with that statement. And this is the experience of the most successful! I know for a fact that it has been true with all my businesses. All my new companies, locations, and operations took this much extra time and money to reach the stability and performance that's needed for a decently operated business. If it were easy, there would be a lot more people succeeding as entrepreneurs. While difficult, my take is that you have a 100 percent chance of success if you get your thinking and habits right. You have a 1 percent chance if your thinking and habits are poor.

A lot of bad things will happen to you, especially in your less experienced days and years. In a new business or location or branch, it takes a lot of time to work out most of the kinks, build a team, learn the lessons firsthand, and get the people and team functioning well. It takes more time than any of us think it will or that even makes sense. I've been involved as an owner in ten locations, plus several sub-businesses or locations at each, and I can attest to this. If you understand this from the start, the bumps in the road will jar you less than they would if they came as a terrible surprise.

The truth is that entrepreneurs (and new businesses) are pioneers, and we should all realize that pioneers endure numerous hardships as they chart new courses—regardless of whether they are establishing a new country, as the American pioneers did hundreds of years ago, or whether they are simply pioneering a new business. In either case, a very strong survival attitude needs to be practiced and displayed by the leader/CEO. It is the CEO's duty to ensure survival, as no one else will do it for you. If you are going to be a pioneer, you'd better develop and embrace a pioneering attitude. We're all pioneers of ourselves if we plan on going far.

Given enough time, most hardworking and industrious CEOs can survive the difficulties of the start-up phase or times of economic troubles. But if you do not have adequate resources to buy enough time, you are traveling a perilous road to ruin. My experience is that most successful CEOs can creatively buy time without having a lot of money. Anyone can spend money to buy time, but it takes real creativity to do it without deep pockets. It is pleasantly shocking how much creativity we develop when we have to. It's always the CEO's duty to control labor, people, costs, and expenses.

When you find yourself and your company truly immersed in survival mode, sweating the other big stuff will help you in numerous ways. I certainly acknowledge that it is difficult to work on nonurgent issues while trying to survive, but the successful do, and so should you. Never say that you are too busy to work on the important, nonurgent work, even if the wolves are baying at your front door.

Survival mode builds your success muscles

Ultimately, I believe that business success or failure is determined almost entirely by the CEO's attitude, thinking, determination, toughness, energy, leadership, habits, communication, relationships, and mental strength. It really is up to you, which can be a rather intimidating reality. But remember that you do not need to be a master of all those intangible qualities right away … or ever. The early survival phase is one of the most important learning times of your career, and the lessons that you learn in this survival can serve you well for the rest of your life. You will never be a warrior if you have never fought tough battles, and you will never be a winner unless you have been in the midst of tough competition and have failed from time to time.

As Oliver Wendell Holmes once said, "If I had a formula for bypassing trouble, I would not pass it round. Trouble creates a capacity to handle it. I don't embrace trouble; that's as bad as treating it as an enemy. But I do say meet it as a friend, for you'll see a lot of it and had better be on speaking terms with it."

Indeed, adversity—or trouble—is good for you, and you truly need it. Just as muscles will not develop without friction and force pressing against them, you will not develop your CEO muscles without combating adversity. We've already discussed this. However, my point is that the adversity-builds-strength concept definitely applies to finances, as well. While no one actually looks for difficult financial times, you should attempt to consider them a blessing when they arrive. They will test you, stretch you, and fortify you, and your PMA will grow exponentially if you maintain an upbeat perspective.

Also, keep in mind that your business is developed best when a lack of money and other constraints force you to tap into your creativity. With little money, you and your team will constantly be forced to think and act in less costly ways to give your customers value, as you will not be able to simply buy results. It's really only then that the genius within you is released. That's how entrepreneurship develops and thrives within you. I didn't appreciate this early in my career when I suffered through problems, but the crisis experience shaped and strengthened me and my business. Smart entrepreneurship doesn't seem risky at all to most successful entrepreneurs. The major risks come from starting blindly, spending in a naive fashion, or thinking conventionally. Those are recipes for failure.

According to business guru Brian Tracy, 80 percent of people who start a business without entrepreneurial experience fail in the start-up phase. On the other hand, Tracy points out that 80 percent of the people who had some previous entrepreneurial experience survive in their new businesses. I believe that the 80 percent who had previous experience knew from their earlier experiences that starting a business requires a serious survival attitude from the outset. It was burned into their brains. They knew that they were in a battle to generate a profit before they ran out of money, and they minimized all expenses. Most of the naive newcomers didn't. Without survival, there's no opportunity and rewards.

Debt matters

Vistage speaker Walt Sutton says that "it's hell to run a business with high debt, while it's easy and fun to run a debt-free business." While that sounds like old-fashioned common sense, I assure you that many businesspeople and entrepreneurs fail to follow this simple principle. It is true that most businesses experience various amounts of debt at times, and as an entrepreneur, you must understand what high or low debt is within your particular industry and budget. But no matter your size or situation, it is certainly good practice to stay away from high debt and avoid using up your safety net from the start like the losers do.

Monitor your debt. Controlling debt takes discipline, good financial thinking, and a long-term perspective. Allowing debt to grow is a form of instant gratification and failed thinking. High debt places business at risk because of interest costs, the reduction of your financial cushion to survive, reduced freedom of action from banks or investors, pressure from creditors, and the dangers of being fired or potential foreclosure. No one tends to think about these risks until they are swimming in a debt hole. Most entrepreneurs tend to operate their businesses under the presumption that their cash flow is about to dramatically improve. I always have. While it is beneficial to think positively, we must always maintain options to survive in case things don't improve dramatically. In fact, it really couldn't hurt to inject a bit of controlled pessimism into the equation. If you act as though your cash flow will dramatically decline, you'll adopt a more conservative approach to your financial management. Take prudent risks. Avoid those that might sink you.

Increasing debt continually reduces your freedom of action, and as I have often mentioned, success and entrepreneurship thrive on freedom of action. Freedom of action built America, and it's built the world where freedom has been allowed to prosper. It's the CEO's duty to limit debt, which allows for more freedom. This duty cannot be delegated. Personal debt prevents most of the people who would be great CEO entrepreneurs from starting their own businesses.

Partners can retard progress. Another form of debt that is not often labeled or discussed in this regard is acquiring partners in a singular entrepreneurial business. Many entrepreneurs want to seek and use partners as a crutch, but this rarely works best in the long run. Instead of using the crutch for a little while and then walking on your own, you often wind up in a wheelchair being controlled by those partners, who push you in one direction or another. It's best to resist this urge. Only one person can be a true entrepreneur or CEO who develops a business in his or her image. Don't get partners. Of course, I'm not necessarily referring to partners who may fit a law, accounting, real estate, or financial-type business which does have a CEO.

Starting out with too much money. As I noted earlier, keeping costs down is essential even when you're not in survival mode and even when your company has become firmly established in the market. It's particularly important when you're just starting out. I've noticed a pattern that's worth pointing out. It's been my observation that when inexperienced entrepreneurs start out with a lot of capital, the business rarely works out as planned. In those situations, there's always the tendency to buy success instead of using your creativity and leadership. Surviving and thriving with little capital develops perseverance, confidence, determination, leadership skills, creativity, and so much more. It forces us to constantly look for more economical approaches and more freedom of action. On the flip side, if you develop habits of merely throwing money at your difficulties, it will lead you to throw money away. Brian Tracy, who is perhaps the world's top entrepreneurial trainer, says that more businesses fail due to starting out with too much money than do those that start out with a shoestring budget. I agree wholeheartedly.

Proven products and services matter

No matter how good an entrepreneur may be, it's rare that a business will survive without proven goods or services for which there's a willing demand. You see some of these unproven businesses open their doors, but they tend to be more get-rich-quick schemes than businesses with a real plan. Successful start-up businesses produce, sell, and market products or services that people need and already buy. There are not many exceptions to this universal rule, but a very few have hit home runs.

Believe me, the odds are against you in starting up with the unproven.

Nothing will put you into financial-survival mode faster than that! It's an extremely demanding task to start up a business with proven services or products, and it's exponentially harder when introducing something brand new into the marketplace. Why put another hundred-to-one odds against yourself by trying to market products or services without a ready market when you haven't even mastered just running a business *with* a ready market? Successful entrepreneurs will nearly always recommend that you wait until you have a successful business before you roll the dice on an unproven product or service. If you do have a new unproven product, try to get it proved out as much and as quickly as you can. You may be the next person on *Shark Tank*.

Bootstrapping matters

The most common form of entrepreneurship is called the bootstrap method. The best formula for success is usually this, and it involves a small amount of start-up money and resources from savings, family, friends, or loans and a product or service that people need or desire. It's called the bootstrap method because, in most cases, you will have to pull yourself up by your bootstraps and do just about everything for yourself—with little or no help from others. A bootstrap entrepreneur normally has little financial cushion to survive, which would seem like a recipe for disaster. But most often, the opposite is true. If you have very little money, you most often develop a tough-as-a-boot mentality, pulling yourself up out of the hole with an old-fashioned work ethic and plenty of creativity and ingenuity. I have never seen anyone master a business unless he or she started from the ground up.

Bootstrapping builds success muscles. Bootstrappers generally do more with less, and their customers receive more for less. Bootstrappers buy survival time by working, producing, and believing in nonconventional success principle thinking. They do what they must do in order to succeed because there is simply no other way. Bootstrapping is the best way to become a successful entrepreneur. The principles are also very effective if you are working for others. I have never had a successful manager or worker who has ever spent his or her way to success with me. All the buyers of success that I have ever known have failed.

In life, most people will not tap into their subconscious mind, their faith, their true confidence, and their infinite intelligence unless they have no other options. It's like that old saying that states, "I didn't realize God was all I needed until God was all I had left." It's very similar in business. Most people will not realize they have the genius within them to succeed at phenomenal levels until they are forced to rely upon their own remarkable talents because there are no other options. If you have a bunch of savings, you will use that to throw money at the problems instead of tapping into your ingenuity and creativity to resolve those problems in a more economical manner. If you have partners with strengths, you will never develop your own success muscles in those areas. We are all geniuses when we are required to be, and we all have unlimited potential if we tap into our PMA brain.

The bottom line is that bootstrappers tend to succeed far more often than nonbootstrap CEOs. When you are required to start from the ground up, you understand all the workings of the business from the ground up. Those who merely buy into a business, inherit one, or are promoted to a CEO often are not equipped to run it because they missed out on so many steps and/or personal development needed along the way.

I liken bootstrapping to boot camp in the armed forces. Soldiers must learn discipline and how to survive long before they can go and lead others. It's very similar in business. When you go through the entrepreneurial boot camp and build your way up through the bootstrapping method, you are a much tougher and more courageous, confident warrior for the major battles that you will face in the future. It works in the military and everywhere else. I highly recommend starting out as a bootstrapper. If you can develop your 80/20 thinking and survive long enough, bootstrappers have a much better chance of long-term success because they develop so many great qualities and success muscles along the way. If you're not an entrepreneur, bootstrap your way through whatever job you have. It's how you will develop your success muscles.

Financial-survival mode at KMCO made me stronger. I am a bootstrapper entrepreneur myself. I started the business with $5,000 each from both a partner and myself. We'd work for free until we could afford to pay ourselves. I then got used equipment dealers to loan me equipment until I could pay them. Then I got seven or eight workers to work for free until I could pay them in three or four months, plus I got my dad and father-in-law to spend their vacations to help get us started. I leased a small, deserted research plant for six months at $1,000 a month until I could pay the owner the rest of $77,000 after I obtained an SBA-guaranteed loan. I learned the business from the ground up and learned to economize. I also got toughened up from plenty of adversities. Tough times started the day after I leased the research plant. The attorney who had bought the plant on a courthouse-steps sale sold the equipment at the plant to a used equipment dealer after I obtained the lease. They showed up with trucks and cranes to level the plant. I had to hold them off.

Another early adversity happened right after I bought out my partner three years after we started, with a future payment commitment of about $300,000. About ten days after the buyout, we had a fire on January 8, 1978, that burned down much of our plant. It was one of the coldest winters in Houston history, and it caused us many problems in rebuilding. It cost us $500,000 to get the plant going again, and we still owed $300,000 to my ex-partner, after also paying him the cash that we had. Our employees couldn't take the cold and rebuilding, so they all quit except for my sales VP, Steve Bordelon, and an injured worker, Marshall Brady, on leave from a motorcycle accident. The bank and most suppliers cut off our credit. We had a lot of problems with hiring good people and with finding good supervision. We got back into limited operation in four weeks and full operation in six weeks, even though we still had about 70 percent of the rebuilding to do. It wasn't easy to find new suppliers and delay payments for ninety days, but we got by.

You might say we were truly in survival mode at that point. Fortunately, by then, I had acquired sufficient experience as a CEO to weather the financial storm. I retained my PMA, worked leaner and meaner, kept my eye on the future, and remained focused on what matters most. Having to go into financial-survival mode is inevitable, especially if you're just starting out in a new business. Expect it. Plan for it. Don't be afraid when the going gets tough. In fact, welcome the adversity as a way to build your success muscles. See it as an opportunity to grow!

Chapter roundup

Most everything you do when it comes to managing and growing a business should involve lean financial-survival skills, especially when you're just starting out and are new to the CEO game. Plan for the inevitable tough times. Understand that economizing and working with less from a financial perspective builds your creativity. It also enables you to offer more value to your customers. Operating with low debt is also an essential part of working in the arena of full financial-survival mode, even when the times are good and profits are up. Remember that nearly all business progress in the world is done by doing more for less and not more for more. Doing more for less is excellence.

Conserve your cash reserves. Without them, you will not be able to buy yourself the time you need to respond to financial distress when it hits. You won't have bought yourself an opportunity to learn from your mistakes and thereby become a stronger CEO. Operating from the standpoint that revenue might plummet at any moment is going to breed financially conservative spending habits when it comes to capitalization, facilities, personnel, suppliers, and marketing initiatives. Obviously, you don't want to lean too far over to the conservative side in that you won't take prudent risks, improve your facilities, and develop your people. Use your master mind group like Vistage to learn and experience others' financial mistakes so as to help minimize your own.

If you save and keep costs down, you'll be nicely positioned to weather the financial storms that will hit your business. Any financial adversity you end up facing will make you stronger. When it comes, embrace it and learn! Harness your creative genius as a CEO!

Remember …

- » Include lean thinking in your long-term planning—and increase lean thinking during downturns. You will need to learn to stop trying to buy success if you are to succeed in the long run.
- » Building sound financial planning and business mindsets will build a cushion for new entrepreneurs to use to learn the ropes.
- » Save, keep costs low, and minimize all forms of debt, even when the business is doing great. You may need to run a marathon on short notice.
- » Partners are often a form of debt and mismanagement to avoid.
- » Analyze your financial habits, and get rid of any bad ones you identify. Listen to the audios to condition, further develop, and improve your financial mindset. None of us starts out with enough good financial thinking. Bad habits include failing to save, throwing money at problems, overspending to start the company in business, high debt, too much of a need for instant gratification, and taking on unnecessary partners.
- » Keep a positive mental attitude even when finances are terrible. Turn the adversity into an opportunity to think more creatively.
- » Operating lean builds your success muscles and creativity over the long term. Develop this thinking.
- » Learn your business from the bottom up.
- » Manage in good times for the bad times. Don't fatten up during the good times.
- » Build your success by always looking to do more for less, or you'll be passed by the competition.

- If you bootstrap a business, be fast to the market with the least amount of money spent. You're in a race to build at least a modest profit before you run out of money.
- Join a business or CEO group where you can benchmark yourself to others and learn from them. You can also watch TV shows on the operation of other businesses, such as *The Profit*.

8

Navigating Your Rivers of Profit

I am the master of my fate: I am the captain of my soul.
—William Ernest Henley, "Invictus"

Nothing is more dangerous than an idea
when it is the only one you have.
—Émile Chartier, philosopher

In many ways, a business is like a boat on a river. You are the captain and navigator of your boat. We can carry the river analogy a little further. Indeed, you can compare your markets, profit, and cash flow to a river. Profits flow in at varying rates, depending on a number of factors, including marketing strategy, the state of the economy, and innovation within the company. At the most basic level, your services or products constitute what we might call your "river of profit." Think of yourself as a riverboat captain. You are ultimately responsible for interpreting the flow of the rivers and navigating the deep waters while steering clear of the shallow streams.

Navigating the profits is fun and exciting

When you're on the river, understand that the profits and sales you are currently enjoying will not last forever. Many rivers of profit will eventually become narrow, bringing your vessel dangerously close to jagged edges of the riverbanks and rock-infested, shallow waters that could leave you shipwrecked. No river stays the same or goes on forever. You will have to look for new profitable rivers to navigate your business on and plan ahead to keep your boat or boats moving in safe waters. We have to normally think and plan well ahead. Planning five or ten years down the road isn't a bad idea. In fact, it's a very good idea! Think from the long-term result wanted backward to where you are now. This is goal setting, which is reverse engineering.

In contrast to narrowing rivers of profit, some rivers of profit could become so wide and deep that you'll need a larger boat to stay safely afloat. You may also need to acquire more big boats to create a fleet to best serve the customers and to weather rough white-water rapids when markets dip and the competition makes inroads. And you must always continue to make real money as you navigate your ship or ships. You are the captain of your ship, responsible for charting a course that will get you where you want to go. This responsibility cannot be delegated, since no one else will have your CEO viewpoint or wisdom.

Navigating the rivers of profit is another CEO duty, a vital piece of the 80/20 principle we discussed earlier. Only the CEO has the thinking, understanding, and responsibility needed to do this job. Only you can embark upon the right strategic planning to account for potential shifts and changes in the market and your business from one to five years into the future. The general rule for navigating the rivers is to use 80/20-principle thinking, which will allow you to follow the larger profits and steer away from low-profit business. We will need to plan ahead for long enough to keep the right boats profitably navigating down long, wide-enough, and deep-enough rivers. You'll need plenty of feedback to continue to navigate well, and you will need plenty of prospecting for new rivers to find the 20 percent of rivers that will give you 80 percent of your results.

Small sales aren't big deals. As you contemplate the concept of rivers of profit and consider where new avenues to profit might exist in the future, keep in mind that you're also looking to execute big deals that will make a positive difference on your bottom line. You no doubt know that, in business, very large sales that are an order of magnitude larger than a typical sale are commonly called *deals*. Some deals are normally needed for growth and success, as a business's small sales are not normally enough to sustain well in times of change, adversity, and new competition. These deals can result in very fast growth and profits or failure that can happen so quickly that it's like flying a crippled jet into the side of a mountain. Examples of what could also be considered deals are mergers, acquisitions, and ultimately the sale of your business at a handsome profit.

Deep down, I am convinced that virtually every enterprising, goal-oriented, and forward-thinking CEO dreams of ultimately making big deals that will drive his or her business to success. That's why most ambitious people go into business. Although genetic researchers have yet to prove it, I think that desire is probably somehow rooted within our CEO DNA. And with every high-profile success story of a "deal done right" that we read about or watch on television, our own drive to make our big deal steadily rises within us like the mercury of a thermometer on a hot summer day. After all, most of us realize that deal making can be, and normally is, an absolutely imperative component to the success of a business. Only you can identify and pursue the rivers of profit that can result in a big deal.

Vistage consultant and speaker Walt Sutton refers to deal making as "critical to CEO success," and I completely concur. We are all the CEOs of ourselves, and we have to live with the deals we make, good or bad, though hopefully the good vastly outweigh the bad! Each deal can either give you great success or enslave you for years. I'll talk more about that when we take a close look at prospecting. Basically, it's the CEO's duty to make the big profitable deals that fit the business and most likely drive profits.

Keep the following in mind:

- » There's opportunity in every business for potential deals and new rivers of profit. Focus on your company's strengths, and build for the future.
- » Deal making is a primary function of a CEO. The CEO can go to the top of an organization to make a deal and avoid the bureaucracy that will kill most deals. Big deals can result in long partnerships, which small deals rarely do. The top person of the other business is much more likely to give a CEO a great deal than the lower managers, who will lowball you into a bad deal.
- » The small sales are normally not enough entirely on their own to carry most businesses to success. Economic downturns, internal adversities, and new competition can narrow a river of profit. Substantial deals in new rivers of profit will propel the company forward even in tough times.
- » Small sales are important because that experience will uncover new markets, customers, and what you do that is so valued by others.
- » Seeking new rivers of profit, excellence, and the best deals within those new waterways is a perfect example of applying the 80/20 principle to your business. It's thinking big. To pursue it, you'll have to let go of the small stuff and only focus on the big stuff. Only seek deals that fit your 80/20 principle unfair advantage.

The CEO is the motor and the navigator of the big stuff

Looking back on my own experience with KMCO, I now realize that, like many CEOs, I had fallen into a trap. I believed that I was the captain of my ship and was firmly in control. After all, I founded the company and ran it. Yet I really wasn't doing the important stuff. I had allowed myself to be enslaved by the small stuff and let sales steer my ship. As a consequence, I was letting the company drift with the current, and I was focused only on the river I started on when I first began the business. I was trying to steer a drifting ship. As you may know, if a boat is moving downstream no faster than the current, the boat is almost impossible to steer. You're not really in control at all. The CEO is like the motor. Without it, the ship will simply drift with the current, only coming to rest in the shallow water. At that time in my life as a CEO, I was distracted and consumed by all the naive, well-intentioned directions our salespeople and managers were suggesting that were keeping us too busy to do the big deals.

Think big, not small. I foolishly thought small (but thought that it was big), which in turn prompted me to green-light taking on customers who were on the very low end of the profitability scale. They were never going to propel KMCO to the next level. Instead, they would hold us back because we'd be spending time maintaining a relationship that was going nowhere other than where it was already. It all sounded good at the time, though. I now understand that many salespeople, managers, and customers will want you to supply some product or service that people need. However, much of this needed work is not to our advantage. I just didn't see it at the time, since I didn't have a CEO's viewpoint.

Bear in mind that everybody thinks that they are bringing you a great idea or a solution to generate more business and make the company more profitable. But they tend to view it from their own conventional, linear, and narrow sales or manager perspective instead of the CEO's viewpoint. The most successful leaders maintain control of their time and the focus of their business by understanding their business and practicing the 80/20 principle in regard to steering their ship along better and better rivers of profit. That's the key idea. Playing to the lowest denominator wastes time and keeps you from focusing on what's important that of seeking out customers who will exponentially grow your business over time. If you do that, you'll be ready when profits from existing customers inevitably dry up or precipitously drop off.

Now, of course, I am indeed the captain of my ship, and I'm only sweating what matters most, such as planning, strategy, culture, people, and marketing. I learned that managers and salespeople can't effectively manage my job, which is what I was letting my people do when I signed off on a bunch of low-end business from customers who would never get us anywhere except in a maintenance-enslaved situation. If you picture yourself as a captain on a river, it may help you as much as it did me.

Do only what your company is good at. I've mentioned this before, but it merits repeating. I've said that it's important to find your niche and to play to your strengths. This is highly important for many reasons associated with your day-to-day operations and profitability, but it's equally important from the strategic perspective of finding new rivers to navigate when the one or ones you're on grow shallow and rocky. When you're out exploring, you may find yourself leaning toward a river of profit that stretches the limits of your company. If you ever have been or are presently in that situation, know that it is natural. The push to grow the company with new business is intense, and if the company is on iffy financial ground, the pressure on you and your sales staff is understandably enormous. Thus, it's easy to give in to the temptation to move into a niche that does not match the strengths of the company.

The huge mistake I see happen far too often is that CEOs veer from the business they know into completely different businesses. This is a recipe for disaster. I've gotten away from my strengths on many occasions, and on nearly all of them, I have suffered. When I vary less than perhaps 20 percent from what I'm successful at doing, it normally works out well. When I vary much more, it rarely works out. You will also stray, but knowing this will teach you a good lesson. I cannot express enough how important it is to stick with what you know and do well in deal making. It's good to expand your realm of thinking, to move beyond your comfort zone, and to strive for personal growth in all areas. But when it comes to new business or actually making deals, stick to your strengths. Only make deals where you have an advantage, and only make deals that play to your company's strengths. I learned this lesson when I took on a lot of business in the early years that I knew exactly how to do. However, our operators and our lab, health, safety, environmental, and shipping personnel didn't. They just knew the chemistry and processing of the simpler chemistries that they were used to.

Make sure that you're ready to do the job. The largest mistake I've made on deals is not having the infrastructure or the right people to execute the deal to the perfection the customer wanted. Keep in mind that large businesses, which are very bureaucratic and perfectionistic, will often crucify you if you start out executing the work or product at 98 percent right. They are very perfection-oriented. You'll normally need strong personal relations and a stronger team than you think to execute big deals and deal with the imperfections that can ruin them.

Focusing on what you do well and avoiding your weaknesses seems like rudimentary, stating-the-obvious type of advice. But throughout the history of business, even well-established and rock-solid companies have made colossal mistakes by simply straying from what they do best. In his book *The 50 Best (and Worst) Business Deals of All Time*, author Michael Craig, a former class-action lawyer who now writes about big business, examines the root inspirations/causes of the brightest and most boneheaded deals of all time. In many cases, the genesis of a disastrous deal was simply the bad decision of a CEO to venture into an area or industry in which he or she had little to no expertise.

Temper expectations. It's been my experience—time and time again—that overenthusiastic CEOs and salespeople generally perceive the large deals too optimistically. I certainly did. Doing these deals is a lot more complex than the concept you agree on with the other party. Murphy's law is also always in effect. It's the real world. Especially for more inexperienced CEOs, my strong advice in making a significant deal is to take your first excited and typically naive evaluation and always add as much to the bottom-line proposal as you can because you are surely going to need it. Resist the temptation to promise the stars at a price that won't even cover the expenses of a trip to the moon.

Here's the reality: if the job were that easy, someone else would be doing it and doing it well. Generally speaking, the customer or client is always going to be expecting a lot more than what you think when the details and demands come in later. Believe me! I've been there so many times that I could practically establish residence in Outlandish Expectationland. Customers will want to take you there, as well, so build extra costs into your budget to cover added expenses before ever making the initial offer. No matter what you're being paid, you need to do an excellent and a totally complete job for your customer. If you're not charging enough, you probably won't be able to do a good job. Your customer will be unhappy with you even if you're saving them millions. I've been there. New "whale" deals are a lot like new businesses in terms of Murphy's law. It will take you three times longer and cost twice as much as you first naively estimate to get it fully implemented. Your customer will most likely expect far more quality, bureaucracy, and service than you could have ever imagined.

Most important, keep your head. Stay cool. Even if you are on the cusp of striking a deal that could be front-page headlines on the *Wall Street Journal* tomorrow, make absolutely certain that the newspaper will be praising your deal-making expertise instead of ripping you to shreds for being a village idiot. As in medicine, the first objective in deal making is to do no harm. Like an iceberg, deal making involves much more than the 10 percent others see above the water. Most of the work and obstacles are in the 90 percent of the iceberg below the water's surface that only the CEO can see. That's why the CEO has to do the deal.

You learn a little bit more and gain more confidence with each deal you make and as you open up new rivers of profit on a bigger scale through solid prospecting and strategic marketing. It's much more than luck or being in the right place at the right time. To be a good deal maker, you need to fine-tune and develop strengths in doing the big stuff so that you have the ability to see the right opportunity at the right time and perform if you make the deal.

You'll need to have made progress on your positive mental attitude and 80/20 thinking to clearly see opportunity and the great deals. Without enough of this thinking, no one can see the opportunity, as any deals look like they are good. Good customer relationships and interpersonal skills will help greatly, but mere intellectual, conventional knowledge of particular customers or how to make a deal will likely not.

You will most likely enter the negotiation process and have to learn from your successes and mistakes, drawing strength from both.

With that said, you might be wondering how to best accomplish the navigation you'll need to identify new rivers of profit and the deals that will ensure the longevity and profitability of your business. Let's take a good hard look at prospecting for new business in a way that applies directly to you as a CEO, not in a way that would apply to a member of your sales staff. We all have to prospect as CEOs. It's an ongoing process vital to the longevity of any company, but there's good and bad prospecting. There are good and bad customers. It's up to you to navigate to the best customers who fit your unfair advantage with good, focused prospecting. In short, you focus on the big stuff!

Targeted prospecting

It's very tempting to take on virtually any new business, no matter what it is. It's logical to think that more business volume will enhance profitability. In a sense, we're hardwired to think that more is better in terms of customers, but that's definitely not true. For instance, at KMCO, the customers who want what we do best and what they most need are the best fit for us both. They'll value what we produce, and they'll value our position as an industry leader. Those are the customers I want. Jack Welch at GE once said that he wanted all its businesses to be either number one or number two in their industry. He wanted only businesses that stuck to their strength and niche (your unfair competitive advantage). The businesses that are number one or two in their industry stick to their strengths. He makes a good point with that concept, and it's one I internalized a long time ago.

I don't want the business that many other organizations similar to mine can do about as well as or even better than we can because the chances are that the jobs won't pay much. I've also learned to stay away from difficult customers and areas of business in which our "boat" struggled. As I said earlier, it's very dangerous for a company to move beyond its area of expertise—its niche, if you will—just to get new business. New business in that area is going to send you hurtling into a river filled with rocks and unpredictable currents. You're virtually guaranteed to slam the bow into a very sharp rock.

Sometimes, the best deal you can make for your company is the one that you *don't* make. It's easy to fall prey to the pressure to take on new business that doesn't produce premium profits or possibly stretches the limits of the company's capabilities merely to get more volume. Resist and muster the courage to say, "Thanks, but no, thanks!" Have the courage to say this to your sales staff, as well, and fully explain why the new business doesn't fit the company's mission. If it's necessary, launch a program to better train staff to focus on the types of prospects that fall into the rivers of profit you've identified and that are likely to produce the big deals you want. Being enslaved by poor business keeps us from developing additional great business.

CEOs are prospectors. In my case, as is the case with your company, I had to realize what kind of ship I had. It wasn't an icebreaker, a rowboat, or a battleship. It was and still is my responsibility to have the right boats, get on the right rivers, and navigate my fleet to enhanced, sustained profitability. It took me a while, but I finally learned that no matter how talented my associates may be, they can't chart the course. The talented people around you can't, either. Nobody can guide you in your life and business decisions better than you can yourself. Keeping an open mind and soliciting advice when needed is essential, but in the final analysis, the buck stops with you. You can't let others steer you. If you do, you may well run into a sandbar or a rock. If you're going to run aground, it's far better if it's your fault because you'll learn from the mistake and grow stronger because of it. The CEO is the chief marketing officer of the business.

Let's drill down on this concept a little further. While it's natural to rely heavily on others for information and strategic planning when considering the development of new business, only the CEO can make the truly strategic decisions effectively, steering away from the shallow rivers that will inevitably cause your business to become stuck. Not every deal is a good deal. In fact, most aren't. A choice between two poor alternatives is really no choice at all. It's a trap. The people below you are far more likely to fall into that trap than you are because they are focused on their part of the company, not the company as a whole. They simply do not see the 90 percent of the marketing iceberg that is below the surface. In most smaller businesses, the CEO has the duty and responsibility of marketing, which can rarely be delegated. The CEO should be able to direct the business to more of the right customers and right business. Sales is happy about getting any business, which my successful CEO friends will agree. Sales shouldn't be allowed to navigate the ship. That's why marketing exists, and the CEO is the chief marketer.

Say no to the good, so you can say yes to the great. I've found over the years that we must work on several times the amount of needed future business in order to choose the best future business we actually need. We must also allow for the business that won't happen. And we have to look for the 20 percent of the business that will produce 80 percent of the profit. I want only the best 20 percent of business for all my business. In other words, we must explore many potential rivers of profit and vessels to navigate them before we find the desirable waterways and vessels in which we should invest our time, energy, and resources. As I've said, it's a dynamic world. It requires targeting the right businesses (river exploring) to get on the right rivers of profit. Success takes a lot of freedom of choice and action. Much of this comes from a lot of creative thinking and prospecting. The CEO will have to push his or her team to look at many customers, markets, and deals. Your salespeople will be excited about the first business/sales they see and want to do it.

Remember this key point: maintainers simply get enough business to keep them busy and afloat. It's what I did when I started. In fact, most CEOs tell me that their business is doing well and that they have a lot of new business to do. That new business is normally just one customer, project, or product that will keep them busy. They do not have much freedom of action to succeed. I see their businesses as very stagnant and drifting with the currents. Their business is often a comfort zone, but it's not a best practice. That's not a rut that I want to be in. This should be the same for you. You probably will avoid that rut with CEO thinking if you can recognize it as one.

You need choices to succeed. I've seen firsthand that having limited choices or choosing between two poor opportunities is not the path to success. I, like all my friends, did a lot of that and had to learn this lesson the hard way. This is true for even the most talented and wisest CEOs. The success of countries, businesses, and people comes from freedom of action. That's why free enterprise and entrepreneurship have excelled throughout the world where they are allowed to exist. In business, we have to explore a lot of rivers to be able to have the freedom of choice to choose the right or best rivers. Use the powerful-goals brainstorming technique to help build a lot of options by opening up your creative genius. The best businesses will rise to the top, and the average businesses will drift with the current at a much lower level of success.

Any business in any field can be built into a billion-dollar business using these principles, if that should be your goal. You need a lot of choices of business if you're going to only choose the best 20 percent or less. As a growing business, you'll be able to easily spot the prospects you can best serve that will yield the highest profits. It's simpler than you think. The CEO should always be looking for big deals that he or she can close in tandem with another CEO. The entry-level employees or even mangers at the business you're trying to close are never looking to give *you* the best deal. They want that for themselves, even if it hurts their business. They don't want you to get good deals. The CEO is usually looking for a fair, long-term deal to satisfy his or her business needs. The best advice I can give is to bypass the entry-level managers and focus on the other CEO's need for a fair deal benefiting both parties.

In sales, the most successful people are also the best prospectors because they're able to work on the best prospects and eliminate the worst prospects. That's what my boss Paul Meyer at Success Motivation International preached when I was attempting to sell his motivational programs. You will be much more successful by investigating various rivers and selecting the strongest ones, as opposed to just floating wherever the water takes you. Prospect, prospect, prospect! And don't be afraid to be highly selective in any new business you finally do take on. The more freedom of choice you have, the more successful you'll be. An average person will greatly outperform the most brilliant people if he or she has a lot more freedom of choice. Value freedom of action, and strongly fight against all your enslavements, as well as those of your people and/or your business.

Keep developing your rivers of profit. Stay in motion, as it's your job to look ahead and to stay ahead of the game. Always keep in mind that most people operate with static, conventional, linear, and short-term thinking, which is somewhat good and needed for maintaining the monthly operation. But I caution you that merely staying the course is a recipe for disaster. No company continues to progress and evolve by simply doing everything it has always done or what happens to come its way. Progress most often comes as a result of exploration, expansion, creativity, thinking, and adaptation. It's a dynamic world, and your business and profits will not last forever, as they are also dynamic. Continue to develop new strengths that are compatible with your business. This should include sales and marketing.

I've been able to see this personally across a wide group of businesses through my involvement in Vistage, an organization dedicated to helping CEOs improve their performance as entrepreneurs. It has been very helpful to me. As a result, I can now understand what Napoleon Hill meant by the master mind group that he talked about in his success bible, *Think and Grow Rich.* Vistage provides me with a great master mind group of CEOs without my having to go out and create one. We all need to get outside our own narrow business and see our world from the perspective of other successful people. It's a much more effective way of seeing our rivers of profit in the right perspective. Being involved in your own master mind group of CEOs will give you a great perspective of this prospecting. You will not go nearly as far in life if you only surround yourself with people dependent on you.

People count. Lastly, don't underestimate building strong personal relationships with the right people in the industries you have targeted for new business development. These people could be officers in a trade association, or they could be officers or CEOs of specific companies you have identified as potential prospects. Business is about trust and relationships that engender mutual respect. Business is about serving a need, and it is people who determine what we need in the market, how that need is fulfilled, and when it is fulfilled. Always think of what the customer wants and needs and how you can give it to them or how you can give it to them in the most economical and efficient manner while maintaining the highest degree of expected quality.

When zeroing in on a prospect that fits your rivers of profitability and is likely to generate profits within that 20 percent upper realm that you seek, make sure to establish early on a solid relationship with as many people as you can in that business. Big deals come when the customer trusts you to solve a problem that the customer can't solve as well as you can. If the people in the power positions feel invested in beginning a relationship with your company and that the relationship will benefit them and their customers, you're on your way to sealing the deal and securing the new business that fits your strategic plan.

You'll have to determine who you have to sell to and what they want. You'll have to determine how you'll overcome or satisfy the deal breaker (there's always at least one). You'll have to figure out how to get around the bureaucracy that could kill the deal. You'll need to have a lot of potential prospects in the process and manage the process. The good news is that a CEO can go straight to the top to explore the possibilities of developing new business. Salespeople can't, though it's definitely more possible for your subordinates to make bad deals that will bury the company in unprofitable busywork. With the right guidance, your sales and marketing team can assist you as you apply the right, nonlinear thinking to the long process of exploring the new rivers of profit that you'll need as existing conditions inevitably change. Just remember that *you're* at the helm, not your staff! It's only the CEO who can see the 90 percent of the iceberg that's below the surface.

Navigating new rivers of profit and making important deals is fun, exciting, and profitable, especially as you see the progress you are making. As the navigator, you should also embrace the challenge of the exploration. No matter how well you are doing as an organization, there are always areas of your business where you can do much better. Just keep moving toward the rivers that are most profitable (80/20 thinking), and always be aware of the fact that those most profitable rivers can lead you in an even more profitable direction.

Why not take action right now? Grab your pen and a legal pad, and write down answers to the following questions:

1. **Do you have your rivers of profit planned or outlined for the next five and ten years?** If not, take some time to start a working draft of your outline. Work on it at specified times. Include this time in your work schedule. Remember, it's the big stuff that counts. Do the five- and/or ten-year objectives before doing the one-year plan.
2. **Do you have enough freedom of action and enough choices to create outstanding rivers of profit?** This one is a little tougher to answer because it requires you to look objectively at your work schedule to evaluate where your time goes. If you're not free to think about issues associated with future profitability and future prospects to ensure that profitability, you're denying yourself the freedom of action needed to get where you want to go. You could also find yourself boxed in because you signed on new business that fell into that nefarious 80 percent or, worse, that lowest 20 percent of your least profitable business. Now you're busy doing busywork that's getting you nowhere and robbing you of freedom of action and choice.
3. **Write down twenty things that you can do to develop better potential rivers now.** Ask yourself what broad areas of market potential exist now, and consider the current trends influencing those markets. Are pressures exerting a downward push on the industry? Conversely, do opportunities exist that bode well for the industry? An industry on a downward trend is not

necessarily in trouble. It could merely be reacting to a cyclical movement that is completely natural. A down industry shouldn't be immediately dismissed. There could be excellent opportunity for future growth.

4. **What are the top-twenty big deals you dream about making? Write them down in detail.** There's a big difference between identifying the twenty new rivers of profit and identifying the top-twenty big deals you'd love to make. Ferreting out new prospects for rivers means that you're looking at entire industry segments for potential opportunities. Visualizing and writing down the top-twenty deals is going to focus you more narrowly on specific companies and more precise missions. Both avenues of thinking big represent exactly what I'm talking about when I say that we as CEOs need to focus on the top 20 percent of our business. I'm not just talking about our most profitable customers; I'm talking about reprogramming our thinking to surge into the nonlinear to tap into our creativity. I'm talking about a focus that can lead to a shift that in turn can take you to stellar success.
5. **Write down twenty things that you can do to build the right boats—or *enough* boats—to navigate your rivers. Are your boats large enough, fast enough, and tough enough?** This question addresses logistics and long-term adjustments that you might have to make if you are to successfully navigate those new rivers of profit that you identified earlier. This is the time to ask yourself how you would serve these new customers and what you'd need to do to deliver what you promise. Do you need to plan on making a large capital investment in your company's infrastructure? For example, do you need to upgrade a plant or build a new one? Do you need more trucks to deliver goods? Do you need more personnel to make sure that you can still offer top-level service when you're twice as busy as you are now?

Chapter roundup

Your rivers of profit are the services or products you offer your customers, and while you must remain faithful to your niche market, you must also realize that the needs of your customers are dynamic. Thus, customers that need you now won't need you later. This, in turn, means that you have to constantly seek out new and more lucrative customers to serve, thereby opening new rivers of profit. You may also happily have to adapt to existing rivers of profit widening into estuaries of wealth and activity that require you to upgrade your fleet!

In any case, apply the 80/20 principle in all that you do. Select new business that functions at the top 20 percent of business that fits your secret unfair advantage. My goal is to always have most of my business in the top 20 percent of business that fits my unfair advantage. After applying the 80/20 principle for years, my top 60-plus percent of business is all about equal. This is where using the 80/20 principle over time will get us. I don't want to have 80 percent of my business yielding only 20 percent of my results. That's what the mass of people achieve. Don't be enslaved by the bad part of the 80/20 principle. The tendency is to get whatever new business you can and then maintain it. That ultimately leads to stagnation. The best CEOs are always moving ahead, steering their companies to new rivers of profit and making the best deals to keep in the black.

Remember …

- » Rivers of profit are impermanent and always changing. Prepare for that inevitability through strategic planning five and more years out. If you don't, your company is in danger of losing most of its profitability the moment things go bad.
- » Apply the 80/20 principle to profitability. Focus only on the top 20 percent of deals. Then reverse the process and get rid of the worst 20 percent of the business.

- Play only to your company's top strengths. Don't get bogged down in foolish forays away from your niche. If you can't play the best game in a given area, move on to one where you'll totally excel. Strive for excellence.
- Call on far more potential prospects than you can actually take on in order to find enough business that fits your top 20 percent and your unfair advantage criteria. Business opportunities will fall through, and others won't meet your criteria. It's all a numbers game. Excellent business prospecting is what the best do. If you don't find enough of the right business, you'll find yourself doing business you don't want. Excellent CEOs are doing great at navigating their rivers of profit. Poor CEOs and businesses are not.
- Always continue to develop and build your sales and marketing so that you can be more and more effective navigating your ship down the dynamically changing rivers of business every year.
- You need freedom of choice and time to best bring in the right new clients from your rivers of profit. Plan for this excellence thinking in your daily calendar.
- Don't let others navigate your ship. Only the CEO can guide the company down the right path to profitability. You're the responsible party, whether you succeed or fail. There is no one else that has your CEO perspective to do your job. You are the captain and navigator.
- Build vital relationships with the most powerful people in industries under cultivation for new business. Pay special attention to relationships within specific companies targeted as potential prospects, and make certain to get the deal breaker invested in your service or product. If you can get the potential deal breaker aboard or neutralized, you are more likely to enjoy smooth sailing. There's always a deal breaker.

» The CEO pretty much has to make a deal with the customer's CEO in order to have a great deal for both. Salespeople and managers rarely can. Big deals are a CEO's duty. Develop yourself into the CEO who is capable of seeing and making great deals.

» Visualize excellent navigation on your rivers of profit, and write down your plan with twenty options for how to get there. To me, the visualizing of navigating my rivers has proven to be an easy way to direct my business.

» It is fun to have a lot of freedom of action to navigate your business.

9

Culture Eats Strategy for Breakfast

Culture eats strategy for breakfast.
—*Peter Drucker*

Building excellence with business culture is very much like building a great sports team. The excellence mirrors the values and attitudes of all on the team. Culture is the personality of the team. It's basically the "This is how things are done around here" rule that governs how everyone within a group behaves and even thinks. Culture has historically been the best leading indicator of future business performance, especially in a nonlinear business.

As such, business culture is a very big CEO duty. It's actually critical in terms of creating the foundation of excellence you as the CEO can build on to get your business or team where you want it to go. Hopefully, your goal will be to build a great culture with a winning attitude similar to a championship sports team. A winning teamwork attitude with "can do," "go to," "do more than you're paid for," and "one for all, and all for one" players and coaches will make a great team. These teams are fun to lead and play for. They also win championships. Doing only what you're being paid for never wins championships! Developing this culture of excellence is the people building and team building needed for great success. Caring people in a great culture are the ones who you want to execute your processes and strategy. A team culture that fits your goals makes doing business very enjoyable and personally rewarding.

After getting ourselves and our strategy right, our performance all comes down to people, culture and process.

If you doubt the validity of placing so much emphasis on developing a performance-based, can-do business culture, consider the results of the following study cited in the insightful management practice book *What Really Works: The 4+2 Formula for Sustained Business Success.* Authors William Joyce, Bruce Roberson, and Nitin Nohria detail their findings on key management practices, including the establishment of a solid and wholesome corporate structure. The study of 160 companies ran from 1986 to 1996. From comprehensive surveys of those companies, the authors correlated corporate performance with the companies' adherence to over two hundred commonly used business practices. Only four of those business practices correlated directly to a high level of business success. Companies they identified as highly successful businesses were excellent in all four of the below-listed primary business practices:

1. Strategy (chapters 1–8)
2. Performance-based culture (chapters 9–10)
3. Execution (chapter 11)
4. Decentralized structure (flat organizational structure with empowerment by all, chapters 9–10).

The results are dramatic. Good performance-based business culture ranks right up there with strategy. In fact, the other two hundred business practices measured beyond the 4+2 formula are, in fact, ineffectual in making a business highly successful. This makes the top four even more important to you as you navigate your business career forward on its rivers of profit. A healthy business culture is essential for major success, and it's necessary for the other three practices to work well. Only doing excellently in three of these practices wasn't enough to classify a business as highly successful. Most of us admire the businesses and organizations that have great cultures of can-do and go-to people who have a mindset like an owner. Great cultures are often described as action-oriented, where everyone is inspired to do his or her best, identifies with the objectives of the business, is empowered to make independent decisions, is urged to seek out ways to improve operations, helps customers have rewarding experiences, and works as a team. Outstanding businesses have this performance-based culture. It's a "we are great" team, instead of an "I am great and you aren't" in a more linear-thinking team. Employees have the freedom to act and release their imagination and energy, and it extends to the entire organization. They become empowered, which requires little management and bureaucracy. This requires you to use more flexible, strategic thinkers who are focused on excellence and the team goals. The more planful people wanting to do repetitive work will not want to be a part of this culture, as they are more compatible with a bureaucracy. The more flexible, nonrigid thinkers have the habit of thinking about the actions they do during each hour and day. They are the strategic people you need. When and where my businesses have had this great culture, the business has been magical, fun, family-like, and extremely profitable. I know firsthand that culture truly does eat strategy for breakfast, as Peter Drucker says.

Let's briefly further define exactly what I mean when I refer to an excellent performance-based culture. Basically, the nutshell definition means that everyone works together as a team to all row the boat in harmony and in the right direction (very rare!), which explains the emphasis on "we" instead of "me" when I discuss business culture. Every player shares the same level of dedication to his or her job as everyone else and views his or her part in the company's framework as vital and important. Thus, the employees in a business tend to work harder with more pride than those employed in a business where they aren't appreciated or rewarded for performing their duties in an exemplary fashion. In an excellent performance-based culture, everyone from entry-level employees to the CEO has a can-do attitude, and all employees are go-to people who listen to their teammates and respond to any problems that arise. This decentralized organization is a nonlinear culture, where people are empowered to handle their duties, which is in harmony with all the dynamic 80/20 principle execution concepts. Very little management takes place, and people love what they are doing. It's what I have always wanted but have not always had. A centralized culture in a conventional-thinking business is not conducive to the culture I'm describing.

Naturally, we should want that kind of culture for our own organizations if we're not in a linear conventional business. When an organization has that culture, it is easy to manage, and it is very much appreciated by its customers and employees. And you will be able to execute strategy well because execution requires a great culture with the right people and good processes. Sadly, few CEOs know how to build such an excellent performance-based culture, and very few are even aware of the need to build and improve culture. Culture is a very soft, vague, and intangible area of nonurgent work that's difficult to get our arms around or define. Each of the highest-performance businesses will require similar but moderately different performance-based cultures. For example, a shipping company is going to have a different corporate culture in some respects than a fashion design studio. What both will share in common is the can-do attitude and dedication to teamwork to accomplish the common objectives of the company. In all likelihood, the fashion design business will need a more nonlinear, creative culture than the shipping company. The shipping company will still require a nonlinear, creative culture. The "we are great" and the performance-based elements of a robust and healthy corporate culture are highly desired in all nonlinear, decentralized businesses and organizations. The more linear, conventional businesses can also benefit greatly from this culture, but obviously it would take a massive amount of time and effort to gradually move a large conventional business in this direction.

A great culture operates at the speed of now through flawless and excellent execution at the worker level. This culture is very cross functional across levels in a business, which keeps it fast and teamwork oriented. People buy into excellence, action, and speed. The leaders walk around in the trenches and interact with those doing the work and see firsthand what they are facing and doing. Bureaucracy and conventional management are strongly resisted and what is done is nearly invisible. Productivity and achievement are celebrated, as is flawless execution. The entire team is committed to the right priorities and continuous improvement. Everyone wants to do more for less, and everyone is rowing the boat in harmony and in the same direction. Strategy is fluid and flexible, since the people who can best determine how to achieve the goals are making those decisions. There are no conventional thinkers in a place or position to ruin the teamwork. This great culture is truly magical.

The majority of this book preceding this chapter is about the CEO's duties, development, and strategy. Culture is all about the excellent execution of the strategy by the people. I've experienced in my plants where people executed poor strategy with a great culture double the results of what a great strategy and poor culture would have achieved. Culture truly eats strategy for breakfast.

Culture as the implementation part of your internal master mind group. A great culture fits Hill's definition of a great master mind group. Hill says that it is the "coordination of knowledge and effort in a spirit of harmony among two or more people for the attainment of a definite purpose." No one person can solve every problem. It truly takes a great culture to have a great business.

Don't be too busy to care. The CEOs of many organizations view themselves as too busy to tackle the soft issue of promoting a healthy performance-based business culture. It frankly doesn't even show up on the radar screen in many cases because encouraging a good performance-based culture is a nonurgent and intangible issue. One reason is that a performance-based culture is largely ignored in conventional businesses. Besides, who teaches culture at business school? And who offers the right nonlinear training on the subject? Not many. The fact of the matter is that many CEOs choose to avoid building and developing the culture they desire because they don't know where to start, and it's too big of an issue to attack from where their culture is. They would probably have to fire half of their people to get it right. I've been there.

It's been my observation that many CEOs who actually address the culture issue will simply try to hire the right hero or HR person to achieve positive culture results for their businesses, like I did at first. I had little luck in getting the managers I hired to embrace and build this culture. I quickly learned that a performance-based culture is the CEO's duty. This is a tough subject for me largely because, in spite of my efforts to build a sound business structure, I've not always been as successful at building and maintaining that culture as I would like due to various harmful management changes. It has also taken me a long time to develop the good performance-based cultures that I have.

An illustration: Early in my career, I hired experienced managers with good resumes who were more compatible with linear, conventional thinking. These highly technical conventional thinkers moved through the management process in a steady, plodding manner from point A to point B. These managers weren't totally wrong, but their linear ways didn't inspire a real can-do attitude that would have employees anxious to work harder and longer to get the job done when the chips were down in terms of a manufacturing challenge or tight deadline. I had anything but a performance-based culture, and my business suffered. Productivity wasn't humming at 100 percent. Turnover was costing us time and money. I had yet to get to a point where I could fully understand what was wrong.

Over time, I learned the hard way that I had to build the culture I needed within my organization. It was all up to me—just as it's all up to you! I couldn't rely on a manager to handle that role even on a limited basis, unless he or she had previously had experience in a performance-based business similar to what I wanted. I didn't want to foster an "I" attitude or the "my job" mentality. I wanted a "we are a team" and "we are the best" mentality that would permeate the entire labor force. Wanting and knowing how to go about something are two different things. I found the best place to start was to think of the people in the company as family. I'd ask, "How would I feel if I were treated that way?" If the answer was "Crappy," then I'd think twice about doing whatever it was I was thinking of doing.

Now, thankfully, I have a lot more performance-based culture, with several (not most) of the right managers who can assist me. But I do have to jump back in often with the new, more linear-thinking managers when the go-to part of our culture starts getting off base. This has happened to me many times. Only the CEO has the perspective and vision to develop and maintain this highly effective culture, but it takes the help of many others. In my case, I encouraged open communication among all employees and an open-door policy between managers and their subordinates. For this teamwork, it's best to do a lot of cross-training between jobs and departments to where people appreciate others' jobs and departments so that you don't have strong department walls. Have more informal, open space, and mix offices of varying departments to develop team thinking. Don't go with big fancy offices. Make your business to where the wrong culture people will not want to work there and the right culture people will. In a great culture, we get our authority through our leadership and not our titles. In a great nonconventional culture, the CEO and workers are all on the same team; they just have different roles. They all know each other. Each has his or her part on the team. There is no "us" (management) and "them" (labor) divide, or at least I hope there isn't. And if there is one, as I suspect is almost always the case no matter what we do as CEOs, I hope the divide is a hairline crack as opposed to the Grand Canyon. We also have to live, act, and perform according to the culture we want, as everyone will look to us. One mistake that I made over the years is that I never painted a picture of our culture goal with clarity for my teams. I need to sell the culture I want to all and to continue to do so over time with new employees. I won't make that mistake again.

When I've been able to develop a good performance-based culture within my organization, most people could see and admire our results, even though they often couldn't pinpoint the intangible quality. In observing the day-to-day operations of my business, I've had numerous people tell me that I obviously know how to sprinkle enough magic on business to make it work miracles. I am flattered by the compliment, but that magic isn't Tinker Bell's pixie dust. Many consultants and customers just can't conceive how we do it.

In fact, it isn't magic at all. It's mostly the result of our culture. I would say that we have a good "work-ethic, informal, teamwork, can-do, go-to" culture. I believe you—or any other CEO—will experience that magic by first building a good performance-based culture. It's the easiest and best way to inspire people to manage themselves. The first mandatory step is to be committed to such a culture. A majority of all businesses do not want this culture, as they are so committed to the conventional management model. But if you are committed to this can-do culture, then you need to hire people with the right attitude, values, nonlinear thinking, interest, and work ethic that fit your culture. The incompatible-thinking people will never fit your culture and will work against you. Culture works hand in hand with obtaining the right people and maintaining flawless processes, which are discussed in the next two chapters. This is where the execution of your business comes together with your CEO duties, strategy, thinking, and personal growth. Without a strong performance-based culture by your team to execute your business process, much of your hard work, growth rate, self-development, and strategy will be diminished.

After over forty years of running my own businesses, I can also testify that it's relatively easy and fun to operate a debt-free business with a performance-based culture. On the other hand, it's pure chaos to run a high-debt business that doesn't have a positive can-do teamwork culture. I know plenty of both the good and bad sides of culture firsthand. The reality is that when an organization does not possess a performance-based culture, it requires far too much micromanagement and bureaucracy to truly operate at even a decent productivity level. Every one of those times, I was enslaved by all their flaws and continuous problems. With a poor culture and the wrong people, the managers and employees do not have the empowerment and freedom to grow and blossom into all that they might be capable of becoming and achieving. Pairing the right compatible people with having enough freedom of action and empowerment is a cornerstone of a performance-based culture and of success. Remember that we can't give rigid, planful, pessimistic, static, linear thinkers as much freedom of action on wide responsibilities, and we can't give nonlinear thinkers responsibilities that are too narrow in scope and expect good performance. Getting that balance right is a CEO duty, and it requires great people-selection skills. For my nonlinear businesses, it has always been the linear thinkers who have hurt our culture, but that may not be the case with you if you have a very rigid, linear business. As a result, I only want to hire people who are compatible with my mindset for my businesses. They are the ones who have dynamic business thinking and habits and like working for small businesses. I can nearly always get them to adopt our nonlinear culture, and it's easy to teach them the best business practices.

A performance-based culture pays dividends

One of the great things about building and developing a performance-based culture is how it continues to build upon itself. It can be passed on from one generation to another, serving as the glue that holds our businesses and lives together. Of course, the same is true for a culture that is incompatible with your business. In business, people want to work in a culture that fits their values and needs. They want to work in a great culture. For a high-performance business, it's where performance is rewarded, values are cherished, freedom of action is encouraged, and creative thinking is promoted. In such an environment, all people who are compatible with that culture flourish, are engaged, and have better relationships with coworkers, clients, friends, and family. People will also work harder and longer and will display more loyalty for an organization that exhibits such a strong culture. And your staff—no matter how large or small—will remain far more compatible in a culture that treats them well.

As I indicated, I was a bit of a slow learner in this regard. I first went through several years of pain as a business owner because I did not initially commit to establishing such a culture, since I was enslaved by crisis. As a result, I allowed the attitudes of some people with the wrong traits to dictate the culture within our organization. A typical mistake, which is made far too often by CEOs, is making hiring decisions based solely on the strength of a candidate's résumé and interview instead of putting far more of an emphasis on attitude and finding people who fit the culture that you want within the organization. I fell short in this way for many years. However, when we finally built a good culture, I went through nearly thirty years with rarely losing a person that we wanted to keep. But it reared its ugly head recently in one of my plants that I sold.

Now I know that a primary key to building a good culture in a nonlinear-thinking business is to only bring in employees who are compatible with a corporate structure predicated on nonlinear thinking and empowerment. I get rid of people who don't fit our culture. The people who conflict with your culture will never work out well in your business, and in many ways, they will damage your business. The people who are in harmony with your culture will nearly always work out well, even if they're a little short on experience or education or skills. People count, and they can learn skills and gain experience. They are your greatest asset as a CEO, so it behooves you to work hard to make sure that coming to work isn't a dreaded experience. You can go a long way toward making your team more productive by encouraging team members to perform at the tops of their games and then rewarding them for excellent performance. If your strength and business requires linear thinkers to be compatible, you will need to hire people who fit that culture. However, I will caution you that there are very few small businesses that would or should have a linear-thinking culture if the goal of the business is growth. And this book is about nonlinear success, so I'll let the linear-business writers cover the linear stuff that does indeed apply to many people and businesses. In fact, all of us need to know a little about the linear world that we have to live in.

Lead by example. My next valuable lesson as a business owner was that the culture of an organization will tend to mirror the culture the CEO displays. Again, I speak with a great deal of personal experience when I say that if you want to improve the culture of your organization, the best first step is to improve your own thinking, habits, and actions. I had to work to minimize most of my negative habits and unproductive thinking, which were negatively affecting our overall culture. The CEO is the leader, and your staff will emulate the example you set on a day-to-day basis. As I have stated before, we only achieve to the level of our personal growth. You simply cannot expect your business to make great strides in its culture and overall productivity without you, the CEO, first making great strides individually. You must focus on your self-improvement when setting goals. Your smallest negative flaws will be magnified. They'll ripple out through the entire company, and they'll keep you from getting what you want.

As the CEO, you must always be aware that how you act, what you wear, what you say, what attitude you project, how you treat people, what approach you take to problems, how you think, how you exhibit honesty and integrity, what time you come to work and what time you leave, and other similar factors will become your culture. Your staff will model your behavior—positively and negatively. Walt Sutton tells the story that he came to work one Friday casually dressed to play golf that afternoon. Then, weeks later, he questioned a worker on his casual dress on a Friday. To his surprise, the worker told him that they were so pleased that he had implemented casual Fridays in the business. He hadn't!

If we desire an organization that exhibits integrity and attracts staff members of high moral caliber, we need to become the best CEOs that we can be, projecting and displaying the right values, management style, strategy, and philosophy. As CEOs, we must also give direction to our teams. Our vision, strategic plan, guiding principles, and mission should be compatible with our culture and should be taught and developed with our team, as they are a part of our culture. Obviously, your business will be best served by the empowerment culture that can best serve the customer.

Work to make the small stuff and procedures your servants, not your master. If you commit to excellence in what matters most and stick to the 80/20 principle in all that you do, you will in time develop a highly positive performance-based culture. However, if you and your business lack discipline and do too much more than good enough or spend too much low productivity effort on the small linear-performance stuff, you will not serve the winning culture you want very well. For best results, you need others' assistance in working on the important, high-value work. Your culture will be hurt if your team is doing too much low-value, linear work or if you have too many people working on the small stuff, which is another reason to minimize it. Everyone in your business wants to feel good about making important contributions, so stick with doing as much of what matters most as you can, and encourage others to do so as much as is practical. The nonlinear culture that's needed to do what matters most is negatively influenced by too much small stuff and narrow, conventional, static thinking. The small stuff is nearly all linear work. We have a choice of choosing to be good at the small, linear stuff that matters least or what matters most. We can't be excellent at both. No business can.

Because the term *business culture* can be such a vague and intangible quality, it is sometimes difficult for CEOs to gain a clear picture of how a performance-based culture could benefit their organization. In this regard, I think it can be helpful to observe and study other organizations or companies with positive, nonlinear empowerment cultures. I've spent many years studying and observing culture at work, and I recommend that you observe these three companies that possess and portray great corporate cultures: Southwest Airlines, Oceania Cruises, and the Ritz-Carlton hotel chain. I enthusiastically recommend reading the book *Nuts! Southwest Airlines' Crazy Recipe for Business and Personal Success* by Kevin and Jackie Freiberg, which details, among other things, the story of Southwest Airlines' unique culture. Consider copying and selling that culture. They do it right. Adopt it to your culture, and look for other businesses with good cultures to learn from. You can probably identify some businesses with good cultures.

It is obviously extremely beneficial for us to create a target picture of the cultural excellence we want for our business. It's easier to hit a target we can see, and it is almost impossible to hit a target if we do not have a clear picture of what we're aiming for. The great American author Napoleon Hill once said, "What the mind of man can conceive and believe, it can achieve." But the first key is to conceive it, to truly visualize it. In terms of developing a performance-based culture, the CEO must conceive and believe it before the organization can achieve it. Yet I've found that there are very few CEOs who have a good picture of such a soft, intangible concept as a great culture in their minds, which is why so many businesses are lacking in this all-important area. Observing these three businesses helped me greatly to comprehend the concepts of a great culture. Southwest Airlines communicates their culture clearly with three values: warrior spirit (work hard), a servant's heart (treat others as you would like to be treated), and a fun-loving attitude (take work seriously, but not yourself). They promote their culture a lot, and their culture is one that you should consider emulating.

A truly effective way to accelerate cultural change is to make virtually everyone within the organization a go-to person. In practice, instilling a positive atmosphere of greater accountability and responsibility within all employees quickly changes and improves the culture within an entire organization. In other words, don't go out of your way to change your organization; it's the go-to people who will change the organization. Having go-to people requires a decentralized organization, which is exactly what all the sources I'm aware of claim is a trademark of a successful business. In fact, a decentralized organization is one of the four things that all highly successful businesses that focus on the big-picture stuff have in common. A decentralized business is also what most businesses under a few hundred people generally have and what most should have. For this, we need mostly nonlinear-thinking people who match up with the nonlinear nature of the business. Linear, conventional, centralized, bureaucratic businesses need mostly the opposite—linear-thinking people—for their maintenance. Maybe they don't *need* the linear thinkers, but they are about the only good workers who want to work for them. Likewise, it's only the nonlinear thinkers who want to work for growing nonlinear businesses.

I've discovered that if you want people to take more pride in their work, the best way is to make sure that they understand how important their jobs are to the overall success of the organization. In my line of work, you don't need an engineering degree to make an impact in our business, and you don't need to be a high-ranking decision maker to influence our overall effectiveness and bottom line. I have tried to stress to entry-level workers that they play a huge role within our organization because they can make an impact on our customers, and they might advance to the top as others have. They also can help the attitude of everyone else. If they understand that, they see themselves as go-to tone setters.

Negativity is your enemy. Below-the-line areas are extremely negative for developing a good culture. These below-the-line areas include punishing employees for failure, fostering a mentality of survival, micromanaging people, giving people only narrow duties, and focusing only on financial performance. This concept really hit the nail on the head for me because I have also discovered that the below-the-line methods of management are very counterproductive to producing a performance-based culture, yet many conventional businesses do utilize these methods. I don't believe in punishing employees, and I don't harp on financial performance directly. I do discuss pricing, excellence, quality, effective production, and customer service. Our emphasis is doing an excellent and efficient quality, high-value-added job for the customer. Don't harp on weaknesses and nonperformance. Likewise, do not try to micromanage people, as this is very harmful to a nonlinear culture. No one wants to be managed. Do be keenly aware of problems in these areas, and respond when you see them. Just be cognizant of how you do so.

Let me give you an example that might paint a clearer picture. Let's say that your goal as the CEO is for everybody within your business to truly take ownership in their day-to-day activities and to make each day as effective and productive as possible. You meet with your leadership team and express this new cultural mission. Everyone nods in agreement, and you begin receiving feedback on the day-to-day time-management tendencies of the hourly workers. It is discovered that many of the employees are habitually extending their ten-minute breaks into twenty- or thirty-minute extended breaks.

Here is where the cultural rubber meets the road. It's been my experience that many managers and CEOs would handle a situation like this by cracking the proverbial whip, making threatening statements and rigid rules. A better plan to implement a performance-based culture, beginning on the ground (or factory) floor, would be to set goals of productivity, time production, and sell your culture clearly. If workers are making their production, a little time wasted during slow days won't kill us. We want to keep everyone productive. We don't want everyone slaving away every minute, and we don't want them to have nothing to do half the time. It's up to the CEO to see that there's a good balance. The long breaks were probably the result of leadership not having the people lined up with enough work balance, deadlines, or expectations. Hiring too many people to do a job is also very bad for culture and productivity. Operating lean makes each of your employees more important, and good people like it. Operating lean also encourages process improvements.

If you want a better way than this, empower your people to each write out ten ways that each of them can add value to the customer and be more productive. Teach them to be more aware of following the compass of purpose instead of being enslaved by the clock. Empowering people takes a great deal of leadership. The main problem I'm always dealing with is working out how we can make everyone a go-to person. It's not always easy to get everybody to take responsibility for a key job that will interest and challenge them. No one is challenged just doing chores or jobs where they don't have much freedom of action or authority. Building can-do jobs requires a lot from the CEO and the leadership. We have to evaluate peoples' go-to progress and design jobs where we can get the performance-based culture working. We also need to try to get the right people on the bus and in the right seats. The right people are nonlinear-thinking people who are capable of handling the wide range of their job duties. Supervisors and managers should be cross-trained enough in the jobs they are managing so that they can appreciate and understand the work being done.

Also, engage your employees by getting them to write out ten ways that they can make decisions on the spot instead of sending problems up to managers. Sending frequent decisions and problems to management is very harmful for your culture, as you'll learn in chapter 11. In a good culture, people doing the work make most (but not all) decisions on the spot instead of involving management, quality control, and other similar individuals or departments. Have a person encountering a problem take ownership of that problem. Have him or her walk it through the process of fixing it without handing it off to someone else. In building a culture, experiences foster beliefs, beliefs influence actions, and actions produce results. In other words, the experiences, beliefs, and actions of the people in an organization ultimately constitute its culture. If their experiences are good, their actions will also be good. If their experiences are bad, well, you get the picture.

A method that often works for culture building is to get every member of your team to teach someone everything he or she knows about his or her job. This sharing will help your teamwork, performance, and culture. Cross-training with people in different jobs helps to build respect. Having supervisors cross-train with their subordinates also works miracles. The leader learns to appreciate the work that their people do and can see firsthand the problems and obstacles they face.

To foster a great team attitude, set up team-building exercises. Consultants can help in this regard. Set up a social committee composed of all departments. With each department represented, it will help to plan the social events. Everyone sees everyone else as an equal team member. Celebrate and recognize as many people as you can. A company newsletter with personal highlights helps, as well. Conducting a company Dale Carnegie course will pay big dividends. I have had many of the Vistage speakers conduct programs at my plants on sales, motivation, and other areas. I've had our people attend large seminars in Houston by

Stephen Covey, Hammer and Company, and others. Cultural seminars in Houston and other large cities can be done in your business. If you are not near a large metropolitan area, a larger group will be needed to conduct the program on site. Oftentimes at Vistage, several businesses go together to have a seminar in order to cut the price for each. This will pay great dividends in showing your employees that you are interested in their development.

Promote your culture by emulating a business like Southwest Airlines. Celebrate everything and everybody you can. Put up signs promoting your culture. Sell empowerment, a warrior spirit, process, problem solving, "one for all and all for one" mentality, excellence, fun at work, employee importance, and completing a multitude of duties. Manage in good times for bad. Think about developing your people to be leaders who focus on what matters most, and they will do the job for you. Empower someone or a team of people to help you build a great performance-based culture. In doing this, you will be a great leader.

It is also very beneficial for the CEO to be a member of the CEO organization Vistage, which works with businesses on improving most areas of their business, including culture. If your business doesn't qualify for Vistage, join another CEO organization. If you're not a CEO, find another way. In a nutshell, a great culture involves an enthusiastic, collaborative atmosphere where all team members feel a sense of importance and feel that they are empowered to take ownership and get things done well. When that occurs, an excellent, performance-based, get-it-done culture ensues, as everybody does what they can to generate great results for the customer. That does take good leadership and the right people. Most of the reason you need the *right* people (and not "good" people) is that they will fit your culture and can continuously improve your processes. I've found that nothing works well in an organization without good leadership and a good performance-based culture to keep the pieces glued together. Get process-improvement and teamwork programs going, and this will help your culture and teamwork greatly. Do it so that it's bottoms up, and you get ownership and buy-in.

In addition to below-the-line areas, there are also above-the-line areas that contribute to an accountability culture. These include such qualities as teamwork, respect, commitment to excellence, strong customer service, a can-do attitude, camaraderie, and other positive traits. As we've detailed, a culture of accountability is the most effective way for a performance-based organization to operate. This accountability isn't just developed; it's achieved from a combination of things: hiring the right people; getting rid of the wrong people; having plenty of the right, all-inclusive social events; generating an atmosphere of caring, training, and empowering people; promoting the above-the-line areas; and developing go-to people and teams. Personally, I think that hiring the right people who will want to be go-to people might be more important than even leadership. I've noticed that Southwest Airlines, Oceania Cruises, and the Ritz-Carlton hotel chain seemingly hire all can-do people. When I started hiring more can-do, nonlinear, flexible people, my team performance and collaboration increased a great deal. Your cultural goal should be to get your team all enthusiastically rowing together in harmony in the right direction and doing more than they are paid for. Many businesses have also hired team-building and culture consultants to help them build their teamwork attitude.

Culture is vital to your success. You set the tone. You uphold the standard. You are the CEO of culture. Develop your plan to build a great, nonlinear, empowered, performance-based culture in your business, and enlist the rest of your team, as well. A good culture is magic! Develop the culture you dream of and want, and let no one ruin it. Only hire people that fit your culture. When everyone is helping everyone else and solving most problems on the spot, you'll go from a "we are great" to a "life is great" culture.

Chapter roundup

Building your business culture is vital to your business's long-term success. It's not something you can afford to ignore. Besides, even if you bury your head in the sand, you'll have a corporate culture, anyway, though chances are that it's going to be negative, which in turn can hurt quality, productivity, profits, happiness, customer service, and the retention of employees. Step up to initiate positive business practices that instill in each employee the idea that he or she is an essential part of the company and that the team is doing worthwhile work. The "we"—not "me"—mentality is what will get you where you want your career and business to go. As the CEO, it's all up to you! You may need to get a culture or team-building consultant to help, as these concepts can be too intangible and complex for quick progress for many. Use every resource you can find to help build your teamwork culture. It takes the right people and leaders who will fit a great culture to develop a great business. Culture is the responsibility of the CEO. In a great culture, the people doing the work resolve most problems on the spot and do not hand off those problems to management, quality control, or customers. Without a great culture of harmony and empowerment, this performance isn't possible. This is when you know you have a great culture.

Remember …

» Culture eats strategy for breakfast, as Peter Drucker said.

» Every chapter is about you developing the most effective mindsets. This chapter is about also having your team develop these mindsets.

» It takes a great, caring and serving leader with a great PMA and solid goals to build a great culture.

» It's the duty of a CEO (you) to nurture the exceptional culture and mindset that you imagine.

» Make your culture the "doing" part of your master mind group that you depend on for harmony and execution.

» You will need to get a strong team buy-in by clarifying and selling culture. Empower someone to help you build your culture. Work hard at it.

» Face your corporate culture, and determine what it is. Then develop a plan to build a great culture of the nonlinear thinking needed for your business. It can take a long time if you don't have the right people and need to part ways with many.

» A positive performance-based culture means that everyone works together for the common good as a cohesive team, all wanting to row together in the right direction and work to create more value for the customer. Foster and build this in your business. Make each person a valued member of the team who is needed and who can handle problems on the spot.

» You are the only one who can truly set the tone for the company's culture, so you should set the example. Your can-do leaders should also play an important role.

» A positive business culture enhances excellence, quality, customer service, profits, and fun.

» A performance-based culture is only one of four major factors that are required for great success in the marketplace.

» You will need to hire and develop compatible people who will fit into and value your culture. They should all fit the degree of nonlinear and can-do teamwork thinking and attitude that fit you and your business. Get the people on your team to willingly row your boat in the same direction. Most planful, too-linear thinkers are dedicated to rowing in the opposite direction, thus hurting your culture. No cynical rotten apples are allowed on the team.

» For high growth and profit, I encourage you to build a nonlinear, empowered culture with people who seek that culture.

» Use cross-department teams and cross-training to help build your processes from the bottom up, which should build your performance-based culture with a lot of empowerment. Teamwork is inevitable when people can understand and appreciate others' work through this cross-training.

- A poor performance-based culture requires too much micromanaging and results in too many conflicts to ever develop into a great team.
- Constantly identify the worst 10 percent of people who don't fit your desired culture and correct or eliminate them the way that Jack Welch did so successfully at GE.
- A decentralized organizational structure is needed for a great performance-based culture.
- A great culture will help build a great business, which an average culture could never do.
- Consider using and promoting Southwest Airlines' three culture values of warrior spirit, a servant's heart, and a fun-loving attitude.
- It's easy to run a business with a great performance-based culture where people manage themselves and want what you want. No one wants to be managed!
- Be the championship coach of your team that empowers each of them to be champions themselves.

10

Getting the Right People on Your Bus (Hire for Attitude and Culture, Train for Skills)

The best CEOs get the right people on the bus and get them in the right seats.
—*Jim Collins, author of* Good to Great

In May 2011, the Dallas Mavericks stunned the Los Angeles Lakers by defeating the defending world champions in a four-game sweep in the second round of the Western Conference Playoffs. In the aftermath of that series, legendary Lakers coach Phil Jackson confirmed that he would not return for another season. Jackson is easily one of the most successful coaches in NBA history—and in all of professional sports, for that matter. He won a record-setting eleven NBA titles and became known across the country as "the Zen Master" for implementing the Buddhist practice of achieving a meditative state in his basketball coaching regimen.

Fascinating coach. Remarkable accomplishments. But I have a

theory regarding Jackson's success that has nothing to do with Zen or the triangle offense Jackson used. I am certainly not an expert on the *X*s and *O*s of the NBA, but I did notice during Jackson's career that he coached Michael Jordan and Scottie Pippen in Chicago. And after leaving the Bulls, he returned to coaching in Los Angeles, where he led Lakers teams that featured stars like Shaquille O'Neal, Kobe Bryant, and Pau Gasol on the rosters. In other words, he didn't attempt to win championships with the fourth- or fifth-most-talented team. He always had the first- or second-most-talented team in those championship years.

When Jackson joined the Bulls, he inherited the world's best player (Jordan) and one of the league's most talented rosters. Ditto with the majority of his tenure with the Lakers. Then Jackson masterfully managed that talent to multiple championships and made the right personnel moves to maintain that high level of talent.

What does this illustration mean to you as a CEO? Simply put, it shows that the team is only as good as its leader. And the leader is only as good as the talent he or she brings in and develops. CEOs should take special notice of Jackson's career and those of many other successful coaches in the world of big-time athletics. I have found that the good CEOs are far more coaches than they are managers or executives and that our best CEO approach to hiring the right people is the approach of a good coach. While I realize that there are exceptions to the rule, the most successful championship-level coaches are typically the ones who inherit, develop, or acquire the best players. It still takes plenty of work and an exceptional coach to lead those players to peak performance. I am certainly not minimizing the accomplishments of a coach like Phil Jackson because he obviously possessed a golden leadership touch, and he established a performance-based culture.

But no matter how great Jackson's methods were, he wasn't going to win championships with a collection of even above-average players. And the same theory applies to you as the CEO of your organization. However, what I see in the real world is that most CEOs (owners, partners, managers) think that their ideas, plans, and management are so brilliant that they can get great productivity and teamwork out of whoever is there. They can't, and I certainly didn't. It took me five years of enslavement and misery for me to learn this lesson. Some genius!

If you didn't inherit the right employees in your field, you need to find a way to acquire them and/or develop them. In sports, it takes prodigious talent to be the best. In business, we all have genius within us that can be developed if we have the right mindsets and right traits to fit the jobs and do the business we need done. In the nonlinear success world, we need the nonlinear thinkers who want the same culture we want. All business practices can be learned by people with the right attitudes if people fit your culture and there's enough leadership to glue the team together. Be wary of most HR managers, who are looking to spend the least amount of effort possible to find one person who might pass your minimum standards to hire and meet their goal. Likewise, most department managers are trying to meet their own urgent needs, and they have lower standards than the HR manager! They want warm bodies now, and they don't want to let go of their poor workers, as they are also considered to be warm bodies. If you use the conventional approach, you're hiring the minimum quality and fit of people you need or worse. This results in a team lacking a cultural fit, a minimum of good talent, and little leadership. It takes a talented coach and leader to build a great team of the right people. Then you must take the time to find outstanding team members who will fit your culture and want to be on your team, who have the potential to be promoted to satisfy your long-range goals—as well as their own—and minimize your turnover. Don't hire the first person you see who has a decent résumé and can interview well. These are mostly the folks who make up the 80 percent of people who only do 20 percent of the value-added work. We need to hire for a lot more than a good, honest, experienced person. With this hiring advice, I'm assuming that you are hiring for a business of a few thousand employees or smaller and that is not predominantly linear and static. But most of these principles are for all businesses.

By reviewing considerably more potential candidates than others did, I was able to identify more leaders and people who fit in with my desired empowerment culture and had a good attitude. By hiring in this more demanding way, my KMCO base plant provided me with the people and leadership that could help me grow my mini chemical empire of seven plants that I controlled but not in a few others where I was a partner. I used this leadership-generating machine to supply people to my other plants. In nearly all the businesses I'm aware of, finding the right people who fit is more important than finding the rare, most talented people like in the high end of sports. All business processes can be learned.

Not hiring the people who fit what you need is a common trap for most leaders. For example, I sold my original plant and a second one to an investment group. The new owners were typical linear thinkers and began to hire employees via the conventional route, buying into the urgency from department managers and unit supervisors. They were not looking for nonlinear thinkers who could be empowered to fit our needs, and they wouldn't let me have any influence. The new owners did not understand my hiring practices and were not open to learning. They believed that since they had been remotely and blindly hiring people for many businesses for years, they knew what was best. In continuing their more conventional hiring practices, they ended up mixing linear thinkers in with nonlinear thinkers. This developed into the toxic mix of nonlinear thinkers conflicting with the linear thinkers, which hurt our empowerment culture greatly. It wasn't entirely their fault, as the plant had started doing this earlier, when I was mostly involved in other businesses and had pulled out the top leadership to build them. If you seek excellence, stand firm in your leadership, culture, and nonlinear thinking, since managers, partners, and others will most often not understand. From my experience with lots of CEOs, only the very best few have excellent hiring practices or understand who they need to hire that will be best suited for their business or a nonlinear business. Most have been trained on conventional business hiring and development. Nonlinear hiring and development is a totally different game.

The cultural fit and leadership of your team will determine the level of your success. No matter how good you are as a leader, motivator, and example setter, your business will never rise to your needed level of performance with a collection of people who don't fit your performance-based culture and aren't led by solid enough leaders. It just won't happen. Leaders need to understand what people can and cannot do well. Please note that I never said anything about experience, education, or grades. Even though I am in a business with highly technical work, I have only found a negative correlation to resumes and performance in the technical and management areas. With the right attitude, traits, habits, and nonlinear work experience, average people can learn all the business practices that they need. Education and entitlement are most often an obstacle in learning better business practices. This is very much like what the most successful people also discovered around a hundred years ago that *Think and Grow Rich* covered. Your goal—or more precisely, your duty as a CEO—always needs to be to find the right people whom you can win with and build your team. Very few businesses obtain excellent people or adequate leadership with a great attitude for achieving outstanding success. It's not easy to understand who the right people are, and it's also not easy to find them for nonlinear businesses.

In the classic business book *Good to Great: Why Some Companies Make the Leap … and Others Don't*, author Jim Collins identifies and evaluates the factors and variables that allow a small fraction of companies to make the transition from good to great. It's really no different from what coaches have done for generations. From doing an extensive study of the best businesses, Collins determined that the best CEOs "get the right people on the bus and get them in the right seats." That may sound simple. It may seem rudimentary. But very few CEOs ever accomplish this task or even try to accomplish it, although it may be as important as the CEO's other duties. Combine the right people with a CEO who sweats what really matters, and that's all you'll need for great business and life success. Notice that Collins says the *right* people and not the *best* people.

At its essence, a growing business or any organization is nothing more than the people working for it while using the business's assets. Sure, you need a good product or service, but ultimately, a business will only achieve up to the level of the sum of what all the people achieve. This is especially true in a nonlinear-thinking business. Your employees will define your business. Your employees will make the most lasting impression on your customers and clients. Your employees will determine your organization's success or failure and will also play a vital role in your overall legacy as CEO. Your duty and responsibility as a leader is to focus on and accomplish the 20 percent of the work (big stuff) that produces 80 percent of the results. The right people are a major part of the big stuff. The right people are also needed to produce a winning culture.

Making sure that the right people board your bus will allow you the opportunity to compete very well. Many of a business's management problems will dissipate when it recruits and retains the right people, and a business must have the right people before an overarching strategy can be fully developed and implemented. From an experienced entrepreneur's point of view, I can verify that this notion is completely accurate. In fact, it's pure wisdom. You can devise and utilize a foolproof, can't-miss strategy for your business, but the wrong people will only take you so far. And it won't be to the very top. This is what has forced me to focus on finding the right people and building the right culture so much in the past thirty-plus years. This, in addition to the processing and problem solving, has become my team job. The rest of the big-stuff strategy is automatic for me as a CEO at this stage.

Identifying your players

In business, of course, it's not typically as easy to identify the impact of personnel additions and strategic applications as it is in sports. We don't see the scores, the statistics, the daily results, the breakdowns from experts in the media, and the performances of our employees as clearly as in the sports world because quarterly and annual updates in business are often the results of thousands of actions and chores by many different people. It's often too complex in business to see how those daily performances by our employees affected the overall success of our team. And on top of that, people are complex. As a result, very few CEOs and managers get the right people on their teams.

However, the solutions to your problems and/or the answers to your business prayers can be uncovered by acquiring the right personnel and placing employees in the right positions on the team bus. The people on your team will need to be far more compatible than the conventional people in most businesses, as the average mishmash team will not help power you to success in the nonlinear real world. It takes a better-than-average team to maintain. But it takes outstanding teamwork to drive growth, development, and success. Your people will need to be better than average in areas like nonlinear thinking, can-do attitudes, work motivation, teamwork, and nonlinear leadership. They don't have to be better in everything; no one is, and no one should try to be. The marketing goal for every business should be to excel in the big unfair advantage you have and only do "good enough" on the rest. No one can be good at everything and have a good business. In fact, the right average people who fit your needs might be optimum. It's actually a major flaw if you try to be too good in everything. No one can. It's best to focus on being good on the key things that really matter while trying to be adequate but productive on the rest. The keys are to learn the right principles and actions to build a strong team, to have faith that these best practices work, and then to actually carry through with these nonurgent action steps instead of becoming enslaved with urgent, more tangible management or worker duties.

In the dynamic real world, we have to depend on dynamic, nonlinear people to keep our strategies dynamic. We can't coast on static strategies with linear-thinking people like conventional businesses. It's the people who make whatever we do a success. Conventional businesses have done all they can in taking most of the people equation out of the selection, which works for them. But the nonlinear business is far more dependent on the right people, since they are working to dynamically build success rather than maintain the profits of a large, static company on autopilot. This is why good entrepreneurs can always build highly successful businesses if they can build a good team with the right people.

Attitude is everything. A performance-based entrepreneur or CEO hires more balanced, self-sufficient people with a can-do attitude at the expense of strong, hardworking, narrow-duty, linear-thinking people with high-pedigree résumés, which seems to fit their needs and culture. The static, linear, conventional business goes more by education, experience, grades, and résumés, which is its formula. The linear business is looking for conventional maintainers to do narrow jobs in a centralized organization. In the free-market, dynamic world, the nonlinear businesses need to find the more flexible, can-do people who also have enough values, production drive, maturity, and wisdom to be reliable on wide job responsibilities. As CEO, you're responsible for obtaining this balance.

After *Good to Great* was published in 2001 and received rave reviews from critics and business leaders, CEOs across the country seemed committed to placing the right people on the bus. But after a few years, it appeared that most CEOs gave up on getting the right people. The problem was that very few people in those businesses really knew how to identify the right people, and they used the old linear thinking of going by the pedigree of people's résumés, interview skills, and persuasion skills that tend to fit linear-centralized organizations. Only a few businesses improved much in finding the right people.

Right is much better than best. Many CEOs assumed that the right people meant the smartest candidates, the experts in a particular field, the best linear managers, or those with the most perfect résumés and interview skills. In reality, though, nothing could be further from the truth in our nonlinear businesses. I've never found those attributes to be of much value. Most of the business efforts were wasted on the wrong people. As a result, much of the effort to get the right people has faded among many CEOs. They never had the culture, leadership, organization, and knowledge to implement the nonlinear principles or the ability or tools to determine who the right people were. Instead of actively seeking the right people, many CEOs resort to the easier alternative of slowly removing the wrong people. However, businesses with a performance-based culture like Southwest Airlines, Oceania Cruises, and Ritz-Carlton hire mostly the right people for nonlinear success. It can be done.

I once hired people the conventional ways I was taught. And even when I firmly committed to hiring the right people, I later discovered that I was not getting enough of the right people. I was making progress, but it was very slow and painful. My best efforts to find the right people did not result in finding people with the attitude, team-oriented approach, cultural compatibility, thinking, work ethic, or leadership that we needed. Of course, I didn't factor in culture, leadership, mindsets, nonlinear thinking, common sense, and so much more that I was unable to judge or measure. At the time, I was so satisfied that I had finally located people who were qualified—by education, experience, and résumé—that I was ready to move forward to the next obstacle or agenda item like most of my fellow CEOs. I didn't have all the right personal assessment tools or the ability to properly use them to help me identify the people I needed. As a result, I was way off base on many of my choices. My largest mistakes were hiring too many planful linear thinkers with a lot of experience and letting others who didn't believe in the culture and attitude I wanted have too much control. Of course, I didn't know that they didn't believe in what I wanted. People won't tell you, and I believed what they told me.

In a good culture, we get our entire team to row our boat in the same direction. The qualified mentality isn't good enough when it comes to key personnel decisions. All business processes can be learned if the attitude is right. We need people who fit the culture of wanting to row our boat in the same direction that we do. We need people who want to do the work the way we do it and be a part of our culture and team, instead of dissipating our efforts in different directions like most businesses experience. We must think like a visionary CEO to find the right people with compatible mindsets to navigate and power our ship, as opposed to the conventional urgent thinking of a manager. We are looking for the right people who can develop into really good team performers. Don't confuse this with the best people, as I don't really think that the best people ever exist in a practical sense in the business world. In the right culture and with the right leadership and business, many of us can be great. But by obtaining the people capable of practicing and implementing the nonlinear success principles, you will build momentum and create the necessary confidence to tackle the all-important duty of assembling a champion-caliber team.

Foster your team culture first, and match the members of your team to that culture. Developing the right performance-based culture to fit your business should be considered the first and most important requirement for finding the right people. If we don't have culture working for us, our employees will never form a strong team and will require an abundance of conventional structure and supervision. People with conflicting personalities, attitudes, thinking, and objectives (wrong culture) are rotten for business, no matter the level of their talent. For instance, we can't mix blind linear bureaucrats with can-do, nonlinear people, no matter how experienced or smart either are. Our goal is to get the people who are compatible with our culture and want to excel and belong to our culture; then all we need is the right leadership to glue them together. So first, we need to evaluate people for wanting to be a part of our culture. Are they flexible enough (but not too much), can-do, want-to, and nonlinear-thinking team players?

As you move forward, don't forget the issue of hiring and developing your team leaders. These are the individuals who will play a vital role in the success or failure of your business. As I've said before, the leaders you work with help provide the glue needed to bind your collection of individuals into a cohesive team that works together to accomplish the objectives you set together. They will also be ambassadors of your nonlinear business culture. Indeed, they will set the tone in the company. Thus, bad leaders will negatively impact your company. Obviously, the leaders must be nonlinear thinkers, flexible, and versatile, and they, like their subordinates, must possess a can-do attitude. No business will ever achieve close to its potential without the right mix of culture and leadership. By leadership, I mean real leaders and not people with a manager title. The degree of nonlinear thinking that you need is the degree that will fit your business. A highly creative business may need more highly creative people than an average business.

At one of my Vistage sessions on finding the right people, Cameron Herold, who is a successful entrepreneur, author, and speaker, told a story about a lesson he learned from his grandfather from duck hunting. His grandfather was specific about the ducks they were after and that they had a limit of six. Cameron kept pointing out different ducks to try to call over, but his grandfather would tell him that he could see that they were the wrong kind from the way they were flying. He knew what he wanted and could spot them from way off. That's the way we need to be when we want to hire. In a nonlinear business, we want to be able to identify the nonplanful, can-do team players small-business habits that will want what we want. This is a CEO's duty.

Promote from within when possible. Find the right employees and leaders to build and develop your team so that everyone is pulling in the same direction. You'll have to achieve all of this while your people will push you to hire a qualified person as quickly as possible, but the best CEOs resist this temptation. It's more important for you to hire employees who are compatible with you and your culture no matter how long it takes. As such, my advice is to always begin your search for the right leaders within your own organization. I've had many leaders emerge from my business, and I have found that they nearly always turn out to be better fits than hiring from the outside. Just make sure they want to be a leader. Most of them do not have the education needed to receive a legitimate interview for a high-level position in other businesses, but since they already understand and fit our culture, they work perfectly in our organization.

Leadership is a scarce commodity that will typically only be found if you're searching for it. So you must always be looking for it and developing who you have, or you will never have enough. Good leadership will make your average employees excellent, just as a good performance-based culture will make an average employee excellent. And I've discovered that if we focus on culture and we then find the good leaders, placing the right people in the other seats on the organizational bus will simply happen over time. That's what leaders make happen. I would like to suggest that when you find a leader, be willing to accept less education and experience, as good leaders are extremely hard to find. Don't put too many extra requirements on them that will reduce your ability to find enough leadership, or you'll never have enough.

When searching for the right people, we must also consider that 20 percent of people generate 80 percent of the value-added results and that nearly everyone in management is incompetent in his or her current job. Recall the basics of the Peter Principle. This may sound harsh, but that's the reality we face as CEOs. Remember also that conventional managers are trained to be maintainers, not currently visionaries like you need. The truth is that we can't hire everyone that we need who are currently high performers. For great success, we're going to need to hire the people with good attitudes and whom we can develop into the people we need. They will be the ones who will excel in our culture. Building your business or life is all about building yourself and your team. Most will not start out as the performers you need right away. At some point, your success turns into being more of a people evaluator, team builder, and people builder. The right people are out there, but it's like fishing; it takes much skill to catch enough of the right game fish. You too must be a fisher of men and women to build your team.

For instance, I had a nineteen-year-old woman who worked out great as an HR manager in leading and getting things done at my original plant. When I had a problem getting things done in the plant through our health, safety, and environmental department, I put her in charge to straighten it out. Then, when our maintenance and construction department couldn't find a way to paint the plant at a decent pace or price, she got it done ten times faster and at a tenth of the cost. She knew our culture and people and was a leader. Then, when I couldn't get much performance or income from a business I bought, she went over there and improved the profits and performance by ten times. She currently runs three of my plants.

Likewise, I had an outstanding employee who worked his way up to running our original plant's reaction area. When I couldn't find anyone who could successfully run our Singapore plant, I had him go overseas to do it. He knew the culture, performance, and leadership we needed, and he has been very successful at building a team and a growing, highly profitable business.

Take heart! There are many businesses that do find the right people, including some large companies with thousands of employees.

Doing business with these performance-based companies can do wonders for your understanding in this area. I've learned to not be such a perfectionist when identifying leaders and strong performance-based workers. I'm willing to take some flaws, and all the best have flaws. After all, nobody is good at everything. We all are a combination of weaknesses and strengths. When I started as an engineer and entrepreneur, I thought that my journey would be building plants and making the right chemicals and deals. Little did I know that what it's all about is finding the right people, organizing them, and developing them.

Of course, it also takes patience on your part to continually search for the people who are a good fit and to persistently work on placing your existing people where they are most likely to succeed. We know that most of the population does not understand where his or her own genius exists, but it is our job as the CEO to recognize and develop our employees' talents. I try to avoid people who have learned their jobs and habits by working for average, static, linear businesses, since it's nearly impossible to change peoples' thinking and habits. I look for people who have worked well in businesses with a wide duty and responsibility culture similar to what I want. Those are small, nonlinear businesses where each person is productive and has already developed the habit of being empowered and working hard to handle wide responsibilities. It is too much of a long shot to change workers' habits. If the habits and attitude are right, we can develop them. These people also seek out the small productive businesses that they want to work for.

Don't get too comfortable

In my early development as a CEO, it took me several years of chaos and constant problems before I could reach a point of being fully staffed with people who had the right education and experience. Reaching a level of stability is a formidable accomplishment that many businesses never achieve. It led us to a functional business that was making a few million dollars a year. I've noticed that this is where many businesses are when they join Vistage.

However, we had a lot of flaws that I didn't like. And we didn't really have the ability to grow, as most of our people were not developing like I expected. I wanted to double our business many times, but I didn't have the team to do that. Brian Tracy says that short-term success is often a major obstacle to long-term success. This definitely applied to us.

Once I was making several million dollars a year, I joined Vistage. The purpose of Vistage is to help the CEO of a decent-sized and successful business to lead and develop his or her organization past good and onto excellent, which it is fairly effective at doing. Vistage's job is to take CEOs from good to great, not bad to good. It removes CEOs from their closed relationships with yes-people dependent on them and gets them seeing and benchmarking other businesses and performances. It works. When I could clearly compare other good businesses like mine to businesses that I wanted to be like, I knew right away that I didn't want to be bogged down in "good." I wanted to be great, like Jim Collins is telling us to do in his book.

I realized that I did not have a team of the right people in tune with my culture and goals all going in the right direction, although I thought I did. I thought that surely these good people I hired would develop over time to be the people I needed. Most didn't want to.

Nevertheless, we were generating very good profits, and I was very proud of our accomplishments. I had visions of this team leading us to great success because we had achieved moderate success previously. I thought that I could teach them. I was at a place where most successful entrepreneurs level out into the comfort zones and stop growing. But as it turned out, I was still a long way from building a team of the right people. I was learning that hiring good, experienced people is totally different from hiring the right people.

To return to the NBA example that we began the chapter with, I had assembled a team that was decent enough to be competitive, but it certainly wasn't good enough to win a playoff series, let alone a championship. My group was not in tune with my desired performance-based culture, in large part because I didn't know enough about how to develop such a culture or how to hire for such a culture. Many of those employees in my early years were only interested in the culture they wanted instead of what we needed. Some were suffering from learned helplessness, and they were not on the same page with me in terms of the company's beliefs, direction, attitude, and needs. We also did not have enough leadership developed. I was depending on my newly hired managers to bring in their extensive management experience that I didn't have, but I didn't realize that most of their experience was with linear-thinking conventional businesses. I didn't know that it was my job to teach them how to be effective and get rid of them if they didn't learn. I had no management experience and felt that I had to hire others to decide how to run my business. I was wrong. CEOs have to go through a lot of on-the-job learning the hard way to run their businesses. As a nonmanager, I didn't know that I had to decide how to manage and lead my business.

Most of my managers were not adequate at performing or even having the slightest idea about what the 20 percent of work that produces 80 percent of positive results was, as much of that productive 20 percent was totally up to me. They had only worked in large businesses doing the small stuff. So while we were making some money and producing some profits, we were in no position to make a run at the elite levels of success that I envisioned achieving. My goal was developing a great business, not just trying to cash in for several million on a perhaps decent business.

There aren't many businesses that actually go from good to great, because there aren't many CEOs who are willing, motivated, or knowledgeable enough to team build the staff from good to great. While that is the objective for many of us, it's not the reality for most. Most CEOs would settle for going from bad to good or bad to stable. Stable businesses can be profitable, but if you stay at stable, you will suffer and eventually become stagnant and slide downhill. Great CEOs must always work on building, improving, and developing the team instead of resting at stable or jumping back to the non-CEO management chores that are so much easier. If we allow ourselves to become enslaved by non-CEO work, the good-to-great dream fades quickly. That's just human nature. I know that our team didn't want to row our boat in the direction I wanted, and there was no way that I was going to get that group to do it.

My advice is to stay ambitious. I believe that we all do better working on long-term team building instead of settling for short-term stability and success. As Ray Kroc says, "You're either green and growing, or you're ripe and rotting." Trying to be the best will take you much further than settling for good, even if you never make it to great. Keep working at it, as most of the highly successful CEOs never make it all the way to great in the real world. And no one can maintain great forever.

Lower-level people are as important as top people

I've learned from Vistage and through my own experience that most CEOs don't pay much attention to hiring and evaluating the performance of the 80–90 percent of the lower-level workers who perform a majority of the work. This is a big mistake. Highly successful, nonlinear CEOs don't make that mistake.

Many, if not most, CEOs tend to believe that they should only be concerned about the selection and productivity of the managers and high-level staff. I disagree. The people who perform most of the work can make the most significant differences. They're the ones who can actually sink a company with its customers or mess up the day-to-day operations through incompetence and indifference. A good CEO is a leader of all the people. It's a lazy mode of leadership for a CEO to run a business by managing a few key managers at the top and then going with the trickle-down theory as applied to personnel. I know that from experience. I've been guilty of falling into that trap, and so have most of the CEOs I know. It is a very common trait. The very best CEOs are concerned about everyone.

The driven and ambitious CEO understands that assembling the right team includes finding the right people at even the lowest pay levels. Those employees could be your future leaders, and they will certainly impact the overall culture of your company. Now I can finally understand why the best business consultants decades ago would visit with the lower-level workers at a business in order to evaluate the organization and suggest improvements. The lower-level workers often provide the best information regarding how well the business is managed. I've found that if the lower-level workers aren't good enough, there are nearly no leaders good enough to lead them. It's nearly impossible to find any leader good enough to lead poor workers. On the other hand, poor leaders aren't good enough to even lead good workers as I have so painfully learned. No one wants to work for a bad leader.

A CEO who only becomes involved with hiring practices when it's a high-level opening for a key sales VP or a CFO inevitably loses touch with his or her overall team and business and never spends enough time becoming a strong team builder or people evaluator. This part-time involvement is a common mistake, and it often leads to filling your team bus with people who are not suited for your culture. Your managers can be involved in the hiring practice, but only the CEO can truly direct the effort of discovering and developing the right people for the right spots. Even most managers are consumed with the demands of today and making the most of the people they currently oversee. With all that short-term pressure, they will hire practically anybody, and they won't get rid of poor performers. It's the CEO who has the long-term perspective—if he or she is performing the CEO duties and not becoming enslaved by management duties.

The 80/20 principle applies to your personnel. In my first several years as an entrepreneur, I couldn't understand the 80/20 principle and how it applied to people. When I worked for others, I didn't see that 80 percent of the workers accomplished practically nothing of high value outside of all the low-value chores they did. I also didn't easily recognize that the highest achievers were accomplishing sixteen times the results of the ineffective 80 percent. This is the most difficult concept that I've attempted to teach to others. But of all the principles of success, this is the one that can most dynamically change a business from good to great.

It's easier to see with your salespeople because it's normally a black-and-white result. With salespeople, the 80/20 principle is oftentimes more like the 90/10 rule, as 90 percent of sales are typically generated from the top 10 percent of salespeople. In fact, Gallup and Harvard polls show that 94 percent of goods and services in the United States are sold by the top 4 percent of salespeople. Having the tools necessary to determine which employees have the ability to be the best in their field can place a corporation in that top 4 percent.

That's easily measured because sales are either made or they are not. There's no credit for the chores that don't produce results. We should view nonsalespeople in the same manner, but hardly anyone can since it's so vague and hard to measure the 90 percent of the iceberg that's below the surface.

Take steps to measure employee performance. Unfortunately, we rarely know how much each employee has contributed, as there is typically much complexity within the organization and no measure of how much value each person has contributed. Even the employees themselves don't know, as nearly all of them think that they're earning their pay, since they do so many chores and go through so many hassles and problems. Nevertheless, it is an absolute truth that in most business settings, 20 percent of the staff is producing 80 percent of the value-added results. That's different from "work." My goal is to get a much higher percentage of people producing high-value-added results. The same 80/20 or 90/10 principle that applies to sales also applies to other workers and managers. Since so many people are performing so many tasks, it's nearly impossible to consistently measure an individual's productivity in most businesses. However, many entrepreneurs can clearly notice how their money is being spent. When it's your money, you'll see this far more clearly than you will with somebody else's money. I certainly did. Try to look at the value-added results that each person does even if you aren't an entrepreneur. Think about it. That will give you an idea of how your employees are performing, even if it's next to impossible to measure an individual's performance, and then put a dollar figure on what those contributions mean to the bottom line. Through the years, I've learned that can-do and go-to people who fit your culture are worth their weight in gold. If you focus on the high-value concepts and minimize the small stuff for your business, you'll attract more of the right people.

Obviously, it's a fact that a lot of low-value work is necessary in most businesses. Not all jobs can be high-value work. However, the best businesses perform a much higher percentage of high-value work than the poor and average businesses, which tends to make those businesses that focus more on high-value work far more profitable. I've found that to achieve more high-value work, the CEO has to push high-value work and minimize the number of people assigned to low-value work. Linear-thinking managers will always want too many people for the small stuff, and many of the nonlinear people will mistakenly also want it as they try to be excellent at everything. Whenever I failed to emphasize high-value work and limit those people assigned to low-value work, I turned around and found less than half of people doing high-value work and twice the number of people doing low-value work. You will too. There is always a great force trying to pull you down to linear, conventional work. It takes a good can-do, performance-based culture team and a lot of good leadership by the CEO to help you fight this dark force that enslaves most. As a CEO, you need to control the number of people doing the small stuff. The small stuff can always be done more effectively with fewer people. Be highly resistant to having more people to do the small stuff! It's your job to keep your managers from hiring too many people to do low-value work. They will not like it, but they will figure out how to do it with fewer people. Of course, few people even know what the small stuff is and that we only need to do good enough on it. Make the small stuff your servant, not your master. It's a CEO duty and responsibility.

Busy doesn't mean best. When assessing your personnel, do not confuse busy people with high-value producers. Just because someone looks busy, works hard, or has a good attitude doesn't mean that he or she is a high producer. As CEO, your job is to build a team that will take your business from good to great. To do that, you must focus on sweating what really matters, while avoiding getting you and your team sucked up by the small stuff. Your job is to find, motivate, and build your good-to-great team. If you're not enslaved by low-value work, you'll be able to do it.

The bottom line is that we as CEOs are ultimately only going to be as successful as the people we hire and train allow us to be. It's like the Phil Jackson example we started with in this chapter. Even a great coach and leader like Jackson will ultimately fail if he is surrounded by mediocre players who only perform at a minimal level. He and his general manager must continually search for the right players, acquiring them through the draft, trade, or free agency. In sports, you don't need a team full of superstars to win a championship, but you do need a roster full of people who are committed to winning and who are willing to sacrifice for the greater good of the team. Chemistry is so important in sports, and it is just as important in business. Good chemistry on a business team involves a performance-based culture and the right empowered people, coupled with strong leadership. The right people in the right culture can grow a company or a team from good to great. On the other hand, even the wrong good people won't grow very much.

Selecting your players

Through years of trial and error, I've found that the better performers possess a can-do attitude, a culture of values that are not too rigid, enough flexibility, some self-sufficiency, a good work ethic, and positive nonlinear thinking measured as nonplanful or disorganized that matches the environment that's needed. I've also discovered that more often than not, less education (to a point) is better. There is a lot of entitlement and linear thinking that goes along with education in today's world. I don't need anyone with a sense of entitlement, and I don't necessarily need someone who has a great résumé or someone who is really smart. I've discovered that "smart" means "no common sense" most of the time. This is very much like Napoleon Hill described in *Think and Grow Rich*. Give me someone who is hungry and driven to succeed, someone who is ready to prove that he or she can produce, and someone who will follow the direction of our compass instead of being a person enslaved by the clock. I want to watch and help my employees grow and excel. Common sense is genius.

The right nonlinear cultural fit is good for most jobs and business.

I've found that if a person has half the traits I need and no fatal flaws, he or she can grow and excel. People don't have to start out perfect for us. Remember that all business practices can be learned. Also, I've figured out after many struggles that one good highly technical person can supply expertise to many. I don't need armies of technical experts, even in my highly technical business. But I do need key HR and other leaders who are working in line with our culture and needs. I can't do it all, and it's the same for you. As I've said, trying to do it all is one of the most common mistakes we CEOs make, especially if we're at the helm of a small business.

Résumés don't tell the whole story. I don't pay too much attention to some aspects of the résumé when I am interviewing or hiring. Résumés hold a lot more weight at conventional businesses. I am more interested in discovering the candidates' habits, passions, and personalities. I'm also interested if they have worked in wider, small business–type jobs, where they had the responsibility to perform at a high level. I am most interested in whether they are committed to succeeding doing the job we have for them in our business. It doesn't take tremendous experience or high levels of education to learn business practices. In *Think and Grow Rich*, Napoleon Hill discusses how Andrew Carnegie was convinced that much of that which is taught in the schools is of no value whatsoever for business success. I've come to develop the same opinion with regard to nonlinear success. It just takes the right attitude, the right nonlinear thinking, mindsets and the drive to do what we need in our culture.

It takes time to really get to know the candidates and to determine how they would fit within your culture. It also takes plenty of effort to learn what traits you need in your jobs and business, but that's mostly a determination testing every few years on your existing people. Great CEOs embrace the challenge and understand that they are looking for one qualified person at a time who can fit with the company's culture and needs. The cost of spending more on hiring is totally insignificant. The cost of even average hiring is off-the-charts expensive.

Learn from your mistakes. The good news about making hiring mistakes is that we learn from them. Even if you are the best of the best in terms of evaluating people, you are going to miss on many people. But the only way a business will find and hire the right people is if the CEO is leading the charge and is willing to accept responsibility for the great hires and the not-so-great ones. We can't delegate this vital CEO duty, not even to HR managers. Most managers will often make the same mistakes over and over, but the entrepreneur CEO is much less inclined to do so with his or her own money. Get good at hiring, and keep developing the process! Even when I worked for Shell Chemical, I found that most of the managers who went straight to the top had arranged to get all the best performers working for them. It took some doing to accomplish this when the big company made nearly all the personnel decisions.

Have faith that you'll find the right person. In the continual search for the right people, it is most beneficial to implement the mental success principle of thinking that there is an abundance of the right people, just as we believe that opportunity is abundant. Both are true if your attitude is right. You must stay in a positive mental state. Like the law of attraction states, "Like attracts like." Therefore, if you want to attract the right person who will fit you, you must believe that you will attract him or her. That may sound insignificant, but it is extremely important. We won't accomplish great things in life without a very strong, positive attitude, faith, belief, goals, confidence, and determination. Your HR personnel and your managers will think that you are being too demanding in your hiring.

Before you ever interview a person, you must have faith and believe that there is an abundance of the right people. I've found that the people who don't have this faith do not hire very well. You must also commit to searching until you find the right people, no matter how long it takes. Look for the positive things you need, and be willing to accept some flaws. Don't settle for an adequate person, as he or she will rarely even be adequate. However, you must realize that the right person will not be 100 percent right. We're relying on our judgment in an imperfect world filled with imperfect people.

So where do you look for good people? Anywhere and everywhere you go. As a guideline, great salespeople and leaders are rarely on the market. For that matter, most of the available people on the market are the unemployed, the underemployed, the disenchanted, the entitled, the spoiled, and those going nowhere, even though they are continually hopping from one job to another.

Employment agencies can be a decent resource for finding people, especially if you are seeking a high-level, linear executive from a top headhunter firm. But the firms are typically expensive, and they are often recycling those middle- and lower-level people who didn't fit in their last spots. For the most part, these firms don't really know who is an exceptional candidate or not for a nonlinear business. They make their money with the mass of people who approach them. They are nearly always good at helping businesses hire the linear thinkers who have good résumés, but that's not what we want. There are many websites where we can search through a lot of people, which makes it much easier now. I look for the more nonlinear thinkers who have worked for smaller businesses where they had to do a wide range of work or it didn't get done, kind of like a jack-of-all-trades. It's up to you to try different approaches as the technology advances.

Some of my employees and I are always on the lookout for promising people, regardless of where we are or what we're doing. When we're talking to clients, vendors, contractors, suppliers, salespeople, and even our own employees, we are always interested in how people interact with us and how they might fit the company's culture and needs. Even in social settings, it pays to be thinking about how a person might fit into your business or organization. When you encounter a person who you think might possess the right can-do attitude and leadership, it's beneficial to remember who he or she is and to make sure you have a way of contacting him or her. The difficult part of this is that a majority of these people won't be the right person on closer inspection, so you'll need to not get their hopes up too much.

Personally, I learned to look for people who have worked in small businesses where they had to perform wide responsibilities in order to survive. They will likely have the work habits and attitudes that will fit our performance-based culture and not be spoiled by too much narrow, linear, conventional experience for our business. It's practically impossible to change a person to meet small-company needs who has practiced centralized-company habits. It's a losing game trying to change someone's habits. Learn what you need, and find those right people and not the "good" or "best" people.

I also look in different industries than my own, focusing on who people really are, as opposed to what their roles have been in the past. In the chemical business, nearly everyone has been spoiled by doing narrow, linear chores. However, I will find some with some chemical experience. I want to determine their attitudes, values, culture, work ethics, team approaches, and energy levels. The key is to always be listening for what is most important to you. If you are always actively qualifying people you encounter, there's a good chance you will find qualified employees and become good at it. We're not looking for the best person or a good worker, and we aren't looking for a perfect fit. If someone is mostly a good cultural fit, that's a great start. Over the years, compensation has rarely been a factor in our hiring. We will elect to pass on someone who is making two or three times the income we are targeting, but that is extremely rare for us.

Of course, it's also important to remember that when you add new key personnel to your team, it is sometimes very important to remove the nonperformance-based culture people. Your new people can be poisoned by people with the wrong attitudes and objectives, regardless of their talent level. It is important to weed out the wrong people so that your best employees and the people who really fit your culture can grow and prosper. Not every employee (or any) needs to be a superstar, but every employee needs to fit your desired culture and be productive. Average employees who work well with others and who fit your culture can be a great asset to any business. A cultural-fit person with a can-do attitude will have perhaps unlimited potential for you.

It takes faith, belief, and perseverance to build a winning team of the right employees. Assembling a staff of the right people will test you more than anything else in business, with the possible exception of overcoming obstacles in your own mind. But great leaders stay focused on acquiring the right people and placing them in the right seats on the bus.

Write down the qualifications you want. I've found that it is such an important part of my overall role as a CEO to regularly write down what I am looking for in people and then twenty things I can do to find the right people. I will write it down every week for a month or more at a time when I really need the right people. Just like the goal-setting principles we discussed, the process of writing down your list on a daily or weekly basis will ultimately lead you to your key people. Doing this helps me determine the type of person I need, and it may help me identify where to find them. It will work. Trust me. This is the most powerful thing you can do. Tap into your genius. Encourage your leaders to do this, as well. It will make you think and open up your creativeness. When you find a great employee, use him or her to bring in his or her recommended contacts if they fit.

Personality assessments matter

To move forward at a rapid pace in building our business, we need to implement the best-people practices instead of the conventional, static, linear-thinking practices that hinder so many. The people evaluations covered in this chapter are among the best practices and can lead you to find the most productive workers who will fit your culture and needs. I have found that personality evaluations can help CEOs avoid many pitfalls and mistakes in the evaluating and hiring process. With the right people feedback, we're all capable of making great people decisions and avoiding many of the mistakes.

Personality evaluations provide much more tangible information and insight about a candidate than nearly any human relations person, manager, or CEO can typically detect. I've found out the hard way that even really good interviewers fail to produce as much information about a candidate as personality tests. It's been our policy to give these evaluations only to job candidates who we think might be good.

These evaluations provide us with good information about who is a good or poor fit for particular jobs. We hire people in many different jobs requiring many different characteristics. We can't be experts at every position we hire for, so we need some guidelines to help us. These assessments allow us to tailor our hiring to the specific needs of various jobs. The feedback we receive from existing employee tests reveals what traits work best for each position. If you don't have analytical measurements on an applicant's traits, it is much more difficult to know how that person will perform in a specific role. But the personality tests provide feedback that allows us to make an educated decision about how a person would fit into a specific role or the organization's performance-based culture. They also identify leadership traits, team-building skills, cultural fits, creativity, work ethic, and so much more. These surveys allow us to learn and improve from our feedback for future hiring.

Personality tests get you thinking about what you need traitwise, and they let you see what traits (best and worst) your current workers have. Without these tests, hiring is far more of a crapshoot. These tests are very valuable tools that can develop your ability to hire more of the right people. If you can't tie traits to peoples' strengths and weaknesses, you'll never be very good at getting the right people on the bus and in the right seats. However, the tests themselves don't tell you whom to hire. They just tell you more about who people are workwise and how they may fit into your desired culture. You learn a lot more from these than you do a résumé. Of course, at some point, you have to know "what kind of ducks you're hunting for." If you are looking for salespeople, you'll need to give them sales evaluations that demonstrate their sales talent. The evaluations I use are not good for sales.

I've tried most all the personality evaluations used to evaluate people for jobs, except for a few of the more recent products, which I understand are very effective but that I haven't experienced. Culture Index, Inc. is excellent and very easy to administer. It's worth trying, but you'll need their ability to read the results. I have firsthand knowledge of three surveys that best fit jobs for business. The first survey that we use for a prospective hire is the PASS III.

Personal Assessment Selection Survey (PASS) III: You can find this test on the web at http://www.persysco.com/Pages/preemployment.htm. This is an excellent test for honesty, alienation to authority, and attitude toward illegal drugs. If a candidate scores very badly on this test, we will have no further interest or discussions. Typically, a fairly average or even less-than-average score on this test is very good. And scoring too well might represent someone too linear. To build a great team, I've found that we must hire people of at least fairly average midrange honesty who do not possess much alienation to authority.

Profiles: The second personality survey that we provide a candidate is a Profiles Performance Indicator personality profile, and it can be found at http://www.profilesinternational.com. It is a personality-style employee performance test. This is the most meaningful and functional test I've ever seen for work performance. The one we use primarily measures a person's traits in the ten most important areas for job performance. Profiles International has many different surveys. However, it's very difficult for a novice to evaluate the results. A CEO must be knowledgeable and experienced enough to visualize the traits and to determine what they mean for your culture and your job. We all have a combination of strengths and weaknesses, and trying to evaluate them is a complex process.

Knowing what traits are best for a job and for your business can be very helpful. Over time, you'll learn what's needed or not needed for your culture and the different jobs in your business. Be wary of seeking experts to help you evaluate these traits, as they generally don't know your business, culture, or the job. I've found that the experts can tell you how a person will perform in a highly structured, bureaucratic, linear job; and they will also give you nice-sounding phrases on the negatives, which will take at least 80 percent of the blunt truth out of the evaluation. Like everything else, I had to learn what these test scores meant from feedback from real people in a nonlinear business. I've never found an expert for nonlinear business hires, although there are surely a few. These personality surveys are a way to know your employees better than you know your customers. It's a way to help get the right people in the right seats on your bus. Most people can be great if we can get them doing what they are great at.

Over time, I learned the hard way that I needed at least a moderate amount of reliability, flexibility, maturity, work drive, and decisiveness traits in the employees and not much planfulness, security motivation, submissiveness, hyperactivity, situational morality, restlessness, immaturity, and cynicism or many friendship-motivated traits for most jobs, which are not very structured or closely supervised. This is what I want for a performance-based nonlinear culture. Most other traits depend on the job, your culture, and your business. I also look for leadership, teamwork, and personal relationship traits to fit our culture and our needs. I especially look for people who are at least somewhat disorganized on the personality traits (perhaps the most 40 percent), as that trait represents broad, nonlinear, more flexible, whole-brain thinking. They make decisions on a wide range of situations, whereas the planful will make the same repetitive decisions on narrow, repetitive work. I've found that these more disorganized people can be and want to be empowered to handle the wide responsibilities needed in a nonlinear business if they have enough strength, a can-do attitude, honesty, and reliability. What I don't want is too much situational morality, which is also nonlinear but too unreliable. The planning side (the most 40 percent or so) represents more narrow, linear thinking, as do many of the more security-minded people. The more planful, cynical, and security-motivated people normally have to go into an already organized and highly structured position to be effective, which is found in mostly large, stable corporations. A nonlinear business cannot add that structure without destroying its primary nonlinear strength.

After this profile, we may have enough information to see that some people won't be a fit for our culture and leadership style. The important thing is that you need to find a personnel assessment that will relate to your needs. For instance, sales organizations will need a sales assessment geared toward specific responsibilities and traits.

DiSC: The third test we give is the DiSC (http://www.onlinediscprofile.com), which shows a candidate's working style and which helps fill in the picture. This allows us to better visualize how the candidate would fit our needs and mesh with the other people in his or her area.

Then the fourth screen is the résumé, application, health, credit, criminal history, and other checks. They don't have to be nearly as perfect and flawless as most linear businesses demand, but we are looking for who best fits our culture and needs.

The interview matters

The interview is the fifth screening, and it is very important. Here's what we want to learn about candidates during the interview:

- What have been their greatest work experiences?
- What have been their worst work experiences?
- What small-businesslike jobs have they worked in where they had to perform wider responsibilities? How did they like these jobs? How did they like any linear jobs they performed?
- Exactly what did they do best, and how did they do it in previous jobs, hour to hour and problem to problem? What obstacles did they have, what did they learn, and why did they do it best?
- What do they dislike?
- What type of work do they want to do in ten years and why?
- How much of a can-do attitude do they possess on difficult tasks?
- Do they really want to work for us or just get a paycheck?
- Do they have a can-do attitude that we want?
- Are they a cultural fit for us?
- Do they feel entitled?
- Do they think nonlinearly? Do they want a wide responsibility job or a narrower, fixed job?

» Do they need to be empowered to be happy?

» Are they production-motivated? Competitive?

The primary purpose of the interview should be to see if the person is a cultural and job fit. This is where everything comes together or where the candidate falls apart for the culture. If he or she has been in the ballpark on most of the other tests and we have a good feeling about him or her at this point, there's a good chance that this person could be whom we want on our team. If he or she looks good at this point, we'll let a local supervisor or manager take him or her around and see if the supervisor thinks he or she will fit our needs. There are two big questions the supervisor needs to answer:

1. Does the person fit our culture?
2. Does the person really want to work for us and do a productive wide job or just get a paycheck?

The personality surveys allow us the opportunity to eliminate most of the people who are more unlikely to improve our team. We are looking to hire people whom we can promote and satisfy in the long run and not just to fill a low-level job now. Candidates have to at least appear to be able to eventually become senior first-class performers in their initial jobs that they enter and hopefully be promoted further. We need to offer them opportunities to improve over their initial jobs with us.

Most of the people you interview will be good for the right organization but not yours. You are not looking for good or bad, so don't get sold on conventionally good like most people do. You are looking for people who fit your culture and who want to grow in your business.

We also need these tests to uncover people who may be in the top level of performers whom we could not otherwise identify. For instance, we've been able to identify many top performers in the personality tests who don't interview well. Many—maybe even most—top nonlinear performers do not interview particularly well because they don't spend much time practicing how to convince people who they are highly qualified. They allow their work to speak for itself. On the contrary, many average and poor performers spend much of their lives practicing the art of persuasion, as opposed to getting things done. They're very good at interviewing and holding on to jobs they're poor at, as it's what they do.

Don't be in a bind for time, as this is where most bad hires are made. To make the best hires, you must be patient and persistent. Practice your evaluations and also constantly look for the right people when you're not hiring, as your future depends on it. Hire a great person when you have a chance, even when you're not hiring. Don't think you can manage poor workers to success (like most managers think), as this never works. Also, the better we hire, the more leadership we bring onto our team and the less bureaucracy and management we will require. Hire people who fit your desired culture, who will follow the principles and direction toward which your compass points, and who will help coach themselves. No one wants to be managed. Make sure that they really want to work for you. Try to find three people that are very hirable and choose one. This will aid you to better hire and will provide you with more leadership, which is a scarce commodity. Your people will think you're crazy, but that's what it takes to build a great team. We're not just trying to hire someone to get by this year; we are looking for long-term team members who fit our culture.

Chapter roundup

A winning team is the muscle behind the company's ability to perform its functions efficiently while delivering a top-quality product or service. Thus, placing the right people in the right jobs is crucial to the success and growth of the business. As the CEO, it's your responsibility to manage the hiring of all employees, including those who are tasked with the routine jobs. Hire with your performance-based culture firmly in mind, select people who are the most likely to fit in, and get rid of those who don't as soon as possible. Use a battery of personality tests to qualify likely candidates before conducting interviews. You will need a strong HR buy-in and belief from nonlinear HR personnel. If you get started with the right objectives, you'll learn the rest that you need to know by doing. We have to obtain the people in our business who mesh well with executing our strategy of doing the right stuff. We especially need to do so to have a really good culture and to build and maintain excellent processes. The people, culture, and processes are your key to the execution of your business. Combine excellence in these with excellent strategy for great success.

Remember …

- » Number one: hire for culture and leadership. Learn how to spot the "ducks" you want. Get the ones who will work in harmony so that they all row your boat in the right direction.
- » The people on your team will determine the success or failure of your business.
- » Get rid of the toxic people, no matter their talent, that don't want to row your boat in the direction you want.
- » The 80/20 principle applies to people. The top 20 percent of employees do 80 percent of the value-added work. Try to make it so that the majority of your employees are working on the important work that generates 80 percent of the desired results. Minimize the number of people you hire to complete the small stuff.
- » As a CEO, you are responsible for hiring the right team. Get involved even with the lower-level employees because they are essential members of your team. They and your leaders need to be culturally compatible with each other for best results.
- » An employee must be a good fit with your corporate culture, and he or she must possess a can-do attitude.

- Get the right, nonlinear, flexible-thinking (less planful) people on your bus who want to work and thrive in your culture. Do not hire the planful, rigid, bureaucratic, security-motivated, cynical types. Hire people who can think.
- Personality tests are an essential screening tool in addition to résumés.
- Promoting from within builds team spirit and retains institutional knowledge and culture that is difficult and time-consuming to replace.
- Personality tests are a way to know your people well enough to develop them more in your business.
- Beware of people with strong conventional backgrounds who are too linear. They'll never be able to lead nonlinear employees.
- Candidates who have worked in small businesses where they were required to think in a nonlinear way on a wide variety of work make the best employees in a dynamic, nonlinear work environment like yours. Nonlinear leaders need nonlinear people in their business to be able to empower them to take ownership over a wide range of duties.
- As CEO, always demand to routinely evaluate many more people that your HR or management teams want to evaluate. The more you prospect, the more freedom of action you'll have, and the better people you'll get. We can never get enough of the right people. Be very demanding, and don't lower your standards.
- You will make many hiring mistakes. They key to excellence is to get rid of the culture and performance misfits as quickly as possible.

11

Embracing Process Excellence

Problems should be solved on the spot, as soon as they arise. No frontline employee should have to wait for a supervisor's permission.

—Jan Carlzon, airline executive

The ability to simplify means to eliminate the unnecessary so that the necessary may speak.

—Hans Hofmann

The *Executioner*'s goal of excellence is to develop great processes, people, mindset and culture with the right strategy and ability to execute the principles that produce great results. If you think about it, a business is made up of its people and the service or product that they produce together for profit in the marketplace. It really is as simple as that, a basic concept that anyone can grasp. Yet if we look more closely at what we mean by *business*, it soon becomes obvious that manufacturing a product or delivering a service that people are willing to pay for is a lot more complex. We only make a profit and stay in business by how well we execute our business processes with people working together in harmony with common goals, attitudes, and strategy. This is where all the strategy, people, and execution of the first ten chapters come together to make or break a business. This is what your customers are paying for and what is producing your profits. The purpose of all our work should be to develop a high level of excellence at performing the smoothest, fastest, most cost-efficient way of delivering high-value-added products and services that our customers want. While this is rare, it is very doable, fun, and profitable.

When I bring up business processes as a key area of focus, what I'm simply saying is that the entire team has to really care about how the proverbial sausage is made. Good people alone cannot make up for poor or even average processes that will enslave them in problems, double work, small stuff, crises, delays, rework, and the like. It takes a great performance-based culture to work in harmony to develop and maintain excellent processes, which then takes the right people and strategy. We have to know how all the various parts of our business function and fit together to accomplish the objectives we establish and to adeptly head problems off at the pass or resolve them quickly when they sneak through. It might sound a little strange for me to say such a thing because you'd naturally assume that a CEO and employees would know these things, but as our business evolves, most of us lose sight of our business processes as they become more complex, remote, invisible, and eventually go off course. It's only the very few best businesses that can develop great processes and then maintain them. This is primarily because there are so few businesses that are able to execute the strategies, mindsets and practices needed. Most CEOs and businesses never develop themselves enough to execute these best principles or even try to. Business processes and problem solving are where sweating what matters most comes together to generate all your value-added results. This is definitely true of most relatively small and complex businesses valued at a billion dollars or less.

Paying attention to the process mechanisms that make your company work is actually much of what matters most. It's not small stuff! I even consider the processes we use on the vast amount of small stuff to be big stuff, as we can't allow ourselves to be enslaved by even these processes. We need to have a great process to handle the small stuff to ensure that it becomes our servant, not our master. I could likewise say that we should strive to also make what matters most our servants. I've found that excellent and effective business processes will result in an ease of doing business and very profitable products, services, and a great environment. Poor business processes mean that you are enslaved by a flawed product or service to sell. Not good.

Keeping Murphy at bay

When I started as an entrepreneur, I certainly was aware of how important my primary chemical processes were. I was, in fact, making custom chemicals, a complex process in itself, and then I was working to create an organization around that central pursuit that entailed gluing together virtually all the basic functions of any business—administration, accounting, sales, marketing, personnel, inventory control, vendor services, and so on. I thought my business was bound for greatness that would distinguish me among my industry counterparts. I thought that it was my chemical process that needed to be great and that the rest would take care of itself. Like practically everyone else, I was planning on smooth sailing. I certainly wasn't planning to have the problems that I saw in most other businesses, but I did—in spades. I was spending double and triple the cost on workers, managers, accounting, and every other basic function that seemed so simple.

I found myself patching up problems, putting off problems, guessing at short-term fixes, fighting problems, not identifying causes of problems, being unaware of problems, depending on others with even less problem-solving talent than I had, and trying the cheapest or fastest fixes for problems. You get the picture. I was also trying to solve too many complex problems in areas where others should have been better suited, so I was essentially just getting in the way. I had too many of the wrong people, and I wasn't effectively using the few right people when they were right in front of me, ready to help! I had bad, flawed processes and the wrong people in key positions. In fact, I had turned the company into a breeder of fiascos. Nearly every problem was dumped on me. I found that I could not effectively babysit a hundred other people plus our suppliers, contractors, and customers and solve all their problems. Yet I foolishly kept thinking that I was talented, proactive, and knowledgeable enough to bypass most of the business land mines I was facing every day. You might say that I had blinders on like most businesspeople. I couldn't solve every problem all the time. I needed the teams to solve most of their own problems on the spot and not involve me or the managers. It's very bad for your future to have most of the problems of a business be dumped on you and your managers or leaders, which will enslave the leadership and not hold all responsible.

Of course, now I know that anyone who has been an entrepreneur or CEO for any length of time understands that in the real world, business is nearly always a constant series of problems, regressions, demands, slow progress, hassles, and delays, most of which we cannot control. Perhaps the most known and accepted business rule is Murphy's law, which says that "whatever can go wrong, will go wrong." In virtually all business endeavors, that law is applicable, especially in terms of running a business. That's why one of the key requirements for an entrepreneur or CEO should be toughness. But not just any kind of toughness; I'm talking about a backbone and robustness that could be labeled pioneer toughness.

The far-reaching, all-encompassing governing power of Murphy's law in business is also why so many people want to go to work in a steady and orderly job at a good company—they won't have to face the many problems of entrepreneurship or high-level leadership. Many people just want to—or need to—go to work and leave all their problems behind when they exit the building at five o'clock. As for me, however, I've learned to fully embrace the battles because I've benefited from both my wins and my losses. I now realize that the losses and challenges were probably more valuable than the victories and smoother times because the trials and errors better prepared me for future obstacles. But I do wish I had learned the lessons much sooner. I'd have had fewer bumps in the road and fewer headaches to go with them.

The best businesses have a program to execute the best process development principles. Within the real business world of disorder and chaos, there are obviously a few businesses that have mostly smooth, nearly flawless operations—with *mostly* and *nearly* being the operative words here. You would do well to pay close attention to winning companies and to copy the processes they use across the board, though with an emphasis on your problem areas. From my research and personal experience, some examples of businesses that currently possess near-flawless operational execution are the Ritz-Carlton hotel chain, Southwest Airlines, Progressive Insurance, and Oceania Cruises. Whenever I've witnessed or read about these high-functioning businesses, it has totally inspired me to duplicate their operational processes in my own business, above even growth and profits. That's how important I viewed, and still view, a keen concentration on the processes and problem solving that make my businesses what they are today.

I finally got totally sick of the flaws I constantly observed in my own business. As I indicated earlier, we had a seemingly endless stream of production, supply, quality, cost, and people problems. On the one hand, it seemed nearly impossible to duplicate the efforts of some of the most well-oiled, smooth-running businesses that I studied. That was frustrating, to say the least! I'd try and try, and I'd always come up short. When I got discouraged, I took solace in the fact that whatever others had done could be duplicated. If you're feeling overwhelmed and frustrated, take the same comfort I did. Remember that all good business practices can be learned. I knew that achieving a level of near flawlessness would give me peace of mind, satisfaction, and a better life, and so I kept working at it. Smooth, more trouble-free operations would be better for our customers and employees too and would eliminate my enslavement of consistently focusing on overcoming flaws, many of which I'd inadvertently built into my own organization.

In the book *What Really Works: The 4+2 Formula for Sustained Business*

Success, authors William Joyce, Bruce Roberson, and Nitin Nohria state that process execution is one of the four business practices that all highly successful businesses perform exceptionally well. In contrast, practically all other businesses do not do this well. It's an ultimate difference maker, a make-or-break quality. It's an essential quality for great success, and it should be a top priority of CEOs and leaders seeking success. It is *that* important. Having good processes is a dynamic 80/20 principle that is highly correlated to success and is definitely the big stuff. However, very few comprehend what a flawless operation is.

Think about it. Common sense tells us that if we are flawed in our execution, we'll be so enslaved by our small-stuff problems that we won't be able to grow and excel at the rate we desire. Conversely, if our execution is smooth and nearly flaw-free, the business hums along, leaving us freer to focus on the other CEO duties. Over the years, I've learned much by doing business with other companies that have their processes down pat. In these companies, most everything seems to operate smoothly, with each employee immediately taking ownership and responsibility for every detail or problem. I love working with companies that embrace excellence like that, and so do others. As part of your evolution as a CEO, it will pay dividends for you to seek out and do business with nonlinear firms that you may want to copy from a process point of view. At the very least, it may open your eyes to new and exciting vistas.

As an exceptional process engineer, second to nearly no one, most would think that I could easily design and operate great business and chemical processes. Why would it take me so long to work most of these out? The answer is that we have to at least somewhat master the first ten chapters before we can master the process execution and problem solving. It takes the right people and a really good performance-based team culture working in harmony to have the ability to execute good processes and problem solving. Then we have to have a good strategy to execute. We need a CEO who is doing his or her CEO duties of CEO thinking, 80/20 principle thinking, goal setting, a PMA, creating enough action, and using good financial wisdom to be doing enough of the right stuff to be able to need the rest. I learned that we can't start out in first grade and skip our way to being a senior in college the next year. We not only have to possess practical, real-world knowledge of what matters most, but we have to also gain experience, and we have to mature. The great mind of the American Revolution Thomas Paine said, "As to the learning that any person gains from school education, it serves only, like a small capital, to put him in the way of beginning learning for himself afterward. Every person of learning is finally his own teacher." Then there's thinking, attitudes, habits, leadership, confidence, teamwork, relationships, and so much more. Process and problem solving are where everything comes together. It takes at least ten years of doing the right stuff to get to the point of being able to do most of this last chapter well. That's why we need to work on our personal growth and mindsets in each of the key areas all the time. But do work on your processes and problem solving now, where you are and with what you've got. Remember that it takes a great culture of harmony to make it work, since a few people can't do it all. You can make a lot of progress now.

Envision smooth operations, and embrace the processes. Once I witnessed near flawlessness in operation, I had a picture—a real vision—for what I wanted it to look like in my own business. It's something that we have to see to believe, and we must believe in it to accomplish it in our own organizations. If you look at how top companies perform in a smooth and relatively trouble-free way, you'll become inspired by what you see and will want the same for your business. I did. Then I took concrete steps to make it happen.

Go for smooth and simple, not perfect and complex

I don't want you to get the wrong idea when I speak of near-flawless operations. In reality, there are no such things as flawless operations. No business operations are actually completely smooth and trouble-free. There is no perfection in the world, and there certainly isn't in business. Many obstacles and problems are put in our way over which we have no control. A business is all about people working together toward a common end, and people aren't perfect. Murphy is bound to show up at the least opportune moment. It's a mistake to strive for perfection, but many conventional thinkers do just that when they envision the processes that comprise business operations. Go for perfect and you'll end up shooting yourself in the foot. Essentially, if you do that, you're setting yourself up to work at achieving a static operation that's expensive to operate and will tie your hands.

As noted, problems come up all the time. But in a company with near-flawless operations, from the perspective of customers, owners, workers, managers, and suppliers, those problems appear to be handled without issue. That's the big difference between smooth and perfect. If you acknowledge that frequent kinks in processes are bound to occur, you can then accept that reality and design your procedures to take it into account. Here's something important to remember: in smooth, trouble-free operations, a business maintains fast, simple, smooth, efficient, and economical processes, with the employees possessing the autonomy to fix problems and make decisions on the spot. This requires a good performance-based culture of working in harmony to pull it off.

Pause here for a moment to think about that.

If that autonomy and culture are in place, the many daily flaws are handled easily on the spot and are rarely passed on to the customers, management, or others. For example, if the person working the front desk at the Ritz-Carlton has been trained to handle problems on the spot—such as reservation errors or rooms not being cleaned—he or she is able to handle customer complaints, concerns, and problems quickly and effectively without involving the management, waiting for the approval of his or her supervisor, pacifying the customer with a standardized, rehearsed response, or generating the ire of the customer. With that type of autonomy, many problems are instantly handled on the spot by the people best able to handle them, as opposed to growing into larger issues by being passed on to management, other departments, and customers who are not equipped to quickly resolve them. These problems can fester for days or weeks. If it's two hundred hours instead of ten minutes, there's a twelve-hundred-times difference in the time it festers—and it's festering with the higher-ups! As a result, the seemingly flawless business has fewer festering problems, since they're resolved quickly when they're small, making it appear as if it is resistant to problems when it really isn't. Then the leaders will be free to focus on what matters most instead of being enslaved by problems.

Here's another key caution area to watch for. When problems are passed along or handed down to others—as they rarely are in nearly flawless businesses—the costs and troubles increase by an order of magnitude, sixteen times if we believe the 80/20 principle relationship. I say perhaps a hundred times because of the time factor of festering and because of the skill level in the higher-ups. Passing along flaws typically leads to a very flawed operation. These nonseamless handoffs are bad for our processes. The reality is that most of the bureaucratic managers and people who are on the receiving end of the passed-down flaws are not good at resolving remote problems created by others or not equipped to deal with them or able to resolve them quickly. That's just terrible for the long-term health of a business, and it breeds bad attitudes.

Fewer handoffs of problems to others are best. In conventional businesses, the manager's typical approach is to add more nonseamless handoffs to quality, technical, management, and the customer, which slow down the process and make it more rigid, expensive, complex, and problematic. This counterproductive action makes the process less effective for businesses. For a huge company with large assembly lines and with little change, the perfect or fail-safe method can result in a practical and stable process at the cost of rigidity, service, poor response to market conditions, and more bureaucracy. Such processes aren't going to be what drives your success as a nonlinear leader or CEO, and they are not best practices that will develop your business. The conventional bureaucratic perfect method to process improvement is a very flawed practice and is not a best practice. It is a high-cost, low-service, low-profit, and low-growth model that is not in harmony with real-world principles. It's the practice that most governments and large businesses use, and it is very costly. It gets so well engrained that the existing leadership cannot do much about it. They get by with it because their competitors are doing the same.

Think of it like this: perfect and nearly flawless are at opposite ends of the spectrum. Striving for static perfection is the stuff of linear, conventional thinking and is very, very flawed and expensive. Pursuing nearly flawless dynamic operations is an inherent acknowledgment that flaws will occur, and so you're going to factor that into the design of your processes. Implementing excellent processes that are nearly flawless generates many times the profits and results than does using the complicated, conventional, perfect bureaucratic methods of policies, procedures, and handoffs. This is a concept that is difficult for most CEOs and managers to comprehend. They tend to think that a remote higher-up bureaucrat needs to approve of the fix, but they don't want to put their necks on the chopping block.

We often have no control over many events that happen each day because there are so many variables from so many sources. And the old adage holds true that what can possibly go wrong will go wrong. That 2 percent can stop or delay ten times more. For example, if you're running a manufacturing plant, a seemingly small glitch can shut down production. Every minute of the shutdown or slowdown costs big money. Talk about a major stressor and a real challenge for a CEO to maintain a positive mental attitude! If you get over the horror-show factor and you keep your cool, you as the CEO will realize that most of these events can be handled on the spot by empowered employees if your processes and culture are good. Handling these on the spot makes most of them nearly invisible and at least one-sixteenth as costly, since these correspond to the 80/20 principle. Stated another way—the glass-is-half-full way—it could be deduced that even with the unavoidable presence of Murphy's law, 98 percent of everything will go right every day. This sounds quite encouraging, but don't be misled. There's enough that goes wrong every day in a typically active business setting to cause plenty of grief and headaches. I know those headaches well.

Growth, especially rapid growth, introduces more problems. The more action we take and the faster we grow, the more problems we will encounter or create. If you are determined to achieve great success, you also need to make certain that you have good methods in place to handle the magnitude of flaws that will be encountered as your company expands. Another of Murphy's laws is that nothing works right the first time. I can now see that my rapid growth and high level of action created such a flawed business that it enslaved me early in my career. I was encountering perhaps at least ten times the flaws/problems/obstacles as a stable business that wasn't growing much. A fast-growing business with new suppliers, new processes, new employees, and new customers will have far more delays and quality problems than a flat, stable business that's more developed. That's something to keep in mind. If you're on a roll, expect headaches. Also expect great rewards. Know that you're on the right track if problems pop up. The problems will result in your building a strong team and opportunity. If everything stays just peachy for too long, that's the time to start worrying. It might mean that you've hit your comfort zone and have lost momentum and more opportunity.

If we can't handle these more frequent flaws effectively, we'll soon find ourselves in toxic crisis-management mode nearly all the time. The problems will enslave us and keep us from concentrating on what really matters most. Reverting to the standard old bureaucracy and a perfectionistic approach will just make things even worse, especially if we're running a fast-growing business. Problems don't scare off ambitious achievers with positive mental attitudes. Successful entrepreneurs and CEOs become warriors by learning to handle flaws well and using the opportunities created to build their success. The most successful have a strong solution orientation as it applies to problems. They are constantly searching for problems to solve. We have to know about problems in order to solve them. Execution is problem solving. Leadership is problem solving. Excellence is problem solving. This problem solving is also very much a part of goal setting, since we have to excellently solve problems to reach our blue-sky goals. These problem-solving basics are equivalent to an advanced course in goals. Make them your habit. The less successful stay weak by either backing away from opportunities or becoming enslaved by the problems. They also complicate their processes by trying to prevent problems that arise from sources over which they have no control.

Be committed to following an organized problem-solving process

1. Take time to think through the cause and effect of a given problem. Evidently, problem solving isn't covered much in business or engineering school, and businesses don't train their employees in problem solving, either, or at least most don't. When problems come up, people get reactive and think conventionally, a big mistake. They want the quick fix, and they go for it whenever possible. They don't think in a nonlinear way, so their solutions to the problems often lack creativity and reflect a path of least resistance. A bad solution is really not a solution at all. At best, it's a Band-Aid. At worst, it's a buried land mine that will explode later and create even bigger problems. It's best to use a systematic teamwork process and to follow these proven problem-solving basics. Learn them and implement them.

If you ask your competent, caring employees these questions, you might really be surprised at the outcome. The people on the front line know what's what, but they will need some good technical and business training and leadership to learn good problem solving. They'll appreciate being asked to join the team to make things work more smoothly and efficiently, and chances are, they'll have more information to help. A good process team approach and training on problem solving works best. It encourages employee empowerment. It is leadership execution. Encourage them by using the process principles of this chapter so as not to stray. You'll empower your subordinates, instead of browbeating them. In short, you'll be actively improving your business processes, and you'll be building a rock-solid, performance-based corporate culture that you can take right to the bank. Problem solving and process development are always best done by the people doing the work in teams from the bottom up. I've found that when I have had a great culture, people were good at teamwork problem solving. When I didn't, the problem solving was horrible. Leaders and the people doing the work should take ownership of their processes. Make an effort to make the process as motivational as possible (e.g., dinners, free stuff, rewards, recognition, etc.). Make it a big deal. Developing problem-solving skills is a vital part of improving your business processes. It will happen with a culture of excellence and won't with an average culture. Use a culture of harmony and purpose to make your people most of your master mind group.

2. It's not useful to define the problem until the priority or importance of the problem is determined. We obviously need to work on the most important or the most urgent problem first. We should strive to prioritize the 20 percent of problems that can generate 80 percent of the opportunity for improvement (except for urgent necessary problems that can't be ignored). Believe me that it takes a great deal of discipline not to work on the 80 percent of problems that only produce 20 percent of the negative results. If you choose to work on those like the linear thinkers, you will not solve the big problems. My experience with linear thinkers is that they will only face small problems and rarely the big ones. Their solutions are nearly always horrible. Have the discipline to prioritize the problems. If you solve the big problems, many of the others will go away. I learned the hard way to focus on good problem-solving techniques throughout my businesses. It's that important to the CEO. It's a CEO's duty. I've always taken the lead in this but have often been at fault in developing my teams. Conventional-thinking people will try to fix every tiny perceived problem that doesn't need to be fixed instead of the large problems that do. Don't let this happen.

3. Identify the real problem, which isn't always easy. People view problems from a variety of perspectives—hassles, delays, disagreements, conflicts, obstacles, goals, failures, situations, mindsets procedures, policies, and decisions. Many things can count as problems, and it's easy to get caught up in all of them. For our processes to work well, we must be able to dig down beyond the symptoms—the effect, so to speak—and pinpoint the underlying causes. Use all members of your performance-based culture team to help spot problems early, including the obstacles that most people don't see as problems. The best problem-solving businesses use many people to identify and solve problems instead of a few. Always state the problem in many ways, as this is very enlightening, and brainstorm many solutions. The problems that most don't see tend to be the process problems and the handoffs, which are the big problems, and those process problems create a lot of other problems. Oftentimes delays, hassles, double work, miscommunication, paperwork, and such are not recognized as problems.

4. A problem cannot be solved effectively unless its cause is known. We must determine what caused the problem before we try to resolve it. It's important that we avoid trying to treat symptoms and unconfirmed causes. Make sure that you identify and confirm exactly what's wrong before proceeding. Take your time to check facts or even to run a study. Think before you leap. A properly diagnosed problem is already half solved. I know this all sounds obvious, but I'm restating it here because, strangely enough, this basic concept apparently eludes nearly all would-be problem solvers!

5. Problem solving is a process. It's best to use a disciplined approach with multiple people. It's too easy for one person—the CEO or a manager, in many cases—to come up with a fast answer that is less than optimal. We also want to involve more people in the process to prevent the CEO or any key person from becoming enslaved and to develop a better team for the future. This requires a really good business culture. Always use a disciplined approach.

6. Beware of a problem that can only be defined one way. Typically, a problem has more than one layer in terms of cause and effect. If the problem appears to be one dimensional, then perhaps it's not really a problem that fits in that top 20 percent that creates 80 percent of the trouble, making it small stuff, not big stuff, unless it greatly affects the bottom line. Great creativity and insight inevitably come from defining a problem in many ways. We rarely deduce the right definition of a complex problem on the first attempt, and we often do not come up with the right fix the first time out of the box. Notice that this creative approach to problem solving is very similar to what we do in goal setting where we write down twenty approaches to reach our goal. Write down ten or twenty definitions of a problem, and then write out twenty approaches to solve the problem. You'll learn a lot. In a very real sense, it's emblematic of applying the 80/20 principle to yet another aspect of our core business philosophy. Always try to define the problem in a multitude of ways. We're looking for the right definition and cause that typically don't get defined in the real world.

7. Write down your idea result. When involved in the problem-solving process, write the ideal desired results on paper and how much those are worth. Don't worry about anything else. Start with the end in mind, and you'll end up seeing if the solution is complete, economical, or optimal. This effort can result in a much lower cost and a more effective process after the problem is solved. Your goal is to devise a better process after the solution, if this is feasible. Most just gravitate to any solution that might work, which is rarely the best solution. This is reverse engineering, which is successful goal setting. Starting from the first is short-term, failure thinking.

When writing the solution, make it as simple as possible. Ask yourself, "Does this solve the problem? Or half solve it economically? For how long? Is it simply a Band-Aid? How much is it worth to solve the problem? How complete is the solution?" Simplifying the process will normally require several peels off the skin of the proverbial onion. This will ignite your genius and creativity to a degree that will amaze you. Write ten or twenty ways you can simplify the solution.

Devise many solutions as in step 6. This will open up your creativity, as well. Write down ten possible solutions or approaches to the problem. Then look at it again the next day and add five more. If it's a big problem, keep writing more solutions until you hit a home run. This effort is guaranteed to bring out more of your genius. Always do this on big problems.

8. Find the right people to come up with as many solutions as possible. Don't sit in your ivory tower trying to come up with the solution all by yourself. While you alone must bear the responsibility for how well or how badly your business processes work, you can and should rely on your entire team for support when it comes to finding the best solution for systemic procedural problems within the business. One goal is to develop them. You're the ultimate decider, as it were, but the more input you can get from the right people, the better. Who are the right people? Bar none, it's the nonlinear thinking ones in a performance-based culture who are performing the work, the ones who understand the process or technology, and the ones with enough leadership ability to lead the troops to victory. It's usually not some remote manager who doesn't own the problem and doesn't possess firsthand knowledge of the issues. The remote manager is going to simply hand off the problem to someone else, anyway, so don't even bother doing this! Don't hand off problem solving on a company-wide level to anybody. It's your job to deal with it. However, I have found that I have sometimes had to seek expert advice from the best people in the industry. It's up to you to make sure that you really solve the problem.

9. A great performance-based culture is essential. People with the right attitude will work miracles with problem solving, as will having good personal relations and harmony with all people in a business. Problem solving requires a lot of this leadership in an organization. It requires teamwork and harmony at a very high level. It's the only environment I have experienced where everyone involved was rowing their boat together in the right direction. Otherwise, it seems like problem solving is political or done with the cheapest, easiest, fastest solution.

Commit to training yourself and your team in the fine art of problem solving. Develop your culture and people to be very solution-oriented. Doing so is integral to maintaining good business processes. The two are inextricably linked. The better you get at dealing almost solely with what matters most across the board in your company, the better problem solver you'll be. I believe that great problem solving mostly takes a positive attitude and a belief that there are great solutions, even if those solutions aren't readily discernible at first glance. I oftentimes solve problems that others don't because I have complete faith that an outstanding solution exists. If you don't think there's a solution to a problem, you'll be much less likely to take effective action. That, in turn, will exacerbate the situation. Use a disciplined approach, and seek others to help because problem solving doesn't work well by the seat-of-the-pants method. Seek the simplest route. There is great genius in simplicity. Embrace it wholeheartedly! Few do.

Sound business processes matter

Using business-process improvement concepts as a path for business success came to the forefront throughout the business world in the 1990s when Michael Hammer and James Champy published *Reengineering the Corporation: A Manifesto for Business Revolution*. The premise of this book is that all businesses are basically a group of business processes. The efficiency, effectiveness, and productivity of these processes will determine the ultimate success or failure of the business. It takes good, simple processes to be smooth and nearly flawless, and it requires at least decent processes to survive.

These processes include every action a business undertakes, such as all paperwork, computer work, telephone calls, meetings, sales, purchasing, shipping, and so on, as well as its primary product process. While all of these processes can be improved, they can also deteriorate, as they are always under assault. It requires a CEO mind-set to understand this concept. Your workers and managers are often too enslaved by their narrower, short-term production work to notice. Acknowledge that, and you're already on your way to improving the business. Remember, problem solving and business processes are bound together. Each impacts the other, and one cannot be addressed alone without taking the other into account.

Here are the comprehensive key concepts for the process-improvement basics that matter most. Developing and maintaining great business processes is as big as anything else we do. It has many advanced elements of goal setting not covered in the goals chapter as part of the process. Developing your goals and processes use nearly all the same principles. Get good at it. This is the PhD level of goal setting.

I've found that the excellence in business nearly all comes from combining a great culture with good business processes. Here are the process basics:

1. Be committed to process improvement. Your major first step is to acknowledge that you can and should improve your business processes to get as close as you can to smooth, excellent, effective, and nearly flawless operations across the board. Be solution-oriented. To do so will require you to have a can-do attitude that has already rippled through the company to create a vibrant and dynamic work environment for your team. We only excel to our level of personal growth and leadership. In other words, a poor CEO with the wrong attitude won't be able to develop good processes no matter how much process knowledge he or she has. Also, people in a poor culture or with poor leadership will likewise not be effective with good process principles. They'll also perform poorly in problem solving. It takes an excellent nonlinear CEO, an excellent performance-based culture with much harmony, and the right nonlinear-thinking people coming together to develop good processes. Linear-thinking businesses that I know have failed at this type of process improvement.

2. Learn and train yourself to practice Occam's razor. Just what is Occam's razor? In the year 1142, William of Occam formulated his theory that "the simplest and most direct answer with the fewest number of steps is usually the best solution to any problem (or process)." This principle forms much of the basis of the highest level of science, even in the twenty-first century. There is pure genius in its simplicity. It takes genius to peel back the layers of the onion and to simplify the process, while any idiot can and will complicate anything. This is a good way to figure out who the nonperformers are. Good nonlinear workers, managers, and entrepreneurs simplify, while the losers will complicate.

Learn to simplify and continually practice simplifying everything. Build that thinking into your business. In most every case, process improvement comes from making our processes simpler by using a small set of process principles that start with Occam's razor. No one will ever master process or problem solving without learning and practicing this theory. You've also got to resist those who try to complicate the process. Sadly, the complication lovers are everywhere! Get rid of them, as any idiot can complicate. But simplify and simplify by continuing to "peel the onion."

> "Great leaders are almost always great simplifiers, who can cut through argument, debate and doubt, to offer a solution everybody can understand." ~ *Colin Powell*

3. Map your processes on paper, especially the ones on which you're currently working. Putting a business process on paper is often half the battle toward actually improving the process. The same goes for problem solving and goal setting. It's basically the same principle as "a problem properly defined is half-solved." Or in the medical world, "an illness correctly diagnosed is half-cured." I've found that most people can easily see how to improve a process once it is properly defined on paper. Michael Hammer and James Champy's book and other process-mapping sources will help a person map his or her process on paper. Just write all the steps down on paper in "process map" form. The map will include delays, hassles, paperwork, lack of cooperation, lack of teamwork, unclear procedures, lack of simplicity, handoffs (especially handoffs to management or quality control), time to perform the work, elapsed time, and steps that are not strongly value-added and efficient.

Mapping can be difficult at first. Every delay and obstacle must be put on paper to enable you to see it clearly, and then you must assimilate the data. It's an area where you may initially want to use a consultant. However, I think that anyone who wants to simplify and develop can put it all down on paper no matter what his or her training is. Just use common sense, and put everything on paper. Everything means delays, hassles, miscommunications, rework, high cost, management slowdowns, excessive paperwork, and the like. What's important is that you have to believe that the process can be improved, just like you have to believe that there is a superb solution for most every problem. As I said, bear in mind that most conventional thinkers want to complicate the process. They do not believe that a great solution exists—a natural inclination, though a damaging one. It all comes down to your attitude and beliefs. It is very important to always simplify processes and procedures as much as possible and to develop a strong resistance to adding complexity and additional steps. The goal is to get every process easy, fast, simple, right, economical, and adding value. We want a minimum of steps. Your objective should be to always minimize, simplify, and reduce steps. Make the small stuff your servants.

4. Continuously refine your business processes. It's easy to get complacent once you've set up your improved business processes. Be totally committed to not letting people add extra steps or complexity to your processes, as I can assure you that there is an army of people waiting in line that are hell-bent to do so! Be committed to excellence and discipline. Effectiveness is all about improving business processes and seeking excellence instead of maintaining. With our processes always under attack, they will always degrade if we are not proactively improving them. Write down a process to improve across all major aspects of the company every quarter or every month or week. It's your duty as a leader. Make all additions to processes go through you so that you have the opportunity to prevent complexity.

Most people, businesses, and organizations will never do anything in this regard until they absolutely have to, which is often too late. Be proactive and in control of keeping all your business processes as flawless as you can. Doing so is priceless, and we owe it to our people and customers. Each wants to know that you care and they can trust you.

5. Minimize handoffs. As previously discussed, handing problems off to others is bound to cause trouble. While some problems obviously must be kicked upstairs, analyze your current procedures for dealing with problems of all sorts, and go to great lengths to eliminate handoffs in favor of giving employees more autonomy to immediately handle the problems as they come up. Handoffs are great on the football field, but they are not good for business processes.

This happens more often than you might think, and it's a real killer from a productivity standpoint. It also ends up costing the company lots of money. In fact, the handoff syndrome permeates most organizations. Be committed to going to great lengths to minimize handoffs. Most well-intended added handoffs are process killers, and they are the result of linear thinkers who don't think workers can be empowered to do their jobs. Handoffs are the number-one part of bureaucracy we want to minimize.

For instance, it's better for three people to perform three steps each on a process than it is to have nine people do one step each. And better yet, have two people do the nine steps. Which approach are you using? Minimizing handoffs normally involves each worker carrying out more steps. Narrow jobs are process killers. Seemingly harmless handoffs to management, customers, or quality control become process killers, as those handoff people aren't trained to correct the problem or to carry out the process. Do everything possible to not hand off processes to management, engineering, quality control, or customers. Keep the workers working instead of the bureaucracy running up cost, delays, and problems. The leaders should be coaching and not micromanaging! Have the people doing the work check with others on questions rather than dumping a problem on others. Once you streamline your processes, you'll really appreciate why I say that you should play your own cards and not let anyone else play your hand for you. Go to great lengths to do wide jobs and to not dump problems on others. Eliminate 90–95 percent of all the problems that are dumped on others. Of course, a great culture of ownership, harmony, teamwork, excellence, and responsibility is required. Learn to stop the bureaucratic dumping!

6. Make all handoffs as seamless as possible. When you do, the next person receiving the handoff doesn't need to check back, fix something that was wrong before he or she received it, or sit around while waiting on something else to be done to address the next step. Don't drop the ball with delays and hassles when making handoffs. No fumbles, since these are process killers! Be cognizant to minimize the inefficiency added by handoffs. Our goal is to add value through better-defined business processes. Keep value flowing, and eliminate most rework and double work.

7. Minimize elapsed time for each step and the overall process. Ever notice how if you're given a week to get a project done, it takes a week, and if you're given three weeks to get the same project done, it takes three weeks? It's a strange phenomenon, but we humans behave this way. It's like pulling an all-nighter just before a big final exam when you could have gotten all the studying done ahead of time. It's very much in keeping with the idea that I've presented in earlier pages, stating that most actions only occur when we have to act, not when we could have acted sooner.

Compressing the time it takes to accomplish a process or a process step will boost productivity. Costs and mistakes inevitably exponentially increase with elapsed time. Perform the work in the shortest amount of time. Handle work quickly, and do not wait for anything to show up before performing the work in assembly-line fashion (unless it *is* an assembly line). Think of the process as a hot potato, and pass it on quickly. Make value flow without interruption. Value-thinker Henry Ford said, "The longer an article is in the process of manufacture and the more it is moved about, the greater its ultimate cost." Napoleon's troops marched at 120 paces per minute, while his opponents marched at 70 paces. In the *Art of War*, Sun Tzu wanted actions completed rapidly because when actions take too long, the chance for errors and unforeseen events increase. Oh, so true indeed! Speed simplifies, since each person is handling less complex work at any one time. Start by trying to cut elapsed times in half for most steps or processes.

8. Minimize handoffs between departments, management, or businesses. These handoffs are much more destructive than those within a department or a team. Use teams of people in different departments, but don't hand off to departments. Department, company, management, or business walls are very destructive to processes. A good performance-based organizational business culture among workers and managers will help minimize the damage of handoffs. Good relationships between people will also help any necessary handoffs to be more effective. What also helps handoffs to be more effective is when people in different departments, jobs, or levels of management understand and appreciate the others' jobs. It pays to spend the time to cross-train and spend time in others' jobs and departments. Do not have strong department walls. Culture, relationships, and the appreciation of others go a long way toward minimizing the damage of handoffs. A linear-thinking manager who doesn't fit your culture will create really serious problems with your process. Watch out for that!

9. Processes should be customer-focused. Think backward through the entire process to add value and trust from the point of delivering the product or service to the customer. This is much more effective than thinking beginning to end, which is the ineffective, conventional, linear approach. Don't be self-focused like poor-performing businesses. Do more than you are paid for by adding value for the customer. Keep the customer and your end goals in mind. It works far better than thinking from the beginning going forward. Perhaps sixteen times! Reverse engineer all processes!

10. Maintain a decentralized, flatter-business organizational structure. This is highly effective for nimble entrepreneurial businesses. The approach will work for large companies, as well, but it becomes infinitely more difficult because of the size, complexity, and centralized culture of the organization itself. Strongly resist adding toxic bureaucracy and levels of management to processes that add no value. Processes should not go through management but should instead just be monitored and coached by management. Through this coaching, employees are empowered to make most on-the-spot decisions, solve problems, and make recommendations. This takes the right people with a good culture and good leadership. In the book *What Really Works*, a decentralized structure is one of the only four business practices that all great businesses have in common, as are also the right (performance-based) culture, flawless processes, and strategy. It's that important!

11. Train managers to be coaches instead of being bosses. A manager intent on maintaining is going to build bureaucratic and micromanagement steps into the process. If you see this happening in your business, take action to simplify and remove bureaucratic hindrances. Simplifying makes it easier for your managers to actually coach and empower their subordinates. Obviously, the manager needs to have been cross-trained to perform the work being done under his or her supervision. Only with that ground-up knowledge can the manager truly understand and appreciate the nature of the job at hand and what challenges its proper execution might entail for employees.

Workers should be trained and empowered to improve quality, adjust schedules, and solve routine problems. They must know when and how to consult with superiors and when to bring a flaw to the attention of management or ask and get advice to resolve issues instead of handing off the problem. Workers should let management know what the problem was and how they handled it whenever possible. Make these checks a near-invisible, two-minute issue most of the time. Managers coach, serve, coordinate, and assist. They don't insert themselves into the process as a handoff, and they should not receive an excessive number of problems to deal with, if possible.

12. Use zero-based thinking on the processes. What is zero-based thinking? It's simply coming at a process as if no process or procedures were in place. Think about how you would perform the process if you had to start over now, which is essentially the concept behind zero-based thinking. Start from scratch, and go from there. What is the simplest and most direct way to solve the problem or get the project done? Don't become tied down or limited to only what has been done in the past, or your competition will pass you in the future. Don't let old complicated processes tie your hands and muddy your thinking. Nearly all processes in even the better businesses could use a lot of improvement. The knowledge of the process now is nearly always infinitely more than when the process was started. You are in a better position to improve the process than you were in the past. This additional way of thinking will in itself bring a great deal of creative thought and improvement to the process. Nearly all processes could be done better knowing what we know now.

13. Use value-added thinking on processes. Question the value of each step. Ask, "Is it necessary? Are we spending too much on certain steps? Could we add more value to steps that will help the customer or generate more profits?" Value-added thinking is very effective. If a step doesn't add value, eliminate it or reduce its time and expense. Determine how to reduce costly steps that appear to cost too much for the value they add. Add more value for the customer when possible, and reduce low-value activities. That's basically what our job is when it comes to establishing more efficient business processes. Can you double the profit by improving the product for the customer or by cutting the operational cost?

14. Strongly resist complicating any process. I know I've already said this, but it's definitely worth repeating and expounding upon here. What happens when you simplify is that others involved in the process will try to complicate it. Maintain a high resistance to managers, customers, employees, suppliers, yourself, and others complicating the processes by trying to add steps or time or cost. Your processes will be under assault by conventional, well-meaning thinkers who don't understand that simplicity outperforms complication every time. Many will try to complicate matters to make themselves appear invaluable to the project at hand. In a vendor relationship, others will do so to boost profits for their own company. My experience is that almost everyone will try to complicate your processes. As a CEO, it's up to you to not let them. Allow no complicating!

Virtually everyone around you wants to double the number of process steps to make sure that something is done right. They don't trust your people doing the work. But remember that it doesn't take long to turn good processes into bad processes. There are very few businesses or managers that have or understand good processes. Most processes in most businesses are not particularly good, even if they are very functional. Good employees can run good processes well. It takes heroes to run bad processes, and they burn out over time. Very few businesses of any size have or maintain good processes.

15. Practice developing your process. Read, learn, and do enough on processes to become process-literate. You don't have to be a process expert like me. Our business processes are a lot of what matter most, and you only need common sense along with these guidelines. It's your responsibility as a leader or CEO to perform well in all areas of the business discussed in this book, and processes definitely count. In a very real sense, the future success and profitability of the business heavily depends on how well you develop your business processes and on how well you adjust them to keep pace with the inevitable changes that will occur as your business continues to grow over time.

16. Always use dynamic 80/20 thinking on processes. What's the 20 percent of the process that produces 80 percent of the value? Can we do more of that work to improve the product or result? And how can we do less of the 20 percent or 50 percent of the lowest-value work, in which we only have to and want to do good enough? What does the customer value most? This can turn a no-profit business to a highly profitable business if you have the people and culture to match.

If we're not working within the 80/20 principle, we won't identify which business processes require our attention, and we won't address the 20 percent of the largest problems in the business that cause 80 percent of the negative results. Much of our efforts will thus be wasted on the small stuff. All of these concepts work together. For example, if we're not taking enough concerted action within the 80/20 principle in terms of building the top 20 percent of the business that generates 80 percent of the desired results, we won't have placed the business in a position to encounter more opportunity. We also need good processes on the small stuff so that it doesn't enslave us. You might call what I've been discussing a philosophy—a cerebral, emotional, and psychological path to the unlimited success that I know lies within us all. The hard part is tapping into it. If you focus on what matters most, you're on your way!

Let's take a look at a tough problem. How can you get your people to implement just doing "good enough" on what matters least so that you can focus on what matters most? Keep in mind that most believe that what matters least matters most. There are only a very few of the most successful CEOs who can get their businesses focused on what matters most. In conventional businesses, the managers and workers are nearly always enslaved by the habit of throwing people and money at what matters least so that they can "be excellent at everything." They think the small stuff is the big stuff. This approach is very flawed, and it results in very little effort and focus being done on what matters most. A general approach I would use is this:

1. Cover the process principles with your leaders on "good enough," and then do this with everyone. Make posters, and write some memos. Study and learn the basics well yourself.
2. Define "good enough" on what matters least. It's hard for most to accept.
3. Start working on business processes to reduce the time and labor on what matters least.
4. Start reducing the number of people working on what matters least. Always control this.
5. Spend more time on what matters most, and greatly increase those efforts. Only the right culture people can do well on what matters most.
6. Put a strong effort forward to build culture, empowerment, and teamwork harmony.
7. Get rid of the people who are fighting these efforts if you can't get them on board. Give them some time.
8. Set team productivity goals on cost of doing what matters least. Make the small stuff your servants. Managers are coaches, not dictators who are handed all the problems.
9. Set team goals on improving what matters most, which are your strengths that your customers value most. Don't hand off the work to managers.
10. Focus your business on what matters most, and don't let your people get enslaved by the small stuff.

11. Realize that this is a difficult job and that it can take a long time depending on your culture.

Chapter roundup

As we've seen, the importance of defined and constantly evolving business processes cannot be overemphasized. It's where all our leadership, excellence, people, and team development come together to give us our end-result goals. Processes and culture are at the core of the company from an operational standpoint. They determine how excellently you deliver your product or service, the quality, the profits, the logistics, and so much more. Mapping out your business processes in writing will help reveal systemic problems you might not have realized were even present, allowing you to take a proactive—as opposed to a reactive—approach in dealing with those problems. Excellent processes require an excellent CEO, an excellent solution-oriented culture, and the right people all striving in harmony for problem-solving excellence. It's the execution part of our products and services. The rest is how we build ourselves, business strategy, and people strengths so that we can execute well.

No matter what you do to define and improve your business processes, problems will inevitably arise. Having in place a can-do business culture where employees feel empowered to wrestle with problems instead of dumping them off to other members of your team will generate superior customer relations, and it will also tend to boost productivity and reduce costs. Attitude is everything when it comes to solving problems. Problem solving requires a solution-oriented CEO who encourages the team to think about solutions in a nonlinear way and to look for long-term fixes that will reduce the likelihood that the problem will arise again in the future. This CEO is always looking to solve problems and improve processes.

Your focus on business processes and problem solving is just as rooted in the 80/20 principle and positive thinking as your focus on goal setting and new business development. Culture, the right people, and process go together especially well to create a powerful blend. Without good processes, you won't be able to have a good culture or keep enough good people. Put it all to use in your business and in your personal life! Do not let people complicate your processes or change them without a strong process person agreeing to the change. It strongly affects your unbridled success! Don't let the process and problem solving scare you. If you can digest and absorb much of it and apply only some of it with your team, you'll benefit greatly from it. Nearly no one does a lot of good process work, so you don't have to master process to reap great benefits. As a result, this is a great opportunity for you to excel, as you won't have much competition. It's really just all common sense when we get our thinking right.

Remember …

» Business processes are used in virtually every part of your business, from administrative to delivering a product or service, and how well you perform them represents your business performance. As the CEO, it's your duty to refine, simplify, and drive effective and efficient business processes that will allow you to achieve a higher degree of excellence.

» A lack of smooth, fast, and empowered business processes will enslave you in too much small stuff.

» Good processes and problem solving builds culture, and good culture builds processes and excellence.

» Develop your team to be your internal master mind group working in harmony toward a common purpose.

» Benchmark winning companies, and learn from their business processes. Join a CEO organization when you can so that you can do this.

» Develop your processes by always using the sixteen-step process basics and the problem-solving process of this chapter. Remember that it requires a good performance-based culture of can-do people to execute the process development and problem-solving principles well. Poor processes can damage your culture, while good processes build culture and excellence.

» Inefficient and complicated business processes reduce productivity and excellence, increase costs, dampen employee morale, and hinder the growth of the company. They will also enslave you by breeding problems that will take you away from your focus on the big stuff.

» Avoid excessive handoffs in problem solving and process management. It's better to have three people do three steps each in a process than it is to have nine people do one step each. The wider and more empowered each person is while avoiding handoffs if at all possible, the better the processes will be.

» Go to great measures to avoid bureaucratic handoffs to management, quality control, or customers. You are running your business, not a bunch of bureaucrats who can't boil water.

» Study your processes, and map them on paper, identifying every area where obstacles and delays appear to be built into the system. Simplify and eliminate problem areas. Map out your major problems, as well, and see how they relate to or stem from flaws in your business processes or problem solving. Don't let people complicate your processes.

» Continuous improvement and refinement of your business processes is necessary to enhance your business's success. This is particularly true for rapidly growing companies, since growth increases the number of problems you will face.

» Go for smooth and nearly flawless processes. Avoid the perfectionist myth, whereby you micromanage and complicate the actions while neglecting the process.

» Assign projects to teams, not departments, and complete work quickly and without delays to increase productivity.

- Processes should always be focused on giving value to the customer. Resist looking at completing work in a linear way, which forces you to start at the beginning and work your way forward. Instead, look at the project from the back, with your focus on delivering what the customer values, eliminating as much of the low-value aspects in the process as possible. Goal setting works from the desired result backward. Process development is process goal setting. There are many advanced elements of goal setting in process improvement that you can use in problem solving. For instance, brainstorm problems with writing out twenty different approaches or solutions. Remember that customers only want four things: fast, easy, right, and value.
- Focus on developing good, disciplined problem solving, which is so rare in business. Problem solving is also goal setting. Reverse engineer problems.
- Empower the people doing most of the work to handle most problems on the spot, instead of handing off the problems. This takes a great culture to execute well.
- Good execution of business processes is necessary for all highly successful businesses that excel.
- Go for team building and empowerment in your process development and problem solving to help build your excellent culture and processes.
- A decentralized, flat, nimble organization with a strong, nonlinear, performance-based culture like yours is a prime candidate for success!
- Minimize elapsed time to complete work. Treat work like a hot potato. Costs and mistakes go up with elapsed time to complete work.
- Good culture and processes of going the extra mile are where most excellence comes from.

» Mastering as much as you can of the first ten chapters is the personal and team development needed to do well in process execution and problem solving. We can't make a silk purse out of a sow's ear.

» Develop a fun and rewarding program in your business to develop people to practice these leading-edge processes and problem-solving principles of excellence. Focus on excellence and giving value to the customer, and the profits will come.

12

Your Journey to Execution Excellence in Entrepreneurism, Personal Success, and Business

Though no one can go back and make a brand-new start, anyone can start from now and make a brand-new ending."
—*Carl Bard*

Focus on the high-value thinking (80/20 principle) and duties of what really works and matters most. From a lifetime journey to achieve success by the nonlinear route of practicing both the intangible success principles and the best business practices, I've learned firsthand how most any of us can more effectively achieve our dream goals and great success in our lives. All of this comes from someone who has done it and not from remote business studies. There is a huge difference. Nearly all of us are capable of achieving greatly by developing who we are. No one else is better than you. Some have just started before you and have different talents.

In the success classic *Think and Grow Rich*, Napoleon Hill demonstrated how the most successful people of the late nineteenth and early twentieth centuries obtained their success. It was essentially starting from scratch and by developing a positive mental attitude with the absence of self-doubt through spending long hours on affirmations combined with goal setting and working in harmony. It's all about improving your thinking, mindsets and habits such that you develop yourself into the executioner. Hill's classic alone has helped at least a few million people become millionaires and achieve other great goals that they would not have otherwise achieved. Today, we now have the advantage of having the best audios and many proven methods that are so much more developed and effective than what people had to work with in Hill's time.

However, it is still all about developing your thinking, mindsets, habits, and actions to be good enough to execute the best-proven principles, thinking, and practices needed for your great success that most aren't doing. This personal growth takes a lot more time and effort than what we're made to believe, but it can be truly worthwhile. I've found that what effort it takes is relatively nothing in the grand scheme of perhaps your next several hundred thousand hours of work. It should be very liberating to you to know that doing much of the right critical principles and practices for ten years will transform you to a much higher state of life, excellence, and achievement. It's not the persistence forever by working hard as we've always been told that hasn't worked for most. Keep in mind that it is no picnic spending your life coasting at a much lower achievement level than what you really want in your heart. There is no easy route. You will be working on something, so why not make it the right-focused principles and practices of *The Executioner* instead of the less effective small stuff? It took much more time than I thought, as I had to personally make all the mistakes, do all the actions, and develop the right thinking myself for me to transform myself to this higher state. I've since learned that it takes us all more time, effort, mistakes, right thinking, and action than we tend to think.

Since schools and businesses consumed by their selfish goals don't teach us much about how to get ahead by the success principles or even conventionally, we have to get this on our own by being the CEOs of ourselves. I've found that it's best, or perhaps easiest, to start on our own with repetitive listening to the success-principle audios to transform our thinking. It takes no time from anything productive if you do it while you travel in the car, when working out, and during other similar activities. How you think and your mindset makes all the difference in the world. Developing the right mindsets and thinking through these audios is the key to your success. Very few people understand this well enough to do it. **Our success depends on our faith in these principles and mindsets because progress is not gradual. We go for long stretches of time with no progress, then our brains accept the mindsets and everything takes off at warp speed. Few have the faith to try long enough.** Most books don't cover the dynamic practices as well. Let others listen to going-nowhere music and read negative newspapers and trash novels. You will transform yourself for great success and a great life.

What I've seen personally of the best of the successful people:

The best nonconventional leaders that I've known in terms of success, excellence, and personal harmony have used the principles of *Think and Grow Rich* in developing their mindsets, habits, and actions as their blueprint for success and excellence. They developed themselves to be people with the right thinking, capable of achieving their goals just like the most successful researched by Napoleon Hill, starting in 1908.

I have adopted the dream that Andrew Carnegie and Napoleon Hill did in 1908 to give everyone who wants to best learn how to get ahead the opportunity to do so. Unfortunately, the world is filled with people whose goals are to enslave others in the linear world. Just as it was over a hundred years ago, it is up to us to get this on our own. Thank goodness we have more tools today to accomplish this.

You have the tools and the guide to achieve greatly if that is your desire. I encourage you to set goals for your heart's desire. These nonlinear success principles, mindsets and practices are the ones that will really work, but you'll have to advance your execution of them beyond an elementary level to the mastery level explained by *Outliers*. Good luck!

Key Needed Audios and Reading for Your Developing Excellence

My life has taken many twists and turns since I started work as a chemical engineer in 1967. Working for Success Motivation International turned out to be a watershed period in my life. I immersed myself in success literature and motivational audiobooks. I habitually listened to the recordings in my car and at home while doing chores. I have listened to each of the suggested audios well over a hundred times. It takes that much exposure to improve our thinking and develop the right mindset for success. Intellectual knowledge alone means nothing when it comes to our positive right thinking and habits. Did you notice I used the word *habitually*? I did so deliberately. Immersing myself in motivational cassette tapes and spending time reading and contemplating the works of some of the best authors in the field prepared me for my eventual success. I still habitually listen to and read motivational books. I've always read, outlined, and reviewed every book where I saw valuable principles and practices, but I did discover, as so many others have, that it's the audios that have had the most lasting effect on my thinking and that of others. It truly takes an unbelievable amount of positive conditioning to get our brains to accept just one great concept or new habit that we already intellectually believe in. I still keep an open mind. I always want to condition my mind with the best thinking and to explore the truly limitless possibilities that are available to us if we only look for them. While there are many ways to positively improve our thinking, I've found that these audios work the best. It's far better to master the universal mindsets in these few audios than to become an expert by listening to too many.

I encourage you to do the same. I believe that if a person who wants excellence will listen to these audios a few thousand hours, he or she will develop his or her mind and thinking to a very successful level. As noted, much repetition is needed to enable the message of these concepts to fully integrate with your habitual thought, your second-nature approach to the world at large. I've seen firsthand what five hundred to a thousand hours of exposure a year of self-improvement thinking can do. There is a world of difference in the people who have spent the effort. That's why you'll want to make it a habit to read and listen to some of the great success authors in the field. Audio learning is the most effective way I've found to condition the mind for more success. It offers us the two things that we need more than other methods—the time and repetition needed to make it a part of our instinctive thinking. Just the intellectual knowledge of these concepts means nothing in the success world. I've taken the liberty of including the best and most effective sources I know on my list for your possible perusal. Seeing all of this from different perspectives does wonders for our minds. Keep in mind that the first two or three thousand hours of repetitive listening may not seem to help much, if at all. It's the transformation to mastery that is your real goal. That takes 10,000 hours of the right stuff (action and mental conditioning). It's not the information in these audios and this book that will help so much. It's your thinking, mindset, habits and actions regarding these principles that will lend to your success. That only happens after 10,000 hours of the right stuff. Have faith.

Recorded gems

Listening to the right success-related audios to build your success mindsets is a major part of the ten thousand hours required for mastery. If you do anything, repetitively listen to these audios. This will improve the way your brain thinks to keep growing and advancing even when you don't have time for anything else. It helps our brains so much to see these principles from different perspectives that will tie these concepts together in your mind. These other audios and books are indeed that important.

Don't let this scare you, but it will only normally work well if we listen to these audios a hundred or two hundred times each. They get better results with each repetition. Just look at the typical advertising model. The more impressions a company can project for a brand across all mediums, the more likely we are to recognize and identify with that brand. The same effectiveness goes for the motivational messages about success—your success! Repeated listening is the key! These audios are not overly expensive. Most can be found on https://www.nightingale.com. They are the greatest source I've ever found. After you have listened to the four suggested audio programs "enough," listen to the audios of the recommended classic books. The process of hearing the messages from different perspectives fills in much of what no one source can. It took every one of these sources to get me thinking right on what matters most and least.

The Executioner by Artie McFerrin
The audio version of my book will make it easy for you to listen repeatedly and internalize the message in many parts of your mind on what matters most; this can be an effective road map for your success. It takes a great amount of mental conditioning on these concepts to improve our success thinking. I hope to have it out by early 2015.

The Ultimate Goals Program by Brian Tracy
As Tracy says, "Success is goals; all else is commentary." Brian Tracy is practical on setting goals that matter and other success concepts in this eight-CD program.

Universal Laws of Success and Achievement by Brian Tracy
This is another Tracy classic well worth listening to repeatedly! It's an old program. If Tracy discontinues it, get another of his similar programs. He's the most practical business-success guru with many great audios. This program covers the foundation success principles to a degree that I didn't have the space in this book to do. It's as good of a program as there is. Brian is also probably the best and most practical overall trainer on conventional business if you need that.

80/20 Principle by Richard Koch
It takes a lot of mental conditioning to free our minds from being enslaved by the small stuff and to get into thinking and acting on what matters most. This six-CD audio set is great! It is very effective at getting you to focus on the big stuff. It did for me, and it's much better than his book.

Other classic reads and great recordings of huge benefit

Think and Grow Rich by Napoleon Hill
When this book came out at the height of the Great Depression, it was an immediate success. The concepts remain largely relevant even today, and it is unsurpassed. This is a classic and the bible in the arena of success literature. Nearly all of the most successful people I know used this as their guidebook. This old audio is great and will provide a better perspective for you.

How to be a No-Limit Person by Dr. Wayne Dyer
On the path of the no-limit person, you achieve anything you set your mind to do. This is a really good Wayne Dyer program and consists of six audio CDs.

Acres of Diamonds by Russell Conwell
This is another classic read, based upon the speech by the same name. Essentially, its central premise is that you already likely possess everything you need to be successful or that you at least have most of what it takes to find your acres of diamonds where you are with what you've got. This is a very short but inspiring book! There is also a short one-CD audio for this book.

As a Man Thinketh by James Allen
This one is a must-read on the power of thinking your way to success in life and in business. It is written in the most beautiful prose of describing a PMA that I have ever read. There is also a great short one-CD audio of this book.

The Magic of Thinking Big by David J. Schwartz
If you can realign your thinking to enable yourself to envision stellar success, you're already halfway there! This book promotes the idea that thinking big can help get us away from the small stuff and that big goals are easier to obtain than smaller goals.

Don't Sweat the Small Stuff... and It's All Small Stuff by Richard Carlson
Understanding the small stuff that enslaves and putting it into perspective was a wonderful experience for me. It takes a great deal of conditioning our minds to gain this wise perspective. This is truly a great book that gave me a great insight and liberated my thinking.

The Seven Habits of Highly Effective People by Stephen Covey
Understanding high- and low-value work and the value of important, nonurgent work is integral to success in business.

Reengineering the Corporation by Michael Hammer and James Champy
Here's another outstanding classic that will help you better understand the importance of defined business processes. A more difficult read, but if my chapter on process isn't enough, this might help.

The Success Principles by Jack Canfield
This wonderful book encompasses sixty-four practical success principles that will get you from where you are to where you want to be. By tackling challenges, it teaches you to grow your confidence, therefore conquering ambitions and goals. Jack also has a really good audio program of the book that is great to listen to repetitively.

ABOUT THE AUTHOR

ARTHUR R. (ARTIE) MCFERRIN is an entrepreneur who owns and operates several highly successful specialty chemical manufacturing businesses serving global automotive, petroleum, and industrial enterprises. McFerrin graduated from Texas A&M University with two chemical engineering degrees. He has worked in the chemical industry for forty-seven years, most of it as an entrepreneur. He was the chemical industry recipient for the Chemical Education Foundation's Vanguard Award in 2009, which recognizes and honors the outstanding efforts of an individual who has exhibited leadership and commitment to fostering the public's understanding of, participation in, and general appreciation of chemistry, chemicals, and the chemical industry.

At Texas A&M University, he is a distinguished alumni, and the Chemical Engineering Department bears his name—the Artie McFerrin Department of Chemical Engineering. McFerrin's success has allowed him and his wife to be major philanthropists. McFerrin wrote *The Executioner* to help people chart a better success principle career.

Success as an entrepreneur has also enabled the McFerrins to pursue their passion for Fabergé eggs and other Fabergé art objects. These spectacular Russian bejeweled eggs were the product of Peter Carl Fabergé's company between 1885 and 1917. Among the firm's best customers were Tsars Alexander III and Nicholas II. McFerrin's private collection is one of the world's most extensive, and it is valued at about $100 million.